Portugal and Africa

This series of publications on Africa, Latin America, Southeast Asia, and Global and Comparative Studies is designed to present significant research, translation, and opinion to area specialists and to a wide community of persons interested in world affairs. The editor seeks manuscripts of quality on any subject and can usually make a decision regarding publication within three months of receipt of the original work. Production methods generally permit a work to appear within one year of acceptance. The editor works closely with authors to produce a high-quality book. The series appears in a paperback format and is distributed worldwide. For more information, contact the executive editor at Ohio University Press, Scott Quadrangle, University Terrace, Athens, Ohio 45701.

Executive editor: Gillian Berchowitz
AREA CONSULTANTS
Africa: Diane M. Ciekawy
Latin America: Thomas Walker
Southeast Asia: William H. Frederick
Global and Comparative Studies: Ann R. Tickamyer

The Ohio University Research in International Studies series is published for the Center for International Studies by Ohio University Press. The views expressed in individual volumes are those of the authors and should not be considered to represent the policies or beliefs of the Center for International Studies, Ohio University Press, or Ohio University.

Portugal and Africa

David Birmingham

Ohio University Research in International Studies
Africa Series No. 81
Ohio University Press
Athens

Center for International Studies
Ohio University
Athens, Ohio

© 1999 by David Birmingham

First Ohio University Research in International Studies edition 2004

First published in Great Britain 1999 by Macmillan Press Ltd
Houndmills, Basingstoke, Hampshire RG21 6XS and London

First published in the United States of America 1999 by
St. Martin's Press, Inc.,
Scholarly and Reference Division,
175 Fifth Avenue, New York, NY 10010

The books in the Ohio University Research in International Studies Series
are printed on acid-free paper ⊚ ™

12 11 10 09 08 07 06 05 04   5 4 3 2 1

Cover art: *Dom Miguel de Castro of Kongo*, attributed to Albert Eckhout and Jasper
Becx. © The National Museum of Denmark, Department of Ethnography.
Used with permission.

Library of Congress Cataloging-in-Publication Data

Birmingham, David.
 Portugal and Africa / David Birmingham.
  p. cm. — (Ohio University research in international studies. Africa series ; no. 81)
 Includes bibliographical references and index.
 ISBN 0-89680-237-X (acid-free paper)
  1. Portugal—Colonies—Africa—History. 2. Africa, Portuguese-speaking—
History. I. Title. II. Research in international studies. Africa series ; no. 81.
 DT36.B56 2004
 960'.09712469—dc22

                                                        2004004405

Contents

Preface

For the past six centuries the south Atlantic Ocean has been open to long-distance navigation and regular links have been maintained between Africa and Europe. The first European nation to occupy itself intensively with African affairs was Portugal. Portuguese emigrants settled on the off-shore islands and captured the on-shore Moroccan fortress of Ceuta early in the fifteenth century. From there they reached down the Africa coast, establishing sugar plantations on the islands and building trade factories on the beaches, until in 1488 one of their sea-captains, Bartholomew Dias, reached Africa's furthest shore at the Cape of Good Hope. For the next 10 years Portugal concentrated on buying gold in West Africa and establishing a missionary bridgehead in the kingdom of Kongo, but in 1498 another sea-captain, Vasco da Gama, rounded the tip of South Africa and opened direct communication between Europe and the city states of the East African coast. The first chapters of this book portray these early years of Portuguese trade in Africa, culminating in the building of the great Atlantic 'slave bridge' which by the seventeenth century ferried 10 000 people a year from Africa to new Portuguese colonies in Brazil.

In 1822 Portugal lost its American empire and slowly began to replace it by an empire in Africa which was territorial as well as commercial. Coffee and cocoa plantations were pioneered and the missionary effort was revitalised, but Portugal was only able to stake claims that did not offend the great powers and its attempt to conquer the Zambezi basin and thereby link its East Coast and West Coast possessions was thwarted by Great Britain. In the first half of the twentieth century, colonial migration was only a trickle and colonial production was severely dampened by the Great Depression and the Second World War. After 1950, however, Portuguese Angola became one of the most dynamic of Africa's colonies. Quarter of a million Portuguese settlers arrived to make Angola the largest white colony outside of Algeria or South Africa and the country produced not only a quarter of a million tons of coffee each year but also several million barrels of petroleum. When Angola collapsed in a long series of civil and international wars the results were devastatingly tragic as is shown in several of the later essays presented here.

Many of the chapters of this book have previously been published in journals and collected volumes and the author and publishers are grateful to the several editors and publishers for permission to reprint them in this form.

Canterbury DAVID BIRMINGHAM

1 Portugal's Impact on Africa

In the year 1488 Bartholomew Dias became the first European mariner to sail the entire length of the Atlantic and reach the Cape of Good Hope in South Africa. A century later Bartholomew's grandson Paulo followed in his wake and disembarked on the coast of Angola bent on conquering an empire in Africa. Five hundred years after the epic voyage a replica of Bartholomew's ship retraced his route in 1988. This chapter, written for History Today *on the occasion of that anniversary exploit, examines the long-term economic consequences of the opening of the Atlantic and explores the origins of modern colonialism.*

Five hundred years ago, in 1488, Bartholomew Dias, a Portuguese seaman, reached the Cape of Good Hope on the furthest tip of South Africa. This was the last stage of the Portuguese exploration of the Atlantic coast and its islands. It was also the beginning of five centuries of often strained relations between Europe and South Africa. Two questions arise out of this turning point in the world's fortunes. The first is how did Portugal, a relatively remote and impoverished land at the far ends of medieval Europe, become the pioneer of Atlantic colonisation? And secondly, what were the long-term consequences of the opening of South Africa to alien influences?

The Portuguese domination of the eastern Atlantic took place in six stages, each of which pioneered a new set of colonial experiments. Bartholomew Dias was the heir to two centuries of trial and error as Portugal sought escape from its chronic poverty. The fact that Portugal was able to succeed in becoming an international power was due primarily to the superb shelter which the harbour of Lisbon provided to mariners on the otherwise inhospitable coast of south-eastern Europe.

Lisbon had been a harbour in Phoenician times when Levantine traders needed a haven on the long haul to Britain. It was also used by the Roman and Arab empires, although their primary interest lay in land-based domination. In the thirteenth century, sea-power revived and Genoa succeeded in breaking out of the Mediterranean into the Atlantic. The great economic centres of northern

Italy and of lower Germany (hitherto linked by land routes through the great markets of Lyons and Nuremburg) were now joined by Genoese on the safer maritime route. Lisbon again became a thriving port. The Portuguese learnt about shipbuilding from the Low Countries and about seafaring from Italy and Catalonia. At one time the Portuguese monarchy hired no less than six Genoese admirals, although the most famous of them, Christopher Columbus, sought fame by transferring his allegiance to the rival port of Seville in Castille.

The rise of Lisbon as the maritime gateway between northern and southern Europe led to the growth of an urban middle class with merchant and banking skills learnt from Italy. It was this middle class which became the driving force behind the Portuguese search for new wealth overseas. It found its patron in the royal prince, Pedro, brother of the vaunted Henry the Navigator. Portugal was unusual in that the nobility, lacking any other source of wealth in a country of agrarian poverty, showed a willingness to engage in merchant adventures. They were greatly helped by the thriving Jewish community of Lisbon, a community spasmodically enhanced by refugees fleeing persecution in other parts of Christendom. Jewish scholars were not hampered by Christian concepts of the world as portrayed in the scriptures and were able to take a much more scientific look at the evidence needed to draw maps and collate intelligence on economic prospects overseas.

The crises which drove Portugal to expansion were always crises over the price of bread. Throughout the Middle Ages Lisbon had been a hungry city. Access to the farm lands of the interior was inhibited by poor river navigation and expensive long-distance cartage. Grain was therefore not sought from domestic sources but from overseas shippers. Both Spain and Britain became key suppliers of wheat to Lisbon, and England built a 600-year alliance on Portugal's need for northern trade. But in the fourteenth century one new solution to the grain deficit was a colonial venture in the Atlantic.

One thousand miles off the coast of Portugal lay the uninhabited islands of the Azores and Madeira. With the development of better shipping they became more accessible to Lisbon than the much closer interior of mainland Portugal. Colonisation and the setting up of wheat gardens were therefore attempted. Concepts of colonisation were learnt from the Venetians, who had established settled colonies around their trading factories in the Near East. The labour supply consisted both of cheap European migrants driven by hunger, and captured slaves raided from the Barbary coast. The necessary capital was raised in the banking houses of Genoa. Patronage was provided by the land-owning nobility under the protection of Prince Henry. The beginnings of temperate cereal colonisation in the Atlantic basin were laid. The system was later to spread to the far side of the ocean, and eventually the Canadian and American prairies became a source of wheat not only for Portugal but also for half of Europe. Stage one of the Portuguese expansion, the wheat-based stage, was successful in the initial objective of supplying bread to overcome the Lisbon deficiency. It was also successful in terms of pioneering a colonial system which carried Europe out into the world.

The second stage of Portuguese expansion involved a more subtle development of overseas investment. Wheat was a comparatively low-yielding agricultural enterprise. A much higher return on capital, on labour and on land could be obtained by turning agrarian produce into alcohol. Alcohol could also be better preserved and could be sold when the price was advantageous rather than when the crop was ripe, as in the case of grain. The second stage of Portuguese expansion therefore attempted to establish a wine industry over-seas. The necessary skills were available in the wine industry of Portugal. But Portuguese domestic wine, like Portuguese grain, suffered from severe problems of cartage to the coast. Even in the eighteenth century, when port wine became a lucrative export, the shooting of the rapids on the Douro river made transport almost suicidal. The prospect of using colonial islands for the growing of vines was therefore attractive. The territory chosen was the Canary Islands, off the Moroccan coast of Africa.

Morocco was known to the Portuguese after a series of raiding wars associated with the militant crusading Order of Christ, of which Prince Henry was the commander. Despite an initial victory in Ceuta in 1415, these wars had failed to capture the 'bread-basket' of North Africa which had once fed the city of Rome. Instead, the conquerors therefore set their sight on the off-shore islands. Unlike the Azores, the Canaries were already inhabited and conquest was necessary before plantations could be established. Once conquered, however, the surviving islanders could be compelled to slave servitude. Migrants from Portugal's impoverished backlands sailed in to create vineyards using both local and mainland slaves. Even when the colony was transferred in 1479 from Portuguese suzerainty to control by the Crown of Castile, Portuguese immigrants continued to provide many colonists for Tenerife.

The Canary Islands were a second, wine-based, stage of Portugal's colonial pioneering. The development of colonial wine industries, for instance in California, South Africa and Australia was slower to take off than the development of wheat colonies. Portugal itself imposed restrictions where the interests of metropolitan producers were put at risk, though Canary wine was extensively smuggled into the Portuguese empire. The Canary Islands were important, however, for another reason. They became the base for the conquest and colonisation of Hispanic America. It was from there that Columbus set sail in 1492, and later a significant proportion of the emigrants who went to the Spanish American colonies were Canary islanders, often of Portuguese ancestry. As a stage in the growth of the economic, political and social ideology of imperialism the Canary islands were of critical significance. The slave vineyards of Tenerife, and the spasmodic raiding of southern Morocco, are a more accurate testimony to the place of Henry the Navigator in history than all the myths about his scientific virtuosity which were put out by the hired praise-singer, the chronicler Azurara.

The third stage of Portuguese experimentation in colonial practices was focused on another set of Atlantic islands, the Cape Verde islands. The Cape Verdes became famous over time for their textile industry. Portugal was almost as severely short of textiles as it was short of wheat. One reason for the development of wine exports was to pay for woollen materials from England. Cotton was also bought in significant quantities from Muslim suppliers in north Africa and, after the rounding of the Cape of Good Hope, from the great textile industries of India. But the Cape Verde islands offered an opportunity to create a colonial textile industry.

Cotton and indigo plantations were established on the islands for spinning and dyeing. Labour was purchased on the West Africa mainland. Craftsmen were also brought over from the mainland to introduce the necessary weaving skills. The styles of textile adopted were those which would sell best in Africa. The industry soon became self-perpetuating. Cloth woven in the islands was sold on the mainland in return for more slaves who would further expand the plantations. The only European input was sea transport. The Portuguese shipped cloth up and down the coast in the cabotage trade. The final profits were taken in slaves, the best of which were carried to Portugal to work on the underdeveloped landed estates of the south. By the sixteenth century some 10 per cent of the population of southern Portugal comprised black immigrants. Many were still slaves but others had married into land-owning families, thus increasing the domestic labour force without having to make reciprocal marriage payments. Blacks also became a significant part of the working population of Lisbon.

Slave-grown cotton became, over the colonial centuries, one of the fundamental bases of European relations with the wider world. From its pioneering beginnings the economic system spread to Brazil, which supplied Portugal, to the cotton colonies of the Caribbean, and eventually to the great cotton belt of Georgia and Alabama. This particular branch of Portuguese colonial ideology played a more direct part than any other in the development of the industrial revolution in eighteenth-century Britain.

The fourth stage of Portuguese progress towards the discovery of the Cape of Good Hope involved a fourth set of islands and a fourth type of colonial plantation economy. The tropical island of São Tomé, off the Niger delta, proved to have excellent soil and plentiful rainfall. The merchant community of Lisbon, and especially its Jewish economic pioneers, experimented with the introduction of sugar cane. Sugar required a much higher degree of organisation than the temperate or tropical crops hitherto introduced into the new Atlantic colonies. Cane had to be grown on a sufficiently large scale to justify investing in a crushing mill and boiling vats. It also required a labour force which could be compelled to work intensely hard during the harvest season to ensure that mature cane was crushed with a minimum of delay. Sugar seemed to be ideally suited to a slave economy and labour was therefore bought from the nearby kingdoms of Benin and Kongo. The industry so flourished that the island soon became too small, and sugar planting began to spread to other Portuguese colonies, notably in north-eastern Brazil.

The success of São Tomé as a pioneering sugar colony was watched with admiration by the European powers which aspired to emulate Portugal's path to colonial prosperity. The Dutch went so far as to conquer the island, and also part of Brazil. The English set up their own black slave sugar colonies in Barbados and the Caribbean in the seventeenth century, and then turned to Indian-worked sugar colonies in the nineteenth century. But the greatest imitator of them all was France, whose sugar island, later called Haiti, became the richest colony of all time. It was also the first one to rebel successfully against the racial pattern of servitude that Portugal had evolved, and create an independent black state out of a white-ruled colony.

The fifth stage of Portuguese colonial evolution was concerned not with planting but with mining. The mines which the explorers aspired to reach were the gold-mines of West Africa. From about 1400 the Akan mines of the coastal forest had begun to supplement gold production in the medieval fields controlled by the inland kingdoms of Ghana and Mali. Information about the trans-Saharan supply of African gold was widely known in the Christo-Islamic financial circles of the Mediterranean and certainly reached the merchants of Lisbon. In 1471 these merchants discovered a back route to the mines by way of the Gold Coast in West Africa. In order to buy gold, however, the Portuguese had to offer prices, and assortments of commodities, which were competitive with those of the experienced Saharan camel caravans. They found, to their surprise, that labour was in scarce supply in the mines and that slaves from their island plantations could fetch a good price. Thus the islands became entrepôts for the selling of slave miners. The business flourished and within a generation Portugal was buying 10 000 and more ounces of gold each year.

The lure of gold became a permanent feature of colonial ambition. The success of Portugal in West Africa became a driving force for all the European powers overseas. All the great gold-bearing regions of the world were explored and often plundered. Africa initially protected its mineral wealth with well-ordered states and effective armies. America was not so strong, and the peoples of the Caribbean died in the Spanish mines while the empires of Mexico and Peru were overthrown and ransacked. Only in the nineteenth century did Africa succumb to the conquering quest for gold by Europeans. Gold lust led to the great Anglo-Boer war of 1899 in which Britain, by now the strongest of the colonising nations, conquered South Africa.

The sixth and last stage of Portuguese expansion before the discovery of the Cape occurred on the western mainland of Central Africa. In Angola the Portuguese made their one and only attempt to create a colony on terra firma and among native inhabitants. The trump card which they played to gain access was religion. By offering to introduce more powerful gods and saints to control the supernatural, the Portuguese were able to build up political allies who protected their commercial interests and allowed a limited development of foreign settlement. Africa's first mainland colony was primarily concerned with the buying of slaves, however, and in less than a century it had been stalled by resistance and overrun by rebellion. The Portuguese therefore adopted Spanish military tactics and sent squads of *conquistadores* to fortify their trading posts. Justification was supplied by accompanying Jesuits who commended armed conversion and established slave-worked plantations to finance their churches and monasteries.

Portugal was initially less successful than its latter-day imitators in achieving territorial conquest. But the Jesuits and the soldiers did cross over to Brazil and began the harsh opening up of the eastern half of the South American continent. The colonists included some three million slaves brought over from Africa against their will. All the previous colonial experiments that Portugal had attempted in the fourteenth and fifteenth centuries – cereal-farming, wine-growing, cotton-picking, sugar-planting, gold-mining – were introduced into Brazil. Sugar in the seventeenth century and gold in the eighteenth proved the most lucrative. Tobacco was added to the cornucopia. By the end of the colonial period in the Americas, the formerly Portuguese United States of Brazil exceeded the size of the formerly British United States of America.

The six stages of Portuguese expansion into the Atlantic were followed in 1488 by the great expedition to the Cape of Good Hope. This was commanded by a common captain called Bartholomew Dias, for whose services the King of Portugal paid an annuity of 6000 reals. Nothing is known of the captain's experience in tropical waters, but in August 1487 he set out with two small exploring caravels, light enough to be beached, and a bulkier store ship of provisions and trade goods. He carried three stone crosses with which to claim territory on the African mainland. His objective, via Mina and Kongo, was the desert coast of Namibia, beyond the Angolan waters explored by Diogo Cão in the three previous seasons. Dias prepared reports on the available anchorages, and conducted a little trade with local Khoi cattle herders. The Portuguese were not welcome intruders, however, and after selling them some sheep and cows the Khoi prudently turned them away. In the skirmish which followed one Khoi was killed by Bartholomew Dias' crossbow. Relations between Europe and South Africa thus began as badly as they were to continue. At another bay Dias left his store ship with nine men instructed to investigate the commercial opportunities of the region. So unsuccessful were these trade emissaries that six of them had been killed before the main expedition returned to base. The store ship itself had to be fired for want of an adequate crew to sail it back to Lisbon.

After these unhappy encounters, very reminiscent of the hit-and-run exploits of Henry the Navigator's men on the desert coast of North Africa 50 years earlier, Dias sailed on towards the greener coast of the south. After many false promises in the deeply indented bays he gradually realised that the coast he was following had turned eastward. The enthusiasm generated by this discovery was slow to capture the imagination of his homesick crews as bay followed bay along the southernmost shore of Africa. No opening towards the north was encountered. Eventually, at Bushman's River, some 500 miles east of the Cape of Good Hope, Dias was persuaded to turn for home. He planted his first stone totem on 12 March 1488, and dedicated it to Saint Gregory. He had discovered no new wealth, no fertile land, and no hospitable islands, not even a source of slaves with which to recompense the entrepreneurial King of Portugal for his outlay of risk capital. Worse still he had not conclusively found the sea lane to Arabia and India, although the direction of the coast had become more promising.

On the homeward journey Bartholomew Dias stopped on Saint Philip's day, 6th June 1488, and apparently planted his second stone cross on the Cape of Good Hope. This was the most famous landmark of his voyage, though not actually the southernmost point of Africa. It was the rounding of this cape which eventually secured Dias his place in history. Dias did not enter Table Bay, site of the later city of Cape Town, but he did enter the Namibian bay later named Luderitz and mounted his third pillar of territorial assertion of Portuguese rights. He finally arrived back in Lisbon in December 1488 having covered 6000 leagues in 16 months.

The international repercussions of the Dias voyage were numerous. In 1491 a major colonising expedition was sent to the kingdom of Kongo, in Angola, which seemed a more promising African political and commercial partner than the sparse communities of coastal South Africa. In 1492 Columbus, no longer in Portuguese service, and armed with absurdly false data on the earth's circumference, sailed on behalf of Castile to find a western route to China, since Dias had failed to find an eastern one round the African coast. Not till 1497, nine years after the Dias voyage and five years after Columbus began to explore the Caribbean, did a new Portuguese king, Manuel I, manage to raise the resources, the men and the ships to attempt another merchant adventure in the far south without guarantee of profit. The expedition of Vasco da Gama, however, did complete the task begun by Bartholomew Dias and opened up the sea route to Asia. Dias himself was called back to royal service and appointed to open a gold-trading factory at Sofala in south-eastern Africa.

Dias had experience of the gold trade. In 1497 he had accompanied Vasco da Gama on the first leg of his journey down the African coast before turning into the Gulf of Guinea to deliver a cargo of trade cloth and merchant goods to the gold factory of Mina. In 1500 Dias was appointed to accompany the great fleet of Alvares Cabral to the Indian Ocean and set up a similar factory at Sofala. The highland gold of the Zimbabwe mines had recently switched from the old ports of southern Mozambique to reach the international market via the Zambezi route in central Mozambique. Manuel of Portugal hoped that Dias, with his little flotilla of four shallow-draft caravels, would be able to close off the traditional gold route via East Africa to the Muslim precious metal marts of the eastern Mediterranean and divert the Sofala gold round the Cape of Good Hope to Christian bankers and the western Mediterranean. Dias, however, failed to crown his career in such a fashion. After an unscheduled stop on the then unknown coast of Brazil, his boat was lost on the south Atlantic crossing. The trading fortress was indeed built five years later but Bartholomew Dias was remembered not as a great gold trader but as the first navigator along the coast of South Africa.

The discovery of the Cape of Good Hope was initially of little intrinsic interest. South Africa had few attractions to men seeking trade, minerals, slaves, vacant land and any other kind of entrepreneurial opportunity which would allow an escape from the barrenness of Portuguese provincial society. Few Portuguese visited the Cape, and then only in order to by-pass it and seek the wealthy sea lanes of Asia. Dias' son António and grandson Paulo Dias de Novais invested their capital and energy not in South Africa but in Angola in Central Africa. In 1571 they claimed the rights of Lord-Proprietor in Angola and four years later founded the city of Luanda on a shore that their ancestor had patrolled on his epic voyage. The Dias family failed, however, to secure their colony and in the 1590s the Habsburgs repossessed Angola for the united Iberian crown of Spain and Portugal. But despite this check, grandfather Dias had, when reaching the Cape, set eyes on the South Africa that was gradually to become the most powerful of all the foreign colonies of Africa. It was also, five centuries later, to be the one which attracted the largest number of Portuguese migrants.

In 1588, a century after Dias visited South Africa, the country had changed little. Black farming and cattle-herding were as prosperous as ever in the east while sheep-rearing and shell-fishing were important in the dryer areas of the west. Portuguese mariners were regularly shipwrecked on the coast and often hospitably received and given food, shelter, clothing and a safe-conduct along the trade paths to a Portuguese harbour in Mozambique. The first signs of the agricultural revolution which was to bring American maize to South Africa as a staple crop may have been noted, but it was not until the eighteenth century that the new farming, and favourable climatic conditions, led to a large demographic increase in the South African population.

By 1688 the seeds of colonial challenge to South Africa's independence had been sown. The Dutch haven at the Cape had begun to be swelled by Calvinist refugees from European persecution. Wheat and vine colonies, reminiscent of the Azores and Canaries, were set up in the fertile plains of Swellendam and Stellenbosch. Settlers already felt restive at the imperial control imposed on them by the metropolitan government of the Dutch West India company. Slavery was accepted as the normal means to acquire labour both in the artisan shops of the city and on the farms. White women were rare among the settlers and concubines of every race were readily accepted and acknowledged as they had been on the old colonial estates of the Portuguese islands. Indeed, the Cape was seen by the settlers as an 'island' and they tried to hedge themselves off from the mainstream of South Africa.

In 1788, 300 years after Dias, the Cape had become a frontier society very strongly linked to the rest of South Africa. The indigenous population of the western Cape had been either integrated into colonial society in as subservient caste, or driven out to the northern frontiers and labelled 'the people of the bush'. In the east settlers had adopted the cattle-ranching, and cattle-rustling, way of life of their black neighbours. Co-operation and conflict between them alternated according to the grazing and watering needs of the herds. Traders cast their eyes on the further horizon and dreamed of fortunes made hunting elephants for ivory. A large creole population of varied racial composition resembled the creole societies which has evolved in all the Portuguese island colonies and in Luanda. Instead of speaking a 'pidgin' Portuguese creole, the people of the Cape spoke a Dutch creole, later known as Afrikaans.

By 1888 South Africa had changed again and was on the brink of a social and economic revolution. Diamonds, gold and coal had been found and the agrarian societies, both black and white, were beginning to be mobilised for the industrial exploitation of their mineral wealth on behalf of investors in Europe. The upheaval was immense and led to the entrenchment of both a racial divide between black and white and a cultural divide between English-speakers and Dutch-speakers. The old Cape population with its mixed heritage, black and white, English and Dutch, was unable to provide a bridge when the demands of industrial profit outweighed the political benefits of reconciliation. The great Boer War and the ideology of racial segregation were the consequences.

Finally by 1988, at the time of the fifth centenary of the first European visit to the Cape, an embattled South Africa had been transformed into Africa's foremost industrial nation. The old black population had become totally overwhelmed by white power. Surplus people not needed for industrial production or capitalist agriculture were carried off to encampments on the remote and dry fringes of the country. The remainder were segregated into urbanised black ghettos with limited economic rights and no political voice. Meanwhile the white population grew in size and prosperity in the fertile heartlands. Its latest recruits were Portuguese immigrants. Like their predecessors, the Atlantic migrants of the fourteenth and fifteenth centuries, they were seeking an alternative to penury in Europe's poorest yet most innovative colonising nation.

2 Colonisers and the African Iron Age

This chapter derives from a Cambridge conference on Rome and the British Iron Age and was designed to explore possible parallels between Portuguese colonisation and the Roman colonisation of an earlier age. It challenged the concept of colonisation as a re-peopling of cleared land and emphasised the importance of the creolisation of indigenous peoples who adapted themselves to new linguistic, religious and material influences which brought Latin culture to colonial enclaves in Africa. Slight revision and abbreviation have modified the version originally published by Barry C. Burnham and Helen B. Johnson in Invasion and Response: the Case of Roman Britain *(British Archaeological Reports, Oxford, 1979).*

When looked at from a distance, one might assume that the impact of Rome on Iron Age Britain was so different from the impact of Portugal on Iron Age Africa as to make comparison impossible. The Romans, according to received wisdom, rolled back the Celts, dug a few ditches to hold them at bay, and brought on the Roman steamroller. The invasion – so it seemed – brought in a nicely synthesised, homogenised, integrated, instant package of coins, villas, roads, settlers, Latin, literacy, gods, laws, political orators and soldiers, all neatly labelled 43 AD. It is therefore stimulating to discover that this stereotype is in the course of fundamental revision and that the interest is now focusing on questions of continuity and change in Roman colonial society.

Some years ago a theory comparable with this caricaturised version of Romanisation in Britain flourished also in connection with the Arab conquest of the North African coast in 642 AD. The theory was a simple one. The Berbers, the Byzantines, the Vandals, the Greeks and everyone else in North Africa were rolled back into Morocco and then North Africa was completely re-seeded with a new Arabic population of good faithful Muslims. This hardy thesis of Arab conquest has gradually been replaced by a much slower and more varied concept of cultural Arabisation. It took years to entrench an 'Allah' who suited the eclectic spiritual needs of the varied cultural strands of North Africa. It took North Africans

12

centuries to learn Arabic, and pass for Arabs, preferably with well-constructed pedigrees. The process of Arabisation began in army camps, spread slowly to the towns, and more slowly still to the cultivators and the nomadic pastoralists. In the end, however, after perhaps 400 years, much of North Africa had absorbed Arabic language, law, custom, culture, art, architecture, faith, dress and cuisine.

With this picture of continuity and change in mind, what was the consequence of 400 years of Portuguese familiarity with the Atlantic seaboard of Africa? At first sight the resilience and adaptability of Atlantic Africa's Iron Age societies might appear to be in stark contrast with the comprehensive Romanisation of Iron Age Britain or Arabisation of Iron Age North Africa. But the contrast between an effective resistance of Atlantic Africa to cultural, colonial and economic transformation and the apparent inert subservience of some parts of Britain in the face of the Roman legions may not form a wholly valid antithesis. Was not continuity more significant than change in the process whereby Iron Age Britain absorbed the Romans? Despite violent hiccoughs, such as the revolt of Boudicca, was not change more gradual and unevenly distributed than hitherto supposed? The matter might be elucidated by a few specific questions which a historian of Africa would like to ask about the history of Roman Britain. Are the answers to the questions about invasion and response in colonial Britain so different from those found in colonial Africa?

To what extent was Roman colonisation an all-male affair and how deep was its cultural impact on domestic life? Portuguese colonisation involved the establishment down the African coast of Portuguese trading fairs which were almost exclusively staffed by men. The effects of this lack of any significant migration of women were obvious. In the year 1683 a venerable old warrior, António de Cadornega, wrote sentimentally about Angola as the country where one's sons were swarthy, grandsons were dusky, great grandsons were completely black and all was darkness.[1] The immigrants were few in number compared with the host populations, only a few hundred a year even in areas of maximum impact. As a result family life and family culture were African rather than European despite a high level of racial consciousness. Although racial distinction had made the differentiation between free and slave easy to determine, black consorts and their children could nonetheless aspire to high levels of responsibility and accumulate significant commercial wealth. The language of the colonial compound was often African rather than Portuguese and the mother-tongue outweighed the father-tongue in most social and business transactions, though not always in legal, ecclesiastical and diplomatic affairs. Are similar questions asked about family life in Roman Britain?

Where did the immigrant military and civilian population of Roman Britain originate? In Africa the first Portuguese merchants, soldiers and settlers came from the metropolis. Visions of wealth, of land, conceivably of freedom, were dangled before them. One striking episode concerns the Angolan silver rush of the 1580s when, after the discovery of the Peruvian mines of Potosi by the Spaniards, Portuguese cosmologists began predicting the presence of rich veins of silver in the same latitude in Africa. Adventurers from all walks of life, led by the grandson of Bartholemeu Dias, sailed for Angola, where they spent 30 years tenaciously inching their way up the Kwanza river in an endeavour to capture the wholly mythical mountains of silver which featured in the report of an early Jesuit explorer.[2] But not all colonisers came from Lisbon any more than all colonisers in Britain came from Rome.

Many Portuguese who went to Africa came from other Portuguese colonies. The overcrowded and impoverished Atlantic islands of Madeira, the Azores and Cape Verde were a permanent source of colonists. Brazilians featured large in colonising tropical West Africa. Beyond the Cape of Good Hope Portuguese colonial personnel were usually recruited from the Christianised communities in Portuguese India. Voluntary migrants were not always the mainstay of the colonial presence. Uncomfortable minorities were sometimes harshly exiled from Europe to the colonies. Jewish sugar planters were taken to the uninhabited off-shore island of São Tomé and supplied with black wives and slaves in a rare example of economically profitable transportation. On the African mainland gipsies regularly featured among the men enlisted in the colonial garrisons. An even greater category of colonists, and one that was extensively used from the 1490s until the 1930s, consisted of convicts. A large part of the Portuguese presence in Africa consisted of men, and very occasionally women, who were banished for fixed or indefinite periods of African servitude. The common crimes for which citizens of the empire were sentenced to transportation were murder, rape, theft, riotous assembly and political dissidence.[3] Did Rome send convicts to Albion after 43 AD?

One big question is why should significant numbers of people have been sent to remote outposts of empire? Historians of Roman colonies seem to be unusually concerned with the protecting of frontier lines. Lines on maps seem to take on an almost mesmerising importance: wall lines, river lines, watershed lines, foothill lines, ditch lines, enclosure lines. In Africa such precise frontiers did not normally exist. Frontiers were fluctuating zones of economic activity, fluid areas of influence beyond the trade beach, the river harbour, the slave baracoon or the wholesaler's fortified factory. Some frontier zones were fixed by mineral resources or exploitable land but most were mobile, the areas of foraging and hunting economies, the ivory grounds, the slaving regions, the tax fiefs which depended on variable powers of conscription, coercion and collection. Were Roman imperial frontiers really as entrenched as they appear to have been?

Four minerals greatly attracted the Portuguese in Africa: salt, iron, copper and gold. Similar mining opportunities presumably enticed Romans to Britain.

Salt-drying was an important industry in Portugal. The charter which was drawn up in 1571 for a lord-proprietor who was granted colonising rights in Angola assumed that his first task would be to take command of the coastal salt-pans and inland salt-mines. By levying an impost on all salt-trading he expected to cover the costs of the venture. With some effort, and thanks to the introduction of matchlock muskets, the Portuguese did succeed in capturing one coastal salt-pan. The event was still recorded in African folk memory 400 years later: the white men had come in ships with wings which shone in the sun like knives and had spat fire.[4] That was the limit of Portuguese success. The great Kisama salt-mines, 40 miles inland, eluded all Portuguese attempts to conquer them for the next 300 years. The invincibility of the local magnates was ruefully reported in a comprehensive economic survey published in 1846.[5]

Elsewhere in Africa the failure of the Portuguese to capture any mines or any zones of mineral wealth was virtually complete. Efforts were made to establish an iron smelting industry by the importation of Basque iron masters. The cost of the skills, and the mortality of the labour, rapidly undermined the experiment. The Portuguese remained dependent either on imported iron or on iron produced by numerous local smiths. In West Central Africa smelting was undertaken in particularly simple pit furnaces, without high chimneys, and yet Portuguese technology was unable to get a grip and transform the industry. Copper-mining was important in two zones on the fringe of both the Eastern and the Western Portuguese spheres in Central Africa. In the East copper ingots 'shaped like windmills' were regularly bought and prized, but in the West the Portuguese had little success even as traders. It was the Dutch who gained an entrée into the copper trade and began carrying small quantities back to Europe.

Gold was sufficiently important in Africa to stimulate especial Portuguese commercial efforts. Extensive mining both in the West African and in the South-East African gold-bearing zones predated Portuguese expansion by four or five centuries. All Portuguese efforts either to conquer the old mines or to discover new ones came to nought. Even entering into commercial relations with existing miners proved more difficult than might have been expected. Portugal had no productive capacity with an obvious edge over their competitors. In West Africa international caravan trade to the Muslim half of the Mediterranean could only be broken into with Muslim-style textiles and clothing suited to the established fashions and tastes of the market. Portugal had the advantage of an efficient maritime carrying system, but could only sell its own wares when they were carefully made up into mixed lots which included the more attractive North African, and later Indian, goods. Despite difficulties, the Portuguese probably succeeded in capturing about half of the gold production of the West African fields and in stimulating increased production by the Akan mine masters. The effect of this was to heighten the demand for mine labour. At an early date Christian Portugal, which had started buying slaves in Africa 'for the good of their souls', found themselves compelled to sell the redeemed men to heathen pit owners as the most profitable way of capturing a share in the gold market.[6]

In south-east Africa Portugal used more militant methods to capture the gold trade. State-registered pirates such as Vasco da Gama disrupted the richer ports with cannon fire, but did not disrupt the flow of gold to India as comprehensively as they should have liked. Two generations later, land expeditions attacked the smaller Muslim trading towns up the Zambezi river, but again with limited effect. The gold-bearing plateau remained firmly under African government. The captains of the out-lying Portuguese trading posts were absorbed into the traditional political structure by being officially given a title as one of the great wives-of-state of the Mutapa emperor. Small pockets of soldier-traders dependent on the power of local kings were a far cry from an all-conquering colonial army.[7]

Iron Age Africa repelled almost all attempts at land acquisition by alien colonists. In this Africa was in striking contrast to underpopulated, pre-Iron Age America. Only in three areas did any colonisation of settlement occur. One was the Cape of Good Hope where a Late Stone Age pastoral population was unable to resist the encroachment of Dutch colonists who needed a base from which to penetrate the Portuguese seaborne empire. Dutch stock-men took over a share of the pastoralist economy and created a bridgehead for nineteenth-century expansion. The second area of colonisation was the already mentioned off-shore islands. Particu-larly important were the Cape Verde Islands. These were colonised with black slave cotton and indigo planters and with African spin-ning and weaving artisans. Colonial entrepreneurs thereby recreated an African industry whose profits could be easily extracted and then invested in mainland trading ventures. The third area of colonisa-tion was Angola, the weak underbelly of Central Africa. Here, however, land-colonising achievements were slight. The largest slave holdings in early centuries were probably those of the religious houses. A few villas, or *quintas*, were created in the coastal valleys, but they were never sufficiently productive to feed the small city popu-lation of Luanda, or the hundred-odd sailing vessels which regularly plied between Africa and Brazil. The alienation of productive land, or the opening of new land, was not a feature of early colonisation in Africa.

One of the more important mobile frontiers in Africa was the ivory frontier. Roman over-kill had wiped the elephant out in North Africa, and East African ivory was firmly committed to the almost insatiable Indian market. Atlantic Africa provided an almost virgin field and the Portuguese crown imposed a royal monopoly on the traffic wherever it had the power to enforce it. Ivory hunting was never a direct colonial endeavour, but another of the economic sectors which responded to indirect commercial stimulus. Coastal elephant herds were depleted in the seventeenth century, and by the nineteenth century the elephant was becoming rare in West Africa. Rising world prices, however, led to a dramatic extension of the trade lines on the Central African frontier. The great ivory hunting societies from the Atlantic side of Africa eventually met up with ivory traders who sold to Zanzibar and the east coast. Each set of routes to the interior covered over 1000 land miles.[8]

Slaves were always more important than ivory in the mobile zones of frontier exploitation that were opened up by ocean navigation in the Atlantic. From the 1440s the buying of slaves was a domi-nant economic activity on the whole Atlantic coast. The last phase of involuntary sea-borne labour movement was not terminated by the Portuguese until the great São Tomé cocoa-planting scandal of 1908. In Atlantic Africa, three distinct fields of slaving evolved, each with its own methods of operation and pattern of local political response. These three were West Africa, maritime Central Africa, and inland Central Africa.

In West Africa slavery predated the Portuguese. The great salt-mines of the Sahara and the gold-mines of the upper Niger were slave-operated. In agriculture there were natural pressures towards the use of slave labour since manpower was scarce and land was not. Political and material wealth depended on man-ownership rather than on land-ownership. There were early external markets for the trans-Saharan export of captives. The advent of Portugal created one more outlet for the sale of slaves, and a new transport network for their transportation. Very rapidly, however, the scale of European buying increased far beyond previous bounds. New African political powers emerged to manage foreign relations, maximise the profits from slave trading, and minimise the risk of European invasion or direct slave recruitment. Inter-European competition for slaves to man the mines and plantations of the Americas enabled the stronger and more astute African front-line kingdoms to prosper at the expense of the West African middle belt, which became a depressed raiding ground.[9]

The maritime slave zone of Central Africa was quite different. In Angola no labour market existed and slaves were obtained by direct colonial initiative. The process went through four stages. In the first, gifts were exchanged between hosts and guests. Foreigners were welcomed for their fresh ideas and for the prestige which they lent to a local court. In exchange for material offerings which enriched and varied the material culture of the court, the tax and tribute systems were used to obtain slaves among the less-privileged members of society: prisoners of war, convicts, aliens, clients, witches, and other lame ducks and black sheep in the clan families. In a second more militant stage, colonial armies penetrated the fringes of the great kingdoms and army captains were set up as local colonial chieftains. Each was given a conquered princeling to furnish his wants. Traditional tribute of food, salt, cloth and shells to land chiefs and shrine guardians was perverted into slave tribute to the colonial captains. From the distortion of tribute, it was but a small step to direct exaction, and the incipient colonial army began to reward itself by the deliberate capture and sale of indiscriminate victims. Finally in a fourth stage, warrior bands of black mercenary allies were recruited to do the slave-catching and bear the risks of war. This indirect raiding by subject armies proved the most extensive, disruptive, enduring, and profitable means of filling the slave ships.[10]

The interior of Central Africa had a third system of slave recruitment which differed both from the commercial one in West Africa, and from the military one in Angola. Here the slave frontier was diplomatic. The traders in this zone were escapees from the convict armies of the small Portuguese coastal colony, they were the brown children of the great colonial families, they were the shoeless retainers of the white trading houses. For their safety, welfare, maintenance, food-supplies, ferry services, carriers, they were dependent on friendly relations with interior kingdoms. They had to buy goodwill with material imports of textiles, tobacco and alcohol. A whole new breed of small broker kingdoms grew up to service the needs of the long-distance slave caravans. They replaced the old kingdoms grounded on more legitimate concepts of land-ownership, of ancestor veneration and of protection for a kin-based social order. Lusitanianisation did not go deep among the broker-kingdoms, but the indirect sphere of influence had a significant legacy: it allowed a much later generation of Portuguese to claim a large swathe of the continent during the Victorian partition of Africa.

What then were the real consequences of the Portuguese impact on later Iron Age Africa? The first one of note was probably in agriculture. Although no important colonial plantations were established, new plants were introduced into the domestic agrarian economies. Many of the cereal-growing regions adopted either the flint maizes of dry Mexico or the flour maizes of wet Brazil to replace the millets and sorghums which had evolved over 4000 years from local grasses. The new cereal had higher yields, greater climatic adaptability, and above all a seed-casing which made it less vulnerable to bird depredation. In the root-growing areas, where indigenous yams had been domesticated and ennobled, new cassava roots were introduced. They had better yields, tolerated poorer soils and contained toxins in the raw state which made them poisonous to rodent predators. Cassava was also an excellent war-time crop. It did not need to be harvested at any particular season, but could be left in the ground for months while the owner was away campaigning or his fields were overrun by enemies. The penetration of new crops was sometimes rapid, but more often it probably percolated slowly along trade routes, used initially to feed caravans and slave columns. Agricultural conservism was particularly noted in the brewing industry, where the traditional cereals, including finger millet, continued to be chosen for the best beer. A number of other tropical crops, and also weeds, invaded Africa once the world sea-lanes had been opened.

World travel also opened the way for the wider dissemination of diseases. Africa suffered from its full quota of debilitating and mortal diseases – yellow fever, malaria, smallpox, sleeping-sickness, measles, venereal diseases, elephantiasis, river-blindness – but not enough is yet known about their origin and spread. The Portuguese un-doubtedly brought unfamiliar diseases for which there was no local immunity, and caught local diseases to which they had no antidote. Malaria and dysentery were the known big killers of settler and soldier, but the army surgeon and mission apothecary had little to offer in the way of prophylaxis or cure. The Portuguese in Africa turned increasingly to African forms of medical assistance. Colon-ists sometimes travelled far to visit well-known shrine priests who were competent herbalists. They thereby caused anguish to the outraged priests and missionaries of their own nominal Christian persuasion.

Religious conversion operated both ways. While Portuguese fron-tiersmen readily accepted the 'heathen' practices of the communities in which they lived, many African societies adopted the new Chris-tian religion brought in by colonial priests and by Spanish and Italian missionaries. In the more centralised kingdoms Christianity became an important new adjunct of royalty. The Kongo monarchs acquired such a broad dependence on imported religious practices and para-phernalia that they constantly endangered their traditional spiritual base of national support. The capital city built several stone churches staffed by both foreign and indigenous clergy. Two hundred years after the first court conversions, a new missionary fervour broke out and spread for the first time, to the rural areas where it caused extensive disruption to village life. New saints emerged from the social and political upheavals; one of them, a Kongo Joan of Arc called Beatrice, became the rallying point for an eighteenth-century national revival.

Colonists who came to Africa not only brought new religious and ideological influences. They also introduced new forms of human self-indulgence. The pattern of leisure in the Portuguese sphere was not modified by the introduction of Roman-style sauna baths, but through the rapid and extensive spread of tobacco smoking. At first, the tobacco consisted of thick ropes of Brazilian tobacco coated with a preserving layer of molasses. This commodity became a prime source of Portuguese purchasing power. Later tobacco became a locally-grown crop and spread to the furthest parts of the interior. An even more important trade item than tobacco was foreign alcohol. Rum, also from Brazil, became a key commercial commodity. It featured in all gifts associated with diplomatic transactions. Brandy, rum and European wines became the usual payment for tolls on country roads, at river crossings and on state boundaries. In addition to gifts and payments, alcoholic bribes became necessary as a means of improving communication and lubricating social intercourse. Although intoxicants were not the only commodities which the Portuguese introduced to Africa, any more than wine was Rome's sole gift to Britain, they nevertheless featured large in trade over a 500 year period. The twentieth-century per capita imports of alcohol into Angola were about 25 times higher than those of British colonies in modern Africa.[11]

Trading in such bulky items as bottled or casked beverages presented problems of transportation in which one might expect the colonial technology to provide innovative solutions. Nothing of the sort happened. The Portuguese in Africa abandoned the wheel overnight and adopted the head porter of local caravan practice. River navigation had already developed craft of the optimum size and left no scope for improvement. Pack animals were prone to disease, though a few riding oxen were used in the dry south, and some experimental camels survived in a wild state though without ever contributing their economic worth. In other technological spheres the Portuguese also adapted to local practice. Their grain was pounded in mortars and an ambitious programme of windmill construction was never ever begun. The result of all this regression was that early colonial Africa was intensely labour-consuming in all fields of production and transportation. The gravest source of conflict between the colonies and their neighbours was the constant demand for hired or conscripted carriers to head-load bales of textiles and barrels of rum to the fairs on the frontier. Where porters could not be obtained slaves had to be used, and the military recovery of refugee slaves was a further source of strain, conflict and constant irritation between Lusitanianised and un-Lusitanianised communities.

Since conflict was so important in relations between the Portuguese and Africa, one might have expected a fast development in weapon technology. In fact change was slow. Cannon mounted on ships and a few coastal forts were an early feature of defence but could not be used for campaigning. Early handguns had a powerful psychological effect on an unaccustomed enemy, but were slow and cumbersome to use. It took 15 minutes to clean a musket and reload, during which time an African archer might discharge several hundred arrows. Mercenary bowmen were preferred in early colonial warfare. A further problem was that guns relied on imported powder and shot, and the supply from Lisbon was slow and unreliable. The first campaign in which guns played a decisive role occurred 100 years after the Portuguese landing in Central Africa. It was 100 years after that before significant quantities of firearms began to find their way into African hands. Once they did, however, their availability created a market for gunpowder which could never be locally met. The Portuguese were constantly divided as to whether the profits to be made from selling guns and powder were sufficient to outweigh the disadvantage of arming local kingdoms which could at any moment turn hostile. The usual solution was for colonial government to ban the sale of weapons and for colonial merchants to ignore the ban.

One might expect a country like Portugal, with a strong tradition of city dwelling, to introduce urbanisation into Africa. It did not do so. In West Africa medieval urbanisation was an important phenomenon in a wide range of different societies and environments, none of them in any way connected with the Portuguese. In Central Africa even the royal towns were small and no significant growth occurred. Despite this general absence of merchant towns, institutions for urbanisation were introduced into Angola, and two municipalities were set up there. Their oligarchic structures were complex, but there was always a chronic shortage of qualified oligarchs eligible for election to their minute councils. Luanda alone eventually developed into a city – the only one on the whole Atlantic coast according to Mary Kingsley, who eulogised over it more than three centuries after its ceremonial founding in 1575.

If towns and technology were not the hallmark of colonisation, one might at least expect such a supremely commercial nation as Portugal to make its impact on finance. Nothing of the sort happened. In Africa coinage was abandoned. Gold continued to be measured by weight or, in small transactions, poured onto the thumbnail in dust form. Local systems of weights and measures were used, modified, extended and perverted by false units and double values, but no gold was ever coined. Other currencies were also absorbed into colonial usage. Salt bars, sometimes encased in wicker, occasionally shaped in hexagons, served as measures of value and media of exchange in Angola. The old shell tribute system of Kongo was modified so that shells came to serve the purpose of coins. In Luanda, that incipient city, there were fierce municipal debates about the advantages and disadvantages of introducing a copper coinage. For many years local squares of raffia textile, sometimes stamped by government with an official seal, served as currency. The major need for money was to pay the military garrison and the escort forces which accompanied caravans and defended the earthen forts that were set up at a few strategic route points. These soldiers were paid spasmodically in textiles which they could then use to become private traders. Speculative commercial profits provided a better revenue to the army than uncertain salary entitlements.

The conclusion one must draw from this African sketch is that the Portuguese had no great cultural impact on Iron Age Africa which might compare with the Arabisation of North Africa or the Romanisation of Britain. And yet in some respects the Portuguese impact was almost immeasurable in its scope. In Angola a miserable, tiny, semi-literate, half-caste crew of sickly convicts managed – in little over 100 years – to extract one *million* black slaves. The explanation of how they did it lies in three broad areas. Firstly they had behind them the rising economic power of Brazil with its seventeenth-century plantations and its eighteenth-century mines and backed by a prosperous set of colonial shipping and banking institutions. There was no need to develop Africa – not even enough to feed the slave ships – when all services could be provided from Brazil. That way the profits were tightly retained in an American colony without danger of leakage into the economies of indigenous neighbours. Secondly Portugal invested enough force in Africa to maintain unequal terms of trade, and to keep most rivals out from at least their southern slaving zones. Whereas later European slavers put most of their investment into material items of trade, the Portuguese persistently invested more heavily in armed force and thereby conquered the only pre-modern colonial territory, albeit a very small one, in the whole of tropical Africa. Thirdly Portugal undermined, and eventually destroyed, the legitimate old agricultural kingdoms of West Central Africa. In their place arose new broker kingdoms of warrior-traders armed with new imported weapons and maintaining treaty relations with Portugal. These warrior kingdoms depended on the slave trade for their merchandise and their firearms, and in exchange gave extraterritorial rights to representatives of the Luanda trading houses. The slave fairs were the cutting edge of Europe's penetration into Africa, but they showed little evidence of European culture, language, literature, religion, technology, currency or any other branch of that ephemeral concept called civilisation.

3 The *Regimento da Mina*

Attempts by Portugal to control the supply of gold mined on the West African Gold Coast were regulated by detailed sets of royal instructions. One of these was the Regimento *of 1529 which outlined the methods used to manipulate the price paid for gold. The fortress of Mina, built in 1481 and stoutly defended until the Dutch captured it in 1637, was the key trading factory in which gold was bought in exchange for textiles, ornamental jewellery and brassware. The Portuguese also sold slave labourers to the Akan gold merchants and mine owners. It is thought possible that Christopher Columbus may have visited Mina while in Portuguese service and before he set out to explore the gold-mining opportunities of the Caribbean on behalf of Castile. This article first appeared in the* Transactions of the Historical Society of Ghana *(Vol. 11, 1971).*

In 1529 the Portuguese had been trading at Elmina for 58 years. They had become an established part of the economic structure of West Africa. This article proposes to examine briefly the commercial activities of the Portuguese and the organisation of their trade. The information is derived from the *Regimento da Mina*, a 90-page handbook drawn up in 1529 by the King of Portugal. A copy of the *Regimento* can be seen in the Furley Collection at the Balme Library in Legon.[1] It gives detailed instructions about trading procedure to the captain and factor of the City of São Jorge da Mina, later known as Elmina Castle. Three years later a second section was added to the *Regimento* concerning the trade between Mina and the Island of São Tomé in the Gulf of Guinea. Since the document is in Portuguese it is hoped that the details given here will be of special interest to English-speaking historians of Ghana wishing to gain a clearer picture of the country's trade in the early sixteenth century.

In 1529 Mina was inhabited by 56 Portuguese citizens each appointed by the crown and each receiving a royal salary. The ruler of this small fortress-city was the captain, a man of substantial importance who received an annual salary of 800 *milreis*[2] and was attended by 10 personal servants. The captain's main strength derived from his wide judicial powers; he could try all civil and criminal cases in both Mina and Axim, whether they involved Portuguese or Africans. There was no appeal from his decisions except where a sentence of death, or the cutting off of a hand, was passed on a senior official or chief; such cases were to be sent to the king in Portugal for confirmation. A secret provision also required confirmation of severe sentences passed on servants of the royal household who went out to Mina.

The second most important person in the castle was the factor whose task was the management of the warehouse. He had four personal employees to help with the heavy work and two highly-paid clerks to keep the books and records. Next in seniority to the factor was the surgeon who cared for the health of the garrison. He was assisted by a barber, who was also responsible for bleeding patients, a male nurse and an apothecary who dispensed medicines which were both imported from Portugal and obtained from the herbalists in the village. Health was a constant preoccupation of the Portuguese at Mina. Mortality from malaria was high and the regulations laid down in detail the line of succession in the event of one or more officers' dying. The citizens also greatly feared the plague which might be brought in by ship. Because of the unhealthy conditions a tour of duty in Mina was limited to two years.

Next to the problem of medical survival was the problem of military survival. The defence of the castle was the joint responsibility of all the citizens, but especially of the two artillery men and the 13 salaried residents. These residents had no special duties to perform but were allowed to live in Mina and to draw their salary on condition that they were equipped with helmets, lances, swords and breastplates. The captain was to maintain a supply of guns, crossbows and shields for issue in times of crisis. During a siege he was even permitted to draw money from gold reserves in the castle coffers to pay the costs of defence. From 1529 it became customary for the persons awarded the privilege of two years residence at Mina to be servants of the royal household.

One of the problems of Mina was the supply of food. The superintendent of provisions was a senior castle official who kept all food under lock and key. The staple of the Portuguese diet was bread. Every month the superintendent entrusted a supply of flour to the master baker, who employed four Portuguese women to knead and bake the bread. These women received a regular salary and were assisted by four other Portuguese women who received their keep but no pay unless a vacancy occurred in one of the four salaried positions. When the bread was baked four rolls were issued daily to each castle resident. Each one also received a daily flagon of wine and once a month was issued with a pot of olive oil, two pots of vinegar and a pot of honey. The catering department was allowed to employ up to six slave women, who could also be allocated to other domestic chores.[3] The main nutrition problem was the supply of meat. Contact with the native population of Mina was restricted and the Portuguese were forbidden to go out in search of chickens to buy, but had to wait for them to be brought to the castle. Since this supply was very uncertain, the *Regimento* gave permission for livestock to be imported from São Tomé. Only sufficient meat to feed the inhabitants of the castle was to be brought, however, and none was to be sold to the village people. Each animal had to be killed and shared out in the presence of the governor.

The spiritual life of the colony was taken care of by a vicar and three chaplains. These priests also attempted the conversion of the people of Elmina village. They were to organise a school to teach the village boys to read and write so that they might serve in the church choir. To encourage conversions the king offered two golden *junto*[4] to the priests for every boy, up to a total of 15 a year, whom they trained as choir boys. The captain would also receive two *juntos* for each boy and one *junto* for each adult converted to Christianity.

The only reason for the existence of this hand-picked Portuguese colony was of course the gold trade. The mining of gold in the Akan forest area certainly began before the sea route to Europe was pioneered. The date at which mining started is not yet known but by the early fifteenth century there appears to have been an established trading system carrying gold overland to North Africa for the European markets. The southern section of this overland route was in the hands of the Wangara, a Muslim trading community from the Upper Niger area. Their routes ran from the Mina coast through the gold-bearing region to Bicu (Bew, Begho) on the northern edge of the forest, and then over the savanna to Jenne on the Niger. From there the gold was taken by canoe to Timbuktu, the terminal of the Sahara caravans.

In 1471 the Portuguese reached the Mina coast by sea and linked their maritime trade network to the overland trade network of the Wangara. In order to participate in the gold trade the Portuguese had to find trade goods which would induce the gold producers to sell gold dust to them at Mina rather than send it to Jenne for the North African trade. Their attempt to capture part of the trade proved so successful that by 1529, when the *Regimento* was drawn up, they controlled a well-established economic system on the Guinea coast.

The most important type of trade conducted by the Portuguese was the sale of cloth and clothing. The main items were narrow strips of coloured cotton cloth called *lambeis*, and Moroccan burnouses called *algeravias*. The fashion in cotton materials had been set on the coast by the earlier Wangara traders and the Portuguese had to meet the existing demand. The main task of the Mina factor was to look after the stocks of cloth and clothing. On arrival the cloth was to be carefully checked. Any which was damaged was to be sent straight back to Portugal together with any surplus material that was not included on the invoice. The king's main concern was to prevent any trade goods becoming available for private trading by the citizens of Mina. The price of cloth was fixed in Lisbon and although the factor was encouraged to seek 20 per cent more than the stated price, he was never allowed to sell below it. The stocks were to be checked every four months and if any cloth was damaged in storage an inquiry was to be held and a fine imposed on the factor if he had been negligent. The factors frequently complained of lack of space for storing and exhibiting their wares. Damage was caused by feet when Africans had to climb over the stocks in order to see what was available.[5] Any stained, torn or unstitched clothing which could not fetch the required price was to be sent back to Lisbon rather than be sold at a discount, which would open the way to private agreements between traders and the factor.

The second important aspect of the Mina trade in 1529 was the exchange of slaves for gold. Ever since the Portuguese first arrived on the Gold Coast they had been selling slaves to the gold-producers. In 1479 Eustache de la Fosse bought slaves on the Grain Coast for sale at Shama.[6] It is possible, although as yet there is no evidence for it, that when the Portuguese arrived they did not establish a new coastal trading system but merely took over an existing one. The Wangara at Mina may already have been buying goods, including slaves, brought by canoe from other parts of the coast.

By 1529 the supply of slaves to Mina was a large, well-organised business. The trade was arranged through the island of São Tomé. The factor of Mina sent requisitions to the factor of São Tomé for the number of slaves needed. A special ship was employed to ply between the island and the city, normally doing about one voyage every six weeks.[7] The *Regimento* frequently stresses that only slaves of the very best quality should be sent to Mina. Slaves who were too young, old or weak were not acceptable to the gold merchants.

Detailed records had to be kept of the number of slaves sent and sworn statements drawn up in the case of slaves who were rejected as unfit. The castle cleaners were supposed to be recruited only from among women rejected by the traders. The system did not work quite as designed, however, since before beginning to trade the citizens of Mina adopted the finest women slaves as temporary wives.[8]

In 1529 the São Tomé slave trade was organised by a contractor or tax farmer called Jorge Erbet.[9] The São Tomé ships bought slaves on the adjacent mainland from the Niger Delta to south of the Congo Estuary. The price paid for slaves was theoretically limited to a maximum of 40–50 *manillas*. The crews of the slave ships were paid in slaves at the rate of 900 *reis* per month; in addition they received one slave per trip, valued at about four *milreis*, to meet the cost of their subsistence. When the slaves were landed at São Tomé they were carefully branded on the right arm with the Guinea stamp to prevent their being exchanged for inferior slaves from the island. One out of three of these slaves was to be selected for the crown. These were to be the best slaves and were to be sent as soon as possible to Mina for the gold trade. The contractor was obliged to supply up to 500 slaves a year free of charge in this manner. If the Mina factor required more than 500 slaves in any year they were to be bought by the crown from the contractor at rates determined before a magistrate. When the best slaves had been selected for Mina the second-grade slaves were to be sent to Portugal, and only the poorest ones were to be sold locally to the São Tomé sugar planters to pay the costs of the factory.

The third item of trade which was frequently stressed by the *Regimento* was the trade in beads and shells. The most important of these, referred to as *coris* and *contas pardas*, came from the coast of Benin. They were bought by slave traders and taken to São Tomé, where the factor counted and weighed them for dispatch in sealed boxes to Mina. The nature of these beads is as yet unclear. *Contas pardas* would seem to mean literally brown rosary beads, which may have been made of bauxite. Pacheco Pereira said that the *coris* were blue shells with red stripes in them.[10] They may, however, have been the blue beads which were later called *akori* beads or *aggrey* beads. This type of trade was also supplied with shells from Portugal but the *Regimento* does not make it clear whether these were cowrie shells or larger, more specifically ornamental shells.

Another item of trade at Mina was wine. The *Regimento* ordered the factor to appoint a reliable wine seller. Since the officers and residents of the castle received a free daily allowance of wine it is possible that the wine was sold outside the castle, presumably in return for gold. Wine was one of the major products of Portugal and was certainly used extensively for the purchase of slaves in Angola so that it would not be altogether surprising if it were used in the Mina trade also.

It is a matter of some disappointment that the *Regimento* does not give more details of the metal wares which were brought from Europe for the West African trade. Ayres Botelho's account of the Axim trade in 1508 gives a list of bowls, chamber pots, kettles and above all brass manillas then in use in addition to clothes, cloth strips and blankets.[11] It seems unlikely that the trade in metal goods should have shrunk or been superceded, but the *Regimento* makes no specific mention of these items and merely enjoins the factor to order the goods he is likely to require in plenty of time so that trade will not be held up by shortages.

Although the *Regimento* says less than one would like about the goods brought to the Gold Coast, it says a great deal about gold and the manner of buying it. When the traders arrived on the coast from the interior they were to be invited to the castle and given VIP treatment. While entertaining them the governor was to enquire discreetly about the source of their gold, the means of production used, the transport system, the quantities of gold currently being mined, the identity of those controlling mines, and the particular needs of the country which Portuguese traders might satisfy.[12] When a friendly relationship had been established, trading could begin.

In a recent issue of these *Transactions*, Albert Ott described the Akan attitude to the weighing of gold.[13] He said that bargaining and negotiation was more important than an exact calculation of weight. Each trader only knew what his own weights were worth and in his transactions had to rely on his trading ability rather than on a precise scale of values. The Portuguese apparently operated in a similar manner. Although they possessed precise scales and weights, the *Regimento* specifically instructed factors to use their scales in the manner which gave the greatest increase in weight without its being remarked by the traders or causing them to take offence. The scales were to be of silver and they and the weights were to be made and stamped with the Guinea stamp in the Lisbon assay office. The unit of measurement was to be the *pezo* of 132 grains and no other unit. The mark (or half-pound) weighed 36 *pezos* and 48 grains and the *dobro* was rather less than two *pezos*. For weighing the factor used a set of 2100 weights, 60 of each denomination from one *pezo* to 30 *pezos* and 10 of each from 30 to 60.

The trading took place across a table on which there was a large chest with a hole in the lid. The gold was poured through this hole into a leather-lined casket inside. Each item had to be sold above the rate fixed in Lisbon and a careful record of the fixed rate and of the actual price fetched was to be kept. An increase of 20 per cent was aimed at. As soon as trading was completed and the traders had gone the officers were to open the chest with their three separate keys, take out the casket of gold and publicly re-weight it in lots of six marks (48 ounces). The increase over the total of the initial weighings was then to be added to the total recorded in the ledger. The re-weighing should be witnessed by the governor, who would then replace the gold in its casket and lock it up.

The major problem with which the *Regimento* was concerned was gold smuggling. Many of the complex and detailed regulations laid down must be seen as attempts to avoid the passage of gold into private hands. This was especially difficult when no currency other than gold dust was available at Mina. The salaries of all officials and residents were to be paid in gold but they were not to receive them while still in Mina; instead the amounts were to be weighed out for them, recorded in a book, and dispatched to Lisbon in the chest with the king's gold for payment on their return from Mina. No one in the castle was to indulge in any trade whatsoever with the Africans, however small the quantity. A special dispensation had to be issued to the governor to allow him to buy six civet cats. Payments due to traders in São Tomé were not to be sent to the island but were to be dispatched in the king's chest to Lisbon, where the bill would be settled. Although the whole emphasis of the *Regimento* was on preventing private gain by the Portuguese living in Mina, a contrary provision did allow small amounts of salary to be paid out – possibly in cloth – for the purchase of food brought to the castle and for individuals to buy necessary items off the ships from Lisbon.

The *Regimento* contains several chapters of detailed provisions about smuggling. It was customary for Mina fishermen to go out in their canoes and contact ships from Portugal before they reached the castle. Out at sea they conducted private trade to the detriment of the crown. Any fisherman caught trading in this manner would in future be whipped and have his ears cut off for a first offence and be hanged for a second offence. Once the ship reached the castle all the inhabitants were to be kept out of the way to avoid any contact between them and the ship's crew. Any African caught speaking to a sailor was to be flogged or fined 20 *pezos* of gold. The unloading and checking of the cargo was to take place in a shelter on the beach. The limited private trade allowed between members of the garrison and members of the ship's crew was to be by dumb barter under the supervision of the governor. The sailors put their goods on the shore and then retired to allow the castle residents to come up and make offers for them. If any of the items had to be paid for in gold, the gold was put in the royal chest for transfer to Portugal. On the last day of the ship's stay the captain was to come ashore and publicly receive the gold chest. He was forbidden to enter any building and once he had received the gold he was to return to the ship and sail at once.

Regulations were also designed to prevent private trading within the castle. It was forbidden for any officer or resident to possess scales or weights. The penalty for such an offence was the loss of one's entire salary. It was also illegal for any Portuguese, including the captain and factor, to entertain any man or woman from the village in his private apartment, the penalty being a fine of 20 *cruzados*. This ban was apparently imposed for commercial rather than for moral reasons. Any goldsmith who was caught preparing bars of gold, which could be more easily hidden than gold-dust, was to be flogged and lose his ears; if he was white he was also to be banished and if he was a non-christian African to be sentenced to death. Finally it was stressed that the Portuguese should not visit the villages around the castle except in cases of emergency, such as the need for medicine, when a reliable person would be sent by the governor. On his return the messenger was to be carefully searched by the gatekeeper to ensure that no illegal goods had been purchased. Any one who resisted searching was to spend 15 days in irons.

4 Early African Trade in Angola

Although the Portuguese were particularly keen to find precious metals in the hinterland of the harbours they frequented in Africa, they also took care to examine any other trading opportunities that might present themselves. The production and distribution of textiles and of salt were among the important trades which they attempted to dominate. Although Angola's silver mines were entirely mythical, real mines produced iron near the coast and copper in the far interior. By way of payment Portuguese merchants could offer exotic cotton prints and glass beads but were reluctant to sell highly-prized military equipment such as firearms. This chapter was first published in Gray and Birmingham, Pre-colonial African Trade *(Oxford University Press, 1970) and is reprinted by permission of the Oxford University Press.*

When the Portuguese first arrived on the coast of Angola in the last years of the fifteenth century, they were seeking trade. It has often been assumed that at this early date they were already wedded to the slave trade. This was clearly not the case. They were interested in any economic pursuit which could show a profit. It has also been claimed that their second preoccupation was with precious metals. This too is an over-simplification. Certainly the discovery of precious metals was the fastest and surest way of attracting investment from mercantilist entrepreneurs of the sixteenth century, but the early Portuguese explorer-traders were quite willing to espouse any commercial undertaking which could show a profit after covering the enormous expenses of reaching out from Europe to the coast of Central Africa. In order to succeed, these early European investigators had to gain as much detailed information as they could about African business enterprise. They had to seek out trading situations in which their skills and products could be offered. On the whole the Portuguese had more entrepreneurial and technical skills than material products to offer to their African counterparts. In particular they had the navigational skills capable of organising coastal shipments on a larger and more economic scale than was previously possible. Illuminating examples of how the Portuguese insinuated themselves into the African trade pattern can be found among their early activities before they had reached the Angolan coast. In Upper Guinea, for instance, they were able to use African labour and African skills in textile manufacture to set up a new cotton-growing and cloth-weaving industry in the Cape Verde Islands. The Portuguese contribution consisted of a small initial investment, partly in iron bars, and the erection of a sea-borne collection and distribution network which brought the labour to the islands and redistributed the finished cloth among the coastal ports. The profits which the Portuguese made out of this venture could then be converted into African produce saleable in Lisbon, such as gold, wax, wood, slaves, and pepper.[1] This situation, in which profit was derived from a very small amount of capital and a rather larger amount of entrepreneurial skill, was often to be repeated in the heyday of the colonial period 400 years later. Another striking example of the way in which the Portuguese were able to use their trading facilities to insinuate themselves into an existing commercial system and stimulate innovations can be seen on the Mina coast of modern Ghana. Prior to the 1470s it is likely that most of the gold exported from this region travelled north to the Sudanese markets, notably Jenne. If any trade took place with the lower Niger region it probably did so in small canoes along the tortuous creeks behind the coast. When the Portuguese and their European rivals arrived they soon discovered that one of the pressing needs of the Akan mining communities was labour. With their sailing ships these Europeans found that they could obtain labour more easily, and transport it from further afield more cheaply, than rival customers for the gold, and were thus able to cut a slice of the trade for themselves. They also found that Benin cloth, food, and beads were in great demand on the Mina coast and that they could carry these more cheaply and efficiently than African canoemen. Thus the Portuguese appear neither to have inaugurated a new trading system, nor to have introduced new material possessions in any quantity, but to have gained their entrée with novel skills in the field of transport.[2]

The most important pre-European trade which the Portuguese found when they moved on down the coast to Angola was probably that in salt. Salt is one of the first commodities which communities endeavour to obtain when they begin to supplement subsistence living with goods exchanged outside. The salt mined in Kisama, south of the Kwanza river and some 30 miles inland from

the sea, was of exceptional quality. It was quarried in square slabs
some two feet across, which were easily transportable and whose
regular size made their sale easily negotiable. In the neighbouring
kingdom of Ndongo, and perhaps further afield as well, these slabs
seem to have been used as a currency; one block of salt would buy
half a dozen chickens, three blocks a goat, and about 15 blocks a
cow.[3] This use of Kisama salt as a currency both in Angola and in
the hinterland was still common in the nineteenth century. The
finish of the salt bars had been somewhat refined and they were by
then presented in tapering hexagonal bars nine inches long and
one inch thick. To improve their handling qualities as a currency
the bars were enclosed in closely woven canework cases.[4] Salt presumably fulfilled not only the first function of a currency, that is of
providing a regular comparative scale of values, but also the second,
of providing a durable means of storing wealth. Most
subsistence produce, mainly foodstuffs, cannot be kept for long
periods, but blocks of rock salt can be stored away as a token
of one's affluence and as an insurance against a lean year. The
large Kisama supply of most valuable salt probably formed the basis
of an important commercial system. Certainly the Jesuit Gouveia,
writing about the trade in 1563, described salt as the main richness
of Angola and said that traders came from many nations in the
interior to purchase it. He referred to a people called Dambia Songe
– possibly the Songo – who lived in a large kingdom 17 days
beyond Angola and came to buy salt; they appeared to be very
familiar with regions beyond their country in the far interior.[5] A
hundred years later, Cadornega described Lunda traders who came
to the fringes of Angola in order to buy salt, which still remained
an important export.[6]

In view of the importance of Angolan salt-production, it seems
likely that the salt trade was one of the major factors which attracted
the Portuguese to Angola. They showed considerable skill elsewhere
in Africa in siting their settlements at key points on existing commercial networks such as Sofala and Elmina, and it seems unlikely
that their business acumen was any less accurate in assessing the
potential of Angola. African accounts of Portuguese activity certainly emphasise the loss of the coastal salt-pans as being the
noteworthy feature of the Europeans' arrival: 'the white men spat
fire and took away the king's salt-pans'.[7] Although the foreign encroachment was resisted, it would seem that the coastal salt supplies
were not as vital to the economy of Angola as the rock-salt mines

further inland, and their loss was not an irreparable calamity which had to be prevented at all cost. When at a later date the Portuguese tried to move inland and gain control of the mines, resistance forces of a far greater magnitude were mobilised. In the last quarter of the sixteenth century several major engagements were fought on the south side of the lower Kwanza, which dramatically demonstrate the determination of those who controlled them to defend the salt-mines and the trade routes into the interior. In all these engagements the Portuguese lost, though precisely to whom they lost is not always clear; it may be that the African control of the trade was changing hands at the time; whoever was in control, however, was certainly able to prevent Portuguese encroachment south of the river and only allowed them to penetrate along the north bank, albeit slowly and painfully even there. This defence of Kisama and exclusion of foreign enterprise was preserved well into the nineteenth century, when Lopes de Lima referred to the salt trade controlled by the 'barbarous powers' as one of the greatest riches of the area.[8]

Salt was undoubtedly the most important Angolan produce geared to market production. Other minerals were of limited scope. The Portuguese spoke frequently of silver in trying to encourage settlement and investment in their Angolan venture, but little or no silver existed and it is hard to believe that such hard-headed businessmen as António Dias and his son Paulo would have put so much capital into a non-existent will-o'-the-wisp. Indeed, the charter which was accorded by the Portuguese crown to Paulo Dias for the conquest of Angola indirectly recognised the prime importance of salt – for all the talk of silver – and awarded the *donatário* a monopoly in the trade of both dried and excavated salt, a monopoly which he and his successors were permanently debarred from enjoying by the prior claim of African entrepreneurs.[9]

Copper was another mineral in great demand. The Portuguese saw it in frequent use, especially as bracelets, from an early date and made great efforts to find and control the source of supply. The colony of Benguela was founded in 1617 for the express purpose of exploiting the local copper deposits, but these always proved very disappointing, ore usually being found in small water-borne deposits containing only a few tons of ore each. The only large copper-bearing region was in Bembe, in southern Kongo, where copper malachite was found at the bottom of a deep valley about a mile long. The ore was extracted by digging irregular pits about three feet across and up to 30 feet deep in the floor of the valley. The process was extremely hazardous, especially as the pits were dug very close together in the more favourable areas and often collapsed into each other, killing the miners. No mining could be conducted during the wet season and each dry season the pits had to be dug anew as they rapidly silted up. The villages which controlled the area allowed some neighbouring peoples in to work the mines on payment of a fee, but others such as the Ambriz were excluded from the area and had to buy the malachite in basketfuls at the crossing on the Luqueia river.[10] Whether this small copper-mine which flourished in the nineteenth century was large enough or old enough to have supplied the whole Angola region in former centuries is doubtful. It seems possible that the copper which early Portuguese visitors saw had often been obtained by trade over long distances. The nearest major copper-mine lay north of the lower Congo river at Mindouli and was probably operated by the Vili from the Loango Coast and by the Nsundi from south of the river. It is not unlikely that some of this copper found its way by commercial exchanges into Angola to supplement the meagre local deposits. By the nineteenth century, at least, Katanga copper in the distinctive cross form was reaching the west coast at Benguela via Lunda agencies.[11] If much of the copper seen in Angola was imported this might explain the Portuguese failure to find viable copper-mines in the seventeenth century. At the same time the failure of the Portuguese to penetrate the Bembe area before the nineteenth century may have been due to effective defence of the copper-mines by the Mussorongo or other interested peoples who generally kept the Portuguese fairly closely confined to Luanda on the north side.

In addition to copper, iron was of course an important mineral sought in Angola. The richest deposits seem to have been along the edge of the plateau a hundred miles inland from Luanda. They had formed the basis of an important industry since before the arrival of the Portuguese. The traditions of origin of the ruling dynasty of Ndongo, whose capital sites mostly lay in this region on the plateau edge, refer to a founder who had gained wealth and prestige from ironworking.[12] The quality of the ores was such that in the eighteenth century the Portuguese built two iron foundries in the area and brought Basque smelters to operate them, though never with any great success owing to labour shortage and high European mortality.[13]

In the sixteenth century the Portuguese were not the only people to be actively exploring the economic potential of Angola. In the middle years of the century a series of Imbangala groups from the Lunda territory were exploring the region at least as thoroughly, and possibly a great deal more thoroughly, than the Portuguese. There has been a tendency to examine the Imbangala migrations in terms of the forces which drove them out of their original homeland. They have been seen as outcasts wandering across the Central African plateau in search of new land, as refugees unwilling to tolerate the burden of Luba overlordship which the hunter-king Kibinda Ilunga had brought to their country. It may perhaps be more realistic to examine the Imbangala movements in terms of what attracted them to Angola rather than what drove them out of Katanga. A first reason for the Imbangala interest in Angola might have been the presence there of the Portuguese. The interrelationship of the arrival of these two sets of peoples needs careful chronological investigation. It is known with some certainty that the Portuguese were trading at the mouth of the Kwanza river by about 1500; on the other side there is no evidence that the Imbangala reached Angola before the mid-sixteenth community and some authorities put it later still.[14] These dates give at least 50 years for news of the Portuguese to have travelled to the Kasai basin and for Imbangala investigators to have followed up the information by moving down to the coast. Such a time-schedule is not impossible. It does not imply that regular caravans were plying between Angola and the Kasai, but simply that commercial news was exchanged between neighbours, including perhaps news about firearms which the Portuguese introduced for the first time.[15] The question of interaction between the Portuguese and the Imbangala movements does, however, raise wider questions. The migrations of the Imbangala were part of a major upheaval in the political alignments of Katanga; could this whole process, which finally resulted in the rise of the greatest of all the Central African empires in Lunda, be attributed to the new circumstances which Portuguese overseas trade had created? The answer is probably that it could, but not as quickly as the traditional sources suggest. The somewhat telegraphic style of oral tradition implies that a revolution took place overnight in the Kasai–Katanga territories. This is misleading. It is, however, likely that the opening to the west was initiated or widened in the sixteenth century and that this new factor gradually had far-reaching effects over the next three centuries, beginning with the Luba movements which brought new political ideas and leadership to their western neighbours. These changes led, by the eighteenth century, to the growth of the full-fledged Lunda empire which owed much of its power to its several links with the trade of the west coast.

Another factor which might have influenced the Imbangala movements may have been the salt trade already discussed. Certainly the Lunda country from which they came suffered from a severe shortage of salt. Early phases of the expansion of the Lunda empire after its rise to power seem to have been associated with the search for salt, for instance during the Kazembe migrations to the east. Later, in the nineteenth century, caravans into the Lunda, Cokwe, and Bashilange regions carried salt, among other things, with which to buy ivory, rubber, and slaves.[16] The proven need for salt in the lands east of the Kwango and the known richness of Angolan salt combine to make one suspect that the trade may have played a role in the Imbangala explorations. The earliest traditions of the Luba arrival in Lunda claim that the Luba hunters were moving westward in search of salt, salt which could conceivably have been coming from Angola even at such an early date.[17] The existence of such a trade would reinforce the theory that news of the Portuguese arrival on the coast could have penetrated to the Kasai fairly quickly and caused exploratory expeditions to set out.

The impression that the Imbangala were particularly interested in supplies of salt is reinforced by the early documentary references to the Imbangala leaders. The most detailed description of the Imbangala associates them with the Kisama region. The chief who most definitively defeated the Portuguese governor Coutinho in his 1602 campaign to reach the salt mines was called Kafushe, a name associated with the Imbangala leadership. Other accounts of the Imbangala describe their success in driving the Mbundu away from Cacuaco, a still flourishing salt-dying village on the coast. This incident again suggests a keen Imbangala interest in salt supplies. Finally, when the Imbangala under the leadership of a later Kasanje retired from Angola to found their own kingdom in the 1630s, they did so partly in order to take possession of the salt-pans of the Holo people on the Kwango river and drive away the Pende, who had earlier gained possession of them when expelled from Angola. It was in this area that Cadornega described Lunda traders coming to fetch salt in the second half of the seventeenth century.[18]

The presence of the Portuguese on the Angolan coast may have stimulated the Imbangala to move there, but the arrival of the Imbangala may in its turn have increased the Portuguese interest in Angola. If the Portuguese were aware that these people came from several hundred miles inland, it would have greatly enhanced the potential value of Angola by opening the prospect of a route into the far interior. The Portuguese had hitherto been conspicuously unsuccessful in gaining entry to the African interior everywhere except on the Zambezi, and their progress even there was strongly opposed. It may therefore be that in deciding to attempt the conquest of Angola from 1575 onwards their prime objective was a route into the hinterland to find out for themselves about the inland resources of Africa.[19] If the Kwanza valley was the highroad used both by old-established salt-traders and by new immigrants of Lunda–Imbangala origin, their choice of a route was clearly not a bad one – at least in theory. The snag of course lay in the effectiveness of the resistance they were to meet. This resistance was both commercial and military.

On the commercial plane the Portuguese were much less successful than they had been in Upper Guinea or in the Bight of Benin in insinuating themselves into the existing trading pattern and supplying a new ingredient which made them welcome to the local people. The best they could do was to initiate, or take from others, the coastal trade in palm-cloth. This cloth was manufactured in the wetter, palm-growing regions north of Angola, and most attractively in Loango. The Portuguese bought it there and retailed it in Angola, where it was in demand not only as clothing but also as a currency which the Portuguese themselves adopted and used for many years. In other forms of local trade the Portuguese had less to offer. The Kwanza was not readily navigable and they could not provide an effective river-transport system to compete with traditional head-porterage, which therefore remained the means of transport until the twentieth century. The foreign imports which they brought to Africa were also not as helpful to trade as might have been expected. Their supply was limited and they were extremely expensive. Cloth and beads were not manufactured in Portugal in adequate quantities and therefore had to be imported from Northern Europe, the Mediterranean lands, or India, before Lisbon could re-export them in the African trade. In their early association with the Kongo kingdom, the Portuguese had overcome this difficulty by offering their services to the court as clerks, masons, accountants, teachers, and even domestic science specialists, in part-payment for the produce and slaves which they received. In Angola attempts were made to establish a similar relationship with the king of Ndongo, although never with the same degree of success on the Portuguese side.

By 1575 the Portuguese had been on the Angolan coast for nearly a century without any dramatic success in establishing themselves as traders. The inauguration of the wars of conquest in that year might then be interpreted as a radically new policy to establish the profitability of the Portuguese presence. They might have decided that the only way to extract a return was by imposing their suzerainty in order that a system of tribute payments could be instituted. The accumulation of commodities through a hierarchy of tributary payments from the subject to the chief, then to the paramount chief, and finally to the king was a central feature of both the Kongo and Ndongo kingdoms. When the Portuguese sought to obtain produce from these regions they obtained it from the kings, who had accumulated both goods and slaves in this manner. The Portuguese, faced with the difficulty of paying for such goods, and unable to earn part of the proceeds by offering skills and services, may well have decided that their only hope was to set up their own political structure which would accumulate tribute in the African manner directly for their own benefit. When the wars of conquest started, therefore, they awarded to their army captains the chiefs who were conquered. These chiefs and their subjects had to keep the captain supplied with all his needs and with a tax in slaves who could later be redeemed for credit-notes drawn on the office of the slave trade contractor who held the monopoly of the export of slaves. For some 50 years the payment of tribute to a military government was the major means of obtaining slaves in Portuguese Angola.

In the long run, military methods proved little more effective than previous attempts at co-operation in obtaining for the Portuguese a position in the economic structure of Angola. Their initiatives met with increasingly effective military resistance, first from the kingdom of Ndongo and, when that began to collapse in the 1620s, from the new and more powerful kingdoms of Matamba and Kasanje. Their dreams of a highroad into Africa, even a short-cut to the Indian Ocean avoiding the perilous Cape of Good Hope, were rapidly destroyed. Once again Portuguese policy had to be changed, and this time increasing emphasis was put on trade. By now Brazil contained a flourishing series of colonies and the Portuguese were relatively well stocked with goods which satisfied African demands. Rum and thick ropes of Brazilian tobacco cured with molasses were especially useful in building up trade once the limits of raiding and military conquest had been reached.

On the African side the response to the seventeenth-century trade developments was even more interesting than the earlier response to the attempts at foreign conquest. It was perhaps not surprising that the Mbundu had been able to erect military barriers of considerable effectiveness when faced with an all-out challenge to their very existence; even so the armies, occasionally reported to number tens of thousands, were massive affairs which must have required considerable ability to organize, even if no central system of supplies was provided and the campaigns lasted only so long as the forces could live off the land. More spectacular than these military achievements, however, was the response offered to the commercial innovations of the seventeenth century. The trading barriers that were erected by Matamba and Kasanje were more sophisticated and effective than any of the old military resistance had been. They triumphantly succeeded in preventing any spread of Portuguese commercial undertakings and initiatives beyond Angola. At times there was a Portuguese commercial factor resident at the Kasanje court, but he had little power other than to settle disputes between rival traders, and if his activities appeared to be contrary to the interests of Kasanje, he was unceremoniously dispatched back to Luanda. Behind the barrier of the Kwango valley states a commercial network was gradually built up which collected the exportable goods from a large sector of Central Africa and redistributed in return foreign goods brought up from the coast. It is this response to the new opportunities of the seventeenth century which appears so remarkable. African trading entrepreneurs succeeded both in excluding foreign rivals and in meeting the demands put upon them to supply the goods. Furthermore they were able to evolve a degree of flexibility in their system so that it could meet changing conditions. When in the later seventeenth century the demand for slaves was rising on the Loango Coast, it was possible for supplies to be diverted there from the traditional lines of communication to Luanda, firstly across the old Kongo kingdom, and later, perhaps, by more direct routes.

From this speculative reassessment of familiar sources relating to the history of Angola it would seem that trade may have played a larger role at an earlier date than has previously been realized.

By the sixteenth century at least the people of Angola were using a form of currency which, if not quite as sophisticated as the Kongo shell currency, was still a major step forward in economic development. The country also had, or rapidly developed, the necessary diplomatic and military services to protect its resources and commercial undertakings from foreign intrusion from whatever quarter it might come. Most important of all, however, some of the Angolan people were able to adapt their political and economic systems in order to carry on a flourishing trade without being destroyed by it. As yet far too little is known about the way in which the slave trade operated from the middle of the seventeenth century. The relative importance of the Portuguese *pombeiros* and the Kasanje entrepreneurs in raising credit, negotiating profit margins, competing for trade routes, is not yet known with any clarity. Even less is known of the specific impact of the trade on communities further afield, about who succumbed and went to the wall and who survived to become masters of the system. All that is clear is that those who emerged on top to control the trading states must have had very considerable commercial acumen. These skills were probably rooted in a long tradition of growing trade specialisation and showed themselves capable of adapting to changing economic conditions over several centuries.

5 Traditions, Migrations and Cannibalism

This paper was originally presented to a university seminar in Dar-es-Salaam in August 1971. It was firmly sub-titled 'an entertainment on the problems of historical evidence'. Unsubstantiated oral tradition would have some historians believe that a variant of it was later read in absentia *to a conference of the African Studies Association of the United Kingdom. There is no written record of either variant ever having been published. It is offered here as a quixotic and fossilised example of the historiography of the era.*

It should be a well-known fact that oral traditions relate to the order of things as they ought to be rather than to historical processes as they actually occurred. In many cases, of course, the historical process provides the most convincing rationale for the status quo and so the requirements of current politics and of historical research coincide. In other cases, unfortunately, there may be discrepancies between the historical growth of institutions and the rationalization of them. An early contrast between rationalised tradition, and historical evidence, concerns the origins of man where the Book of Genesis gives the rationalisation of the oral traditionalist, while the historian tends to favour the evolutionist theories of Leakey and company.[1]

Although the problems of interpreting oral traditions are now fairly clearly understood, there are still well-known cases where historians have accepted tradition unquestioningly at its face value, and then proceeded to construct theories and models around it. This has often led them to accord exaggerated importance to migrations. In these accounts of traditional migrations there is often a perfunctory reference to the fact that perhaps not all the people came from a distant land, only the majority or the most influential, or the most devout, or the strongest, but the important question of continuity in the society is usually not discussed in detail.

Theories of migration have commonly been succeeded, among the more analytically courageous historians, by theories of political diffusion associated with conquest-states and the spread of cults, shrines, military methods and royal paraphernalia. Clearly we should not despise and reject all traditions of migration, and all diffusionist theories relating to aspects of political culture, but for myself I think it might be useful to revisit some early research ground with a more sceptical and questioning attitude of mind.

The traditions of origin of the Kongo kingdom are exceptional in that they were encapsuled in documentary fossils some 300 years ago and have not developed new rationalised explanations since the mid-seventeenth century. This has caused historians – Ihle, Van Wing, Cuvelier, Birmingham, Vansina, Balandier *et al.* – to accord them a special reverence which has distorted our vision. At the time they were recorded, the Kongo traditions related to a large, centralised, kingdom with a highly visible ruling class which had developed economically and culturally through its contacts with the trading nations of the Atlantic. The traditions of origin referred to past history nearly 200 years old. These traditions should, there-fore, be accorded the circumspection one would give today to traditions relating to the mid-eighteenth century. They should not be accepted as almost words from the horses mouth because of the antiquity of their recording. These traditions had in fact under-gone 200 years of evolution just as the institutions to which they related had undergone 200 years of evolution.

What Kongo traditions said, at a dateline of about 1623, was that the Kongo kingdom had been created, about five generations before the 1483 arrival of the Portuguese, by immigrants from the kingdom of Bungu. The twentieth-century gloss of more recent tra-ditional interpretation, then goes on to explain how this intrusive ruling elite spread out to govern the whole area from the Atlantic to the Kwango, 300 miles inland. The interpretive historian has then moved in and seen these 'foreign "Bakongo" migrants' as im-posing a state-building model – variously described as Sudanic, Luba, Mongo-Bolia, or other – and setting up a fifteenth-century state capable of receiving European cultural influences without struc-tural alteration. The political system, it was implied, merely adapted to the occasional stresses until a new 'migratory invasion', funda-mentally that of the Jaga, altered the situation 100 years later.

The implication that Kongo was similar in size, and structure, in the fifteenth century, to what it had become in the seventeenth century, is clearly unsound. But the evidence relating to the early history of Kongo is unfortunately sparse. We know that it had a capital city, Mbanza Kongo, of some significance since reports of it reached early Portuguese traders 100 miles away on the coast.

We can assume that the fertile plateau close round the capital was administered by the Kongo king. We can surmise that this king was linked into a network of trade routes which supplied him with copper, iron, salt, sea-shells and possibly even more mundane items like dried fish. We suspect that trading had become sufficiently specialised to develop a system of relative values, based on the *nzimbu* currency shell, though this shell was probably more important as a token of value, and a store of treasure than as a 'coinage' for daily use.

What we cannot do in Kongo is presume that the size of the kingdom was comparable to that described a century later by Pigafetta. In fact the evidence suggests that Kongo was at war with peoples barely 50 miles from the capital, and called on Portuguese ships to sail up the Congo River to afford them assistance.[2] We can also not assume a specialised political structure with a hierarchy of governors, chiefs and sub-chiefs. Least of all can we assume a class division between 'foreign' Bakongo immigrant rulers, and 'local' subject peoples. It has frequently been repeated that the local peoples who were subjected by the 'Bakongo invasions' were Mbundu, but this strikes me as unsound.[3] The word 'Mbundu' apparently means 'slave' in Kikongo – which is not surprising when most slaves were captives, and the nearest neighbours to the Kongo were the Mbundu. When the Kongo rulers referred to their subjects as slaves – a thing that kings are wont to do – they naturally used the word Mbundu.

Since we have rejected the traditional account of the Kongo kingdom, as the creation of an immigrant group of conquerors, who settled at the centre, and fanned out geometrically over the whole country, setting up provincial capitals of the new rulers, we must attempt some other explanation for the kingdom's growth. I should favour an explanation which looks more closely at the grass-roots of the society.

It is commonly said that the kingdom is endowed with a peculiarly rich ecological environment in the well-watered savanna which fringes the equatorial forest. A recent journey through the northern part of the kingdom has shown to me that this is only partly true. Large tracts of the kingdom are dry and rather sterile land with a sparse grass covering. The rich areas apparently consist of limited pockets of fertile country along river valleys and on the tops of small plateaux. It is likely that in such fertile, but restricted, areas systems of kingship would have arisen to control land-usage and allocation. One of the more extensive and wealthy of these local regions was obviously the plateau of Mbanza Kongo and its chief, the Mani Kongo, was a figure of considerable power. At what period his power began to spread to bring other Kikongo-speaking peoples into his sphere of influence is not known.[4] It seems likely; however, that whatever the date at which the expansion of political scale began, it was influenced and extended by the opportunities created by overseas trade after 1483. This overseas trade was jointly managed by the chiefs and by small groups of expatriate entrepreneurs. Although these groups vied with one another for the dominant position, they essentially worked together, and the most significant development of the early period of Portuguese contact was the emergence of a wealthy, urbanised, elite who controlled the towns and the trading axes and made occasional forays into the countryside. This elite of the chiefs and their entourage developed a court culture of distinctive ostentation, displaying imported wares of Asian and European manufacture, and toasting their gods in exotic brandies. They became a separate, highly-visible, section of Kongo society. But they were not immigrant conquerors, but rather a successful indigenous elite.

This interpretation brings us to the fundamental point of this paper. Why should ruling groups, in their traditions, accord to themselves a foreign origin? Why should they describe their emergence in terms of migration? How does one explain this particular pattern of rationalisation? This is not an isolated example, but a pattern which occurs over and over again. Indeed Kongo may not be best illustration since the traditions are in themselves rather dubious. The ruling immigrants allegedly came from Bungu, a place which has begun to appear on historians' maps with disconcerting firmness. It is alleged to be a small state north of the Congo estuary. I wonder if such a kingdom really existed, or whether 'Bungu' is not a term which signifies the ancestors? It is curious that among the Lunda, far to the east, the earlier chiefs emerge among the 'Tubungu', the chiefly ancestors. Is this not the same Bantu word?

The traditions of Kongo not only explain the origins of kingship and of the whole political hierarchy in terms of migration. They also explain the first period of severe disruption in terms of migration, infiltration and conquest. This was the period of the Jaga Wars from 1569 to 1574. The Jaga have been seen, in traditions, in contemporary records, and in historical writings, as foreign conquerors. Their foreignness was deemed to be proven by their strange customs:

they were thought to originate in some remote part of the interior, perhaps even Luba.[5] This concept of an exotic origin for the Jaga was particularly enhanced by their cannibalism.[6] Cannibalism, however, is an extremely hard phenomenon to document; it is widely alleged to be the practice of others, but is never found among informants. Where an apparently documented case does exist, as among the Caribs, shortly before their extinction at the hands of the Spaniards, or among the Azande, during the height of the nineteenth-century ivory-wars, it appears to emerge in situations of acute tension. Cannibalism, real or alleged, ritual or marshall, is not a cultural trait whose diffusion can be plotted. It is a response to an extreme set of circumstances.

In the Kongo kingdom such extreme circumstances certainly existed in the 1560s. The overseas slave trade was growing, raids on neighbouring peoples were increasing, and the disparity of wealth between the rulers and the people was increasing. To add to the tensions, the security of the kingdom was threatened on its northern border. In this situation of growing stress, an uprising by those most severely oppressed might be expected. And the Jaga 'Wars' can probably be more satisfactorily explained in terms of rebellion than in terms of invasion. The rebellion – if such it was – began in the eastern part of the country. This is not surprising, as it is likely that the pressure to capture unprotected individuals for slavery was greatest in the east, and the material benefits which diffused along the trade routes from the Atlantic were most limited in that zone. The Jaga appear to have attacked first the provincial capitals, and then the central capital, from which they drove the king, the traders, and their entire urban entourage.

The evidence that the Jaga were local rebels, rather than conquering immigrants as traditionally understood, is not very good. But it is better than the almost non-existant evidence for a foreign horde. When the Jaga were driven out of Kongo, and settled, under the name Yaka, in the Kwango forest, their culture and language were essentially Kongo. Furthermore the behaviour of the Jaga appears, to all intents and purposes, similar to that of other violent rebel groups who attacked centres of wealth, and furthered their cause by deliberate atrocities.[7] But the strongest reason for looking at the Jaga in terms of local rebellion, or resistance to the growth of slave-trading, is to be found by studying a similar, and contemporary, movement among the neighbouring Mbundu of Angola.

This Angolan movement was known as Imbangala. The Imbangala were essentially a series of local Mbundu armies which rose in rebellion against their own king, and against the trading interests which were permeating Angola in the same way that they had permeated Kongo. The Imbangala spoke Kimbundu, just as the Jaga apparently spoke Kikongo, and when they were eventually driven out of the Portuguese sphere of influence, they too settled in the Kwango valley where their society showed marked Mbundu cultural characteristics. The two movements were, of course, quite separate phenomena emerging in two quite separate political and economic spheres. Because of their similarities, however, they were frequently lumped together, and the Kimbundu-speaking Imbangala were commonly referred to as Jaga by the Portuguese. By this time, however, the term 'Jaga' had come to be very vague, denoting an enemy, a nomadic warrior, a hostile chief, an alleged cannibal. Later still, when numbers of Imbangala were recruited into the Portuguese armies, their mercenary captains came to be known as 'Jagas'.

This argument – that the Jaga and the Imbangala were two un-related resistance movements of a similar kind – runs into renewed problems of oral tradition. For the Jaga we have virtually no evidence about the leadership, about the immediate cause of the outbreak or about possible foreign participation in the initial attacks on the towns of the eastern provincial governors. For the Imbangala we have considerable evidence about the leadership, as interpreted by 10 or more generations of Imbangala rulers. This traditional evidence takes us right back to the theories of migration, infiltration and conquest.

The Imbangala traditions are associated with a folk-hero from Lunda several hundred miles to the East. This folk hero died at an early date, but one of his captains led the men into Angola to become the 'invading horde of Imbangala cannibals'. Traditions associated with Lunda immigrants are common throughout Angola and Zambia. The dispersion appears to have begun in the mid-sixteenth century. Its interpretation presents some very real methodological problems to the historian of Africa.

Firstly, was there any migration of people who traversed several hundred miles of savanna and crossed a number of great rivers, all in the course of a single generation? If so why did they go? Did they follow established trade routes? Had these routes by the mid-sixteenth century begun to relay exotic foreign wares into the very heart of Africa? Were the alleged migrants fleeing from political turbulence in their homeland, for instance from a Luba invasion? This seems unlikely, firstly because refugee movements do not usually maintain momentum for so long, and secondly because the evidence from the Luba traditions for any large-scale expansion and conquest in the sixteenth century is suspect.[8] The concept of a large-scale, or even small-scale, diffusion of peoples into and beyond the sparsely populated regions of the Congo–Zambia–Angola borderlands is inherently unsatisfactory. And yet the oral traditions of many peoples refer to this migration, and even break the migration down into two streams, led by two Lunda brothers who had quarrelled with their father and each led his own exodus to the west. Can an explanation be found?

I now begin to think that stories of a great conquering hero, of a legendary founder-father, of an ancestral patron-saint, can be diffused from camp-fire to camp-fire as disparate and isolated societies' search for a prestigeous tribal pedigree. The fact that most of the people of the south-western savannas have heard of the great Lunda prince Kinguri, and wish to be associated with his name, does not necessarily mean that he or his captains passed through, settled, or conquered. It may mean that stories of Lunda's budding political power caused many people to seek affiliation to the new empire. The oral traditions establish such an affiliation and give it a respectable ancestry. For the most part, we do not have versions of the traditions collected before the nineteenth-century, by which time Lunda was at its height, so we have no means of knowing when Lunda stories became current in the various local histories. The key to the problem, however, may be found by going back to the Imbangala, to see if seventeenth-century evidence, as opposed to nineteenth-century evidence, can be found to link the Imbangala leaders with Lunda. I would only expect the link to creep into the traditions in the latter part of the seventeenth century, when the Imbangala states began to establish trading links with the incipient Lunda empire.[9]

6 Iberian *Conquistadores* and African Resisters in the Kongo Kingdom

This chapter consists of a lecture presented at the international congress of historians held in Madrid in 1990 and it was published in the two volumes of congress transactions. The topic was shaped to reflect the Spanish tradition of land-hungry colonial conquistadores. Although the Portuguese commercial tradition of seafaring colonial activity was very different from the Spanish military practice, the Portuguese empire in Central Africa was nonetheless deeply influenced by Spanish custom in the century from 1568 to 1665.

It was not until the 1560s that firearms became a significant factor in the search for power in the Kongo kingdom, but thereafter guns played a significant role. Horses, on the other hand, were never of the same significance in the military expeditions that the Iberians led to Africa as they were to be in the conquest of Mexico or Peru, though cavalry based at Luanda played some role in the wars of the southern marches of the kingdom after 1574. Neither of these military innovations should be excessively emphasised, however, since conquest and resistance were primarily based on medieval-type weaponry and tactics. Unlike medieval Central America, medieval Central Africa was well provided with blacksmiths who could smelt iron of adequate quality to forge javelin-points, arrow-heads and stabbing spears.

If new technology was slow to influence the struggle between invader and resister in Central Africa, religion rapidly became an ideological weapon of the first order. In Africa, as in Europe, religion was crucial in legitimating political power. In Europe, however, temporal and spiritual power were more or less firmly segregated, albeit with such exceptions as Prince Cardinal Henry of Portugal, who briefly became king when the dashing Sebastian disappeared in a cloud of Morocco dust during an ill-judged 'crusade' into Africa. Early European visitors to Africa, nurtured on legends of Prester John, the priest-king of Ethiopia, hoped to find the key to an integrated power structure encompassing temporal and spiritual authority. In Kongo they were not to find it and instead they introduced their own religion and attempted to use it to manipulate the royal factions in support of their own cause.

Even more important than religion in the Iberian intrusion into Central Africa was commerce. Indeed the first foreign entrepreneur to make his mark on the Kongo kingdom was the Lord-Proprietor of the plantation island of São Tomé, off the coast of Nigeria. São Tomé was colonised by male convicts, dissidents, deserters, and persecuted religious or racial minorities, all of whom needed concubines and labourers from the African main. Some of them they bought in Kongo, thus establishing a trade in marketed prisoners of war, debtors, convicts, and, increasingly, of legitimate but defenceless citizens from the margins of society. Initially the management of this traffic was in the hands of the Kongo political authorities. In time, however, the merchant initiative passed into the hands of creole families of mixed cultural or racial ancestry, who dominated the wholesale import–export business of Kongo and became a semi-autonomous factor in the international relations of West Central Africa.

The fourth factor which profoundly affected the Iberian invasions of Kongo was the union of the Portuguese and Spanish crowns and the subsequent revolt of the Netherlands. The incipient ideologues of capitalism at Amsterdam, many of them wealthy Jewish refugee bankers escaping from the new inquisitorial power that Spain imposed on Lisbon, reached the shores of Kongo in the last months of the sixteenth century and became a permanent force for change. Their weapon technology so outstripped the quality of previous arsenals that they gradually enabled the Nsoyo province of coastal Kongo to claim independence from its suzerain. The Netherlands traders brought such a wealth of new trade goods, and offered such attractive prices for commodities additional to slaves, that they gained a permanent foothold in the intercontinental business relations of the Kongo region. They also brought Calvinism, however, and this so threatened the Papacy that the Popes of Rome effectively annulled a Portuguese monopoly on mission and introduced Italian Capuchins to the field. The Capuchins not only repelled Protestantism but also took an active part in court politics and spread Catholicism out from the city to the provinces and the villages.

The year in which Kongo was first opened to seaward, as opposed to landward, foreign relations was 1483. By then the rising kingdom had probably acquired several generations of stability. The state grew from the power of the towns which dominated the poorer villages but the towns themselves were in turn subservient to the capital city. The control of surplus produce – mineral, agricultural and processed – passed through the system of loyal tribute and reward. The result was that wealth was both the source of power and the source of envy, conflict and challenge. Those who challenged for power in Kongo did not normally do so in order to break their power-base away from its relations with the centre, but to capture the centre and enhance their own interests at the capital.

The first clear evidence of major conflict associated with the advent of foreigners occurred in 1506. The prince of Nsundi claimed the right to the Kongo throne on the death of his father. He apparently had no legitimate title to the throne but he did have a wealthy power-base astride a trade route to the copper-mines. More significantly still, his provincial headquarters had become the refuge for Christian missionaries who had left the capital disillusioned by their lack of initial proselytising success in the 1490s. The attempt to put a mission supporter on the throne, by giving him a false, European-style legitimacy, by recruiting power-brokers from his mother's line, and by calling on Christian saints to help his military cause, was successful. At least one horse may have taken part in the battle, and use may or may not have been made of firearms. The key feature of the battle remembered in folklore and disseminated in propaganda was the symbolic power of Saint James whose assistance routed the traditionalists. The converted usurper, Afonso I, held power for almost 40 years.

One of the most lasting and significant features of Afonso's reign was that it brought European and especially Christian attributes to the power system of Kongo. A beautiful, and presumably powerfully influential, coat of arms was accorded to the new king in 1513. European-style titles were devised to enhance the traditional power of office-holders, or to legitimate their otherwise dubious claims. Key elements of ancestor worship were incorporated into the new ideology as the Christian cult took responsibility for the royal graves. In order to destroy the old grave cults Afonso tried to acquire guns to defeat the shrine guardians, but when they failed to materialise he proceeded to cut down the shrine groves and build chapels without firearm protection. At the same time the new royal cult was redefined and instead of being a spiritual force it became a material force relating to wealth and governed by methods that incorporated traditional witchcraft.

The European alliance had to be paid for by the new political order, but Afonso's transformed nobility had difficulty in raising the necessary numbers of slaves to satisfy their creditors and reward their priests. Disintegration threatened in the 1520s as rivals sought to capture the central systems of Kongo, but Afonso was able to expand his slave-supply network beyond his north-east border into the Malebo Pool area. Traditional copper-caravan managers and controllers began to buy slaves from the Teke and so push the slaving frontier forward on its first great lurch into the interior. The slave revenues were used not only to hire European priests, but also to send prospective African priests to Europe for training and ordination. The success of Afonso, and of his grandson Diogo I, was such that they reigned for half a century. Thereafter, however, the kingdom was torn apart by the Jaga invasions from the land and the Iberian counter-invasions from the sea.

The fall of the Kongo kingdom in 1568 was apparently triggered by the uprising of slave-trade victims in and beyond the eastern provinces. The virulence of the Jaga attacks on power and authority probably encouraged oppressed rural peoples in other parts of the kingdom to join the uprising. The rebels terrified their enemies, who believed them to be cannibals. The king and his retinue fled westward and took refuge until he could summon up a European army to rescue him. The expeditionary force, commanded by the Captain-General of the Portuguese Island Colony of São Tomé and consisting of 600 men, some of them armed with guns, was able to reconquer the kingdom, restore the devastated capital and re-enthrone the king. The invasion was the first major campaign fought by Europeans in tropical Africa. It led the way for several others in West Central Africa and a few in East Central Africa, but it did not set the agenda for a European partition of Africa. That had to await the industrial revolution of the nineteenth century and Africa did not follow down the path of American history. The arrival of the *conquistadores* of 1568 nonetheless had significant consequences.

The first effect of the conquest of Kongo was an enormous increase in the slave trade. The frontier moved deeper into Zaïre across the lower Kwango river as the new mercenaries demanded payment in slaves for their services. But the increase in the slave trade also strengthened the restored monarchy. The king became surrounded by his retainers, many of them slaves dependent on his patronage and given positions of influence at court, and owed as much to them as to the web of kinship alliances that had traditionally held the kingdom together. From being a kingdom based on the duties of kinship, Kongo became a kingdom in which the 'kinless' gave power to their patrons, sometimes as royal soldiers. The availability of slaves, and the expansion of literacy, facilitated the integration of the kingdom when slaves could be used as relay runners to carry orders to the provinces and hammock bearers would carry officials on tours of duty without delay or recourse to horses, which were rare, expensive and subject to forest diseases.

The second transformation that the invasion brought was the establishment of a nationwide network of *conquistadores* who settled at the nodal points of political authority and commercial exchange throughout the kingdom. The settlers, primarily mercenaries who did not return home after the Jaga campaign, were political allies of the king and yet had autonomous interests of their own, particularly in matters of commerce. Some of them established large, polygynous, families of mestizo children as well as recruiting communities of loyal retainers. This budding community of Luso-African creoles was simultaneously a source of strength to the king and a potential fifth column. The interests of the creoles could never precisely be predicted by the rulers. So long as the colonial state to which they related was the off-shore island of São Tomé, some distance away by unreliable boat service, the creole trading communities were reasonably careful to maintain good relations with the Kongo crown and not push their economic demands to the point where they might trigger a new invasion or rebellion of the Jaga type. In 1575, however, the position of the settlers was altered by the creation of a second Portuguese colony in West Central Africa. This was the on-shore colony of Luanda Bay, which was rather closer to the Kongo capital than São Tomé and lay just inside the furthest southern frontier of the kingdom.

The establishment of the proprietary colony of Luanda, chartered to the family of Bartholomew Dias, significantly altered the perceptions of the creole community in Kongo. The new colony was capable of expanding the southern slave trade that already flourished there beyond the effective limits of either Portuguese or Kongo control and taxation. Creole traders inside Kongo might have expected the market for slaves who had been marched down from the Zaïre interior to expand, albeit under the control of a new customs house. The new colony might also have been seen as a potential ally in the event of conflict between the Kongo creoles and the indigenous princes. At the same time, however, the new colony was a rival to Kongo, a rivalry that was to break out into warfare on several occasions over the next 100 years. In those wars the creoles and settlers were divided in their loyalties, some supporting the Kongo king, some pinning their faith in the new colonisers, and many being held hostage or even killed for their ambivalence at times of war.

The rivalry between Luanda and Kongo was conspicuous not only in commercial matters but also in the struggle over the control of spiritual power. The first bishop ordained for West Central Africa – with the title of Utica, a lost see in Muslim North Africa – was a son of Afonso I of Kongo. The establishment of a regular diocese of Kongo was delayed for almost a century until 1596. Within a few years, however, the colony had captured the bishopric and effectively moved it from the city of São Salvador in Kongo to the colonial headquarters in the city of Luanda. The colony thus gaining powerful leverage over the Christian cult on which Kongo kings and their provincial lords had become so dependent.

While state-related religious power was growing in Kongo a quite new Christian tradition reached Africa in the shape of the Jesuit Order, the shock troops of the Counter-Reformation in Europe. The Jesuits were convinced that the Church could only make progress under colonial authority, and not in the creolised hybrid culture that had evolved in Kongo. The fact that other religious traditions were dominant in Kongo, and therefore initially excluded them, may also have encouraged their belief in conquest as the best route to conversion. The first Jesuit fathers of the 1560s paved the way for an Iberian conquest of the southern savannas that lay just beyond the effective reach of Kongo authority. Jesuit missionaries provided political and military intelligence on the region and fabricated economic inducements in the form of reports on wholly mythical silver-mines. The myth of silver grew out of the wholly unscientific cosmological belief that if silver was to be found in such abundance at Potosi, a few degrees south of the equator in South America, then surely silver ought to be found a few degrees south of the equator in Africa.

The Jesuit crusade into Angola, backed by the Lord-Proprietor in the 1580s and by the Spanish Crown in the 1590s, did not have great success. It naturally failed to find the mythical silver-mines, it had enormous difficulty in conquering the very real iron-mining zones which were heavily protected by the kings of Angola, and it utterly failed to capture the real mineral wealth of the region which lay in the mines of gem salt quarried south of the river. Gunmen did succeed in driving off coastal salt-makers, who emigrated into the far interior carrying vivid memories of the weapons that spat fire, but even horses were not sufficiently powerful to overcome the rapid fire of bowmen ranked against those who tried to penetrate the much more important salt-mining zone of the interior. Only a frail chain of little fortresses along the north bank of the river could be won and held. The concept of colonisation with agricultural settlers and ranks of well-taxed windmills grinding colonial corn was soon abandoned.

The partial failure of Luanda and the Angolan colonising venture led to a new Habsburg plan to conquer parts of the Kongo kingdom and take over its mineral wealth and long-distance trade in textiles and slaves. The mineral wealth consisted of small deposits of copper well defended by the Kongo provincial authorities but coveted by colonial propaganda which made them into gold mines comparable to those found on the opposite shore of Central Africa. In East Central Africa the Mutapa kingdom had been undergoing assaults from Iberian *conquistadores* and militant missionaries similar to those attempted or envisaged for West Central Africa. In Kongo the king tried unavailingly to get the Pope to protect his mines from Christian agressors. The city of Luanda also aspired to capture the water meadows along the rivers of south-west Kongo in order to establish food farms to feed the city and its slave ships. In 1615 these territories were annexed without declaration of war. Seven years later formal war did break out when Luanda grasped the opportunity of a change of reign in Kongo to invade the kingdom more deeply. This war of 1622 seriously undermined the power of the king and led to the death in one battle alone of 90 members of his nobility. It also led, however, to a change of alliances when the Jesuits found themselves on the Kongo side defending the rights of a Christian kingdom and opposing the colonial *conquistadores* whom they had initially sponsored. The Jesuits established a college at the capital, though they took care to distance it from royal patronage, and began training both Kongo and mestizo clerics. The college remained under the authority of the monastery at Luanda and did not last many years.

The wars that began in 1622 were associated with the steady rise of Netherlands influence. The Dutch trade on the Nsoyo coast had very mixed consequences for the Kongo kings. Positively it provided a rival trading partner through whom to improve the international terms of trade and increase the price of slaves. It also provided a potential European ally against the rising pressure of the Luso-Hispanic *conquistadores* on the southern frontier. On the negative side, however, Kongo trade with the Dutch was a powerful factor in driving the Portuguese to invade and cut off the supply of Dutch goods which was spoiling their market. Furthermore trading with the Dutch could be seen as a sign of disloyalty to the Catholic Church, which had become so important to the preservation of aristocratic rule. A third problem was the role of the Dutch in undermining the central power of Kongo. So long as most trade could be controlled by the king his economic power was enhanced by foreign trade. The Dutch, however, did their trading in Nsoyo in such a way as to minimise the opportunities for royal control. Nsoyo could thus weigh up the relative advantages and disadvantages of loyalty to the king at its leisure. All these calculations, however, were thrown into temporary turmoil when the Dutch themselves turned *conquistadores*.

The capture of Luanda by a massive force of 2000 Dutch troops in 1641 brought to an abrupt halt the latest Portuguese plans for a campaign against the new Kongo king, Garcia II. The fall of Luanda also led to a spate of attacks on Portuguese traders in the Kongo provinces, who were robbed or murdered. The Luanda garrison and its commercial and administrative associates, some 600 in all, were evacuated and eventually survived in cramped exile in a municipal outpost 200 miles up river. Kongo resolved to wipe out the remnants of Portuguese colonial power, but the Dutch hesitated, believing that a small inland community of Portuguese and Luso-Africans would be useful both as suppliers of provisions and as slave-trading partners. Kongo's opportunity passed and the Portuguese exiles were rescued by a new force of *conquistadores*, coming this time from Rio de Janeiro. On being restored to the control of Luanda the colonisers were more determined than ever to gain revenge and reward by invading Kongo yet again. They once again laid claim to the copper-mines but their real booty was to be counted in prisoners of war.

Ironically the advent of Netherlands power in Africa had temporarily strengthened the Kongo Church. The bishops and the Jesuits had both been a disappointment to the crown because of their subversive attachment to Luanda. When the Papacy saw Catholicism threatened by Protestants, however, it sent into Africa a new Vatican-controlled mission staffed by Capuchins from Italy. This was an effective response to Dutch Calvinism. It was also, however, a means of furthering evangelisation without reference to Lisbon which had broken its ties with the Vatican on the occasion of the rebellion of 1640. The Kongo king expected that his new missionaries would be beholden to him and not to his troublesome colonial neighbour. His hopes were in vain, however, and when the Dutch were expelled from Luanda the Capuchins found themselves compelled to come to terms with the restored colonial authorities in spite of the papal interdict on Portugal.

The greatest long-term threat to the integrity of Kongo in the seventeenth century may not have come form the Luanda colony but rather from the pretensions to political autonomy entertained by the coastal 'earldom' of Nsoyo. The capital of Nsoyo, together with its adjacent ocean port, had a population of 15 000 and was the second largest town in the kingdom. The ruling dynasty of Nsoyo was the House of da Silva which prospered because it was permanently rooted in Nsoyo and not liable to be moved around the provincial capitals by the king. Outside the court and capital the counts had been able to build up the local agrarian prosperity, based on the work of slave labour awaiting sale and the consumption of provisions by slave ships which provided a ready market. As Nsoyo became more secure in its independence it acted as a haven of refuge for Kongo leaders who lost power in the factional conflicts over royal succession. By the time the new ultra-militant Brazilian *conquistadores* had seized Luanda in 1648, Nsoyo had acquired a real degree of autonomy which threatened the viability and integrity of the whole Kongo kingdom.

The long-drawn out skirmishes between Luanda and Kongo in the 1640s and 1650s concerned land, trade routes, slave fugitives and mineral deposits. The land over which the most acute conflicts occurred was the populous mountain region of Ndembu on the frontiers of Kongo and the old native kingdom of Angola. One of the most important of the principalities in contention was that of Mbwila, where the culminating battle between the two regional powers eventually occurred. But land and people were not the only factors undermining the viability of Kongo. The restored colony of Luanda no longer depended on Kongo to supply it with raffia cloth from the eastern forests to provide the basis of its currency. The management of the raffia trade had been a major feature of Kongo royal power, but the Portuguese now brought their raffia squares by sea from the coastal kingdom of Loango, north of Kongo, and no longer depended on Kongo supplies. Worse still, from the Kongo perspective, the loss of Luanda meant the loss of the shell fisheries that provided the nzimbu shell currencies which the king controlled and which were widely used for social and political payments throughout the kingdom. To compound the loss of coastal shells, the kingdom also lost control of coastal salt, most of which came from the now detached province of Nsoyo. The whole basis of the royal network of exchanges was thus fundamentally undermined even before the Portuguese started making new claims to control the copper mines and to recover allegedly fugitive slaves who had escaped from Luanda to the free lands of Kongo. Conflict was endemic after 1648.

The long-running hostility between Luanda and Kongo culminated in the battle of Mbwila on 29 October 1665. It was the most famous of the set-piece battles of conquest in West Central Africa. The core of the Luanda army consisted of no less than 450 musketeers led by the famed Luso-African commander, Luis Lopes de Sequeira. The core of the Kongo army was slightly smaller at 380 musketeers, including 29 Portuguese, and was also under the command of a Luso-African, Pedro Dias de Cabra. The Luanda force had brought two pieces of light field artillery into the mountainous battle zone. The Kongo irregulars who had been mobilised for battle may not have numbered quite the 100 000 peasant conscripts that was claimed but a huge hoard of camp-followers carried sacks of food and drove herds of cattle, sheep and goats to sustain them. António also took into the field with him bales of currency cloth to pay for the campaign, 14 chests of precious possessions and two boxes of jewellery that he did not want to fall into the hands of his rivals. To forestall claims to legitimacy by potential rebels back home he also carried his state archives and ensured that the major pretenders to the throne were included in the task force rather than being left at home to make mischief.

Despite all his preparations and expenses António I was unable to defeat the Luanda army. His troops were much less skilled and experienced than the Portuguese-controlled black army which had been in the field intermittently since the Brazilians arrived in 1648. The Luanda shock troops still included regiments of Imbangala which had been conscripted into the Portuguese forces since the early days of the slave wars in the Luanda hinterland. The battle was decisively won by Luanda and the king was killed along with his African Capuchin chaplain, 98 titled nobles, and 400 armoured knights. The Kongo crown and sceptre were sent to Lisbon as trophies, and the king's severed head was buried at Luanda with great pomp.

The defeat of António I of Kongo provided the restless province of Nsoyo with an opportunity to increase its bid for power either as an autonomous state or as a broker in the royal affairs of Kongo. It began by adopting the latter course and imposed a king of its own choice on Kongo by force of arms. Nsoyo did not have adequate authority among the provincial and court nobility to maintain its nominee in power, and a spasmodic civil war ensued as the central forces competed with the Nsoyo forces. By 1670 the central forces, from the dwindling and repeatedly sacked royal capital, decided to call on Luanda for help. The central authorities offered Luanda money, mineral concessions and the right to build a fortress in Nsoyo to keep out the Dutch. Luanda immediately seized the opportunity to try to conquer the north coast.

The colonial army that was raised in 1670 was the most powerful that had yet been seen in Central Africa. It consisted of 400 musketeers, but also a detachment of cavalry, four light cannon, some naval vessels, the auxiliary Imbangala, and the accustomed cohorts of irregular bowmen. The first battle, in June, was won by the Portuguese who broke the Nsoyo army despite its matching firepower of four artillery pieces. The second battle, in October, had quite a different outcome. The regrouped Nsoyo forces, reequipped by the Dutch, comprehensively destroyed the Luanda expeditionary force. Portuguese who were not killed on the battlefield were drowned fleeing across the river or captured and, so legend would have it, offered as white slaves to the Dutch. The Portuguese did not attempt any further military incursion into Kongo for many years.

After two centuries of spasmodic military intervention Luanda gave up trying to conquer territory in Kongo. Since their prime interest, however, was in buying slaves they did not need to conduct further campaigns of their own. Their wars had so fragmented the kingdom that warfare had become endemic and slaves could be drawn off without the need for direct military intervention. The

Portugese campaigns had, moreover, been largely inglorious, whether
in restoring friendly monarchs as in 1568, or in destroying unfriendly
ones as in 1665. By 1670 Kongo lay in ruins and only 30 years later
did a new and much smaller kingdom arise from the ashes; it survived until the second half of the twentieth century, when foreign
war once again devastated the homelands of the Kongo peoples.

7 Angola and the Church

This chapter, the most recently researched essay in this book, was presented in Portuguese to a congress hosted by the Angolan National Archives in the parliament building at Luanda in August 1997. The participants were not only old freedom fighters, seasoned politicians, administrators from the Ministry of Culture, and university academics, but also a new generation of young Angolan undergraduates. The paper attempts to encourage this rising generation of scholars to widen its range of social history to include the religious dimensions. A rich diversity of published and archival material spans 500 years of Angolan experience. This English-language version was published in the Neue Zeitschrift für Missionswissenschaft *vol. 54, (Immensee,* 1998) Number 4.*

There are many ironies in the history of the church in Angola. On four occasions, in 1640, in 1834, in 1910, and in 1975, the church was almost outlawed, and yet it remains a very powerful influence among the people. Throughout five centuries of contact with Africa Portugal tried to claim a monopoly of mission activity in the Angolan field and yet the most influential missionaries have rarely been Portuguese. The 'official' church in Angola has normally been the Catholic Church but this church has often been deeply divided by bitter rivalry between several traditions. Although the colonial power in Angola was a Roman Catholic one some of the most powerful strands of church influence during the formal colonial century between, 1875 and 1975, were Protestant. The rival practices of both Catholics and Protestants have had a deep and varied impact on the peoples of Angola. They have also affected the ongoing pattern of conflict and collaboration between the church and the state. Sometimes willingly, but quite often reluctantly, the various missions were conscripted into a collaboration with Europe's grand imperial designs. The Portuguese state expected co-operation from Catholics but often found them to be subversive; and Protestants imagined themselves to be divorced from politics yet continuously found themselves being drawn into the affairs of both the colonial and the postcolonial state.

In 1508 a party of 12 Blue Friars of the Order of St John the Apostle was sent to the Kongo territory of northern Angola to begin the long tradition of proselytising by the monastic orders. Little evidence of their impact has so far come to light but over the next 100 years other monastic orders competed fiercely for the privilege of sending monks to Angola. The Augustinians, of the Lisbon monastery of São Vicente da Fora, aimed to steal a march on their rivals by providing the bishop of Central Africa, a suffragan to the Archbishop of Madeira with a residence on the off-shore island of São Tomé. Their main opponents in the early contact years were the Franciscans. There may be some interesting work to be done in comparing the ideologies of the two orders and their differential impact on Angola. The Franciscans may have laid greater emphasis on the vow of poverty than did the Augustinians. It would be interesting to know how different the behaviour of the early mendicant friars was from that of any secular clergy that fell under the command of the bishops. Did the tithes of the priests, for instance, fall more heavily on the people than the alms demanded by travelling friars? Despite their vows of poverty some Franciscans did run into trouble over worldly wealth and were accused of accumulating personal property during their service overseas. In 1616 the Franciscan order instructed that any Franciscan friar returning from Angola with wealth beyond that which satisfied his immediate subsistence needs should have his belongings confiscated and handed to the church.

Another important order of friars to reach Africa was the Black Friars of the Dominican Order. Although a preaching order, like the Franciscans, they seem to have been keen rivals of the Augustinians and of the older monastic tradition. When Angola was ecclesiastically detached from the see of São Tomé in 1597, and when a new bishop's seat was established for Angola at Mbanza Kongo, the Dominicans claimed the right to nominate episcopal candidates. In 1604 a Dominican Friar was elected bishop of Angola and Kongo and four years later the old Augustinian monks appear to have been chased out of the city of Mbanza Kongo, or São Salvador as the Christians preferred to call it. It would be fruitful to know more about the rivalry of the Dominicans and the Augustinians and it would be fascinating to know how each was perceived by ordinary seventeenth-century Angolans, by Angola's ruling aristocracies, and by the royal court of Kongo. One unpopular Augustinian, Bishop Gaspar Cão, was charged with 'scandalous behaviour' though whether the alleged scandal was fiscal, theological or moral will require further research in the ecclesiastical archives.

Late in the sixteenth century, after the Habsburgs had added the crown of Portugal to their possessions, other applicants sought the right to open missions in Angola. The new dynasty apparently favoured the White Friars of the Carmelite Order. On 10 April 1584 three 'barefooted' Carmelite priests with two accompanying brothers set off for Angola. Their journey was hardly comfortable, the rotting boat in which they sailed had a defective rudder, and the seas were infested with French and Moroccan pirates. They did, however, eventually reach Luanda and King Alvaro of Kongo is said to have 'jumped for joy' at the news. The Carmelites belonged to the mendicant tradition of preaching friars and the newly reformed branch of the order was noted for wearing simple sandals rather than ostentatious shoes. Their outreach into society may have been rather different from that of the Augustinians of the episcopal tradition. Once in Angola, however, the Carmelites faced angry challenges from rival missions despite the welcome that was accorded to them by the people. The king of Kongo asked for more Carmelite White Friars but the colonial authorities refused and decided to send instead more Dominican Black Friars. In 1610 three Dominican priests and one brother embarked for the Kongo mission. At the same time that the Carmelites were being refused a Portuguese licence to preach in Kongo, they were also being challenged in Luanda. In 1606 the church which the Carmelites had built in Luanda was confiscated and transferred to the Franciscans. The Vatican had strongly favoured the Carmelite mission in Angola but when it came to colonial politics the royal patronage over the colonial church which the papacy had granted to Portugal still held firm in the early seventeenth century. Only 40 years later, when Portugal had been virtually excommunicated in punishment for its rebellion of 1640 against the Habsburgs, did the Vatican succeed in putting its stamp on the Angolan mission enterprises.

The new generation of historians of Angola will want not only to unravel the differential effects of rival monks and friars on Angola, but will also ask questions about the militant church orders. Three of these, the Order of Christ, the Order of São Tiago, and the Order of São Bento appear to have been attached to the crown of Portugal. The Order of Christ had helped to finance early military expeditions into Africa and the order's habit seems to have been awarded to members of the nobility in any African kingdom which established diplomatic relations with Portugal. Assessing the significance of this tradition on the evolution of the nobility, and on class relations, in the kingdom of Kongo will continue to be an interesting task. The old 'crusading' tradition of militant orders was, however, largely replaced in the years of the Counter-Reformation by the new Society of Jesus. The history of the Jesuits in Angola is very widely documented and has been very widely studied. There is, however, surely room for a more careful interpretation by African scholars inside Angola into the role of this powerful colonial institution. In the scale of Portuguese imperial history the Jesuit missions to Angola were apparently of only minute importance judging by the sparse references to them in Dauril Alden's monumental history of the Portuguese Jesuits (*The Making of an Enterprise*, Stanford, 1996). From the point of view of Angola's domestic history, by contrast, there is much to be discovered about the relations of the Jesuits with the kings of Kongo, with the governors of Luanda, and with the rival mission traditions of the friars. Some of the relevant data is, of course, published in the 14 volumes of Father Brásio's *Monumenta Missionária Africana* which provides scope for re-interpreting the history of mission influence and for exploring the prospects for finding new evidence.

Baldly stated, the Jesuits were noted for their belief in the need to conquer mission fields by force of arms, by their emphasis on establishing diplomatic relations with African kings, by their commitment to educating the elite of both colonies and kingdoms, and by their success in accumulating wealth and investing it in land, buildings and slaves. Some of their activities and attitudes may not have been very different from those of their Augustinian predecessors but the scale of their enterprise was much greater and their mission priests were reasonably well paid by the state. Their economic enterprise, however, overshadowed their religious activity and in 1618 a report on Angola complained that although the Jesuit mission received a subsidy of 2000 *cruzados* a year, its priests no longer engaged in evangelism. The complaint may have been exaggerated, or biased, but the report powerfully argued that the mission field needed to be revived with a new generation of mendicant friars. This new generation was recruited among the 'Bearded Friars', or Capuchins, a strict new variant of the Franciscan tradition that had been founded in Italy.

The history of the Capuchin missions to Angola is probably even more important, in terms of local social history, than the history of the Jesuit missions. The Capuchin missions were also very well documented and many selections from the archives have been more or less faithfully reproduced in published collections. But the Capuchin mission immediately raised one of the great problems of Angola's ecclesiastical history: were Christian missions a branch of the colonising enterprise or were they an independent venture with their own policies and priorities? As far as Portugal was concerned the missions came under the authority of the crown's patronage. As far as the Vatican was concerned this patronage was acknowledged only when it served the interests of the Catholic Church. The conflict between the two over the Carmelites may have had more to do with the fact that the Carmelites were of Spanish national affiliation than with the effects of Carmelite religious distinctiveness. Similarly the attempt by the Vatican to set up a Capuchin mission with personnel from Italy was delayed from 1620 to 1645 by the nationalistic sensitivities of the Portuguese. In 1640, however, Portugal rebelled against the most loyal of the Vatican's dynastic supporters, the Habsburgs, and the Portuguese church was placed under a ban. Between 1640 and 1668 no bishops could be appointed either in Portugal or in the colonial mission fields and Portuguese church affairs were increasingly managed by lay administrators. During this 'excommunication' of Portugal and its empire the Vatican enabled the Capuchin order to gain a hold over Angola. They managed to keep their dominant position for the next 200 years despite the fact that Portugal was restored to good standing in the church in 1668 and despite the fact that most of the friars sent to Africa were Italian rather than Portuguese.

For imperial and ecclesiastical historians the national affiliation of missionaries and the bitter conflicts between rival Catholics were important. For social historians, however, the important questions concern the changing nature of mission penetration into Angolan society. Capuchins travelled throughout the northern half of Angola maintaining a living Christianity in many communities until the early nineteenth century. They gained a familiarity with village life, tradition, belief, custom and economic practice which provides one of the best insights into early modern history available for any part of Africa. The Capuchin archives have been perceptively exploited by some of the most original historical observers of the continent, Louis Jadin of Belgium, Anne Hilton of Britain, John Thornton of the United States, and yet there remains ample scope for further research by fresh generations of historians from Angola or from Portugal or from Italy. Among the many books about, and editions of, Capuchin writings there exists a complete list of several hundred missionaries who went to Angola between 1645 and 1834, the year in which Portugal dissolved its religious orders (Graziano Saccardo, *Congo e Angola*, 3 vols, 1982). The Capuchin documentation, and the commentaries upon it, provide profoundly perceptive analyses of the impact of Christianity on Angola. Curiously, and incidentally, they also provide an interesting light on the first Protestants to play an active role in the history of Angola.

From a purely theological Portuguese perspective the Dutch traders in the seventeenth-century Atlantic were Calvinist heretics. From a commercial perspective, however, they were powerful merchants who could be valuable trade partners. Officially the 'heretics' were excluded from the field as political, diplomatic and strategic rivals, but pragmatically the Dutch were included in the commercial activities of the Portuguese. The ecclesiastical records, both Portuguese and Italian, are liable to be quite misleading in their account of the role of non-Catholics in the affairs of Angola. It is ironic that when Queen Nzinga wrote to the pope in Rome her letter was carried by an Italian Capuchin travelling on an English ship trading to Angola out of Bristol, captain Thomas Heath. The English trade was normally fairly invisible, but the Dutch quite openly became the main traders at Mpinda, the largest harbour in the Congo river estuary. Although the traders were Calvinists their customers, the dukes of Soyo, remained staunchly Catholic. Attempts by Catholic priests to spread a fear of 'heretical' propaganda, of outlawed vernacular Bibles, and of pernicious moral codes, were of little avail in curbing the activities of Protestant traders. It is likely, moreover, that many of the so-called heretics were covertly Jewish rather than Calvinist in their religious practice. In Amsterdam the merchant community contained a powerful contingent of Jewish émigrés from Portugal. These religious exiles contributed their skills, their knowledge and their capital to the Dutch domination of the seventeenth-century Atlantic.

It was not only the Dutch who were dependent on Jewish commercial expertise in Angola. This expertise, derived from the need to make a living without being permitted to own landed estates or to practise agriculture, also became a necessary part of the Portuguese colonial tradition. The Portuguese crown gave licences to Jewish merchants to operate in the empire despite the monopolistic religious claims of the Catholic Church. In the sixteenth century the Lord-Proprietor of Angola, Paulo Dias, had been given permission to take with him six Jewish merchants to foster the economic prosperity of the chartered colony. At the same time the *conquistador* of Kongo, Francisco de Gouveia, was accompanied by at least one, and probably many, Jewish entrepreneurs. The famous one was Duarte Lopes, a trader, traveller and explorer who supplied the Renaissance scholar Pigafetta with detailed information about Angola in the late sixteenth century.

Not all the Dutchmen who worked in Angola were Calvinists or Jews by religious practice. Some of those who became most closely integrated into Angolan society were Roman Catholics. One Dutch settler, who served as quartermaster of the Dutch garrison in Benguela in the early 1640s, changed sides during the Luso-Dutch war of 1641 to 1648. He left Benguela, walked overland to Massangano, the besieged Portuguese garrison town of the interior, married a white Catholic wife, and fought against his Dutch compatriots until they surrendered the harbour-city of Luanda. He was subsequently rewarded by being re-appointed to Benguela as the sergeant-major in charge of the once again Portuguese fortress. Another long-term 'Dutch' resident in Angola was Balthasar Van Dunem who arrived in Luanda in the 1630s. He served as Portugal's slave trade contract manager in the 1650s and was exempted from the expulsion of foreigners when he claimed that, despite his Dutch name, he had come from the Hanseatic ports of north Germany. The Portuguese agreed to grant him citizenship and he presumably become the ancestor of the great congerie of black Catholic families called Van Dunem.

Religious pragmatism and toleration were not widely publicised as an aspect of the cultural history of Angola. In reality, however, those travelling to and from Angola crossed many cultural and religious boundaries. The Portuguese rarely confessed their pragmatic toleration in matters of religion but were heavily dependent on their Protestant trade partners. The Dutch, although rebels against Catholic Spain, were so tolerant that Angola's Capuchins could freely walk the streets of Amsterdam wearing their monastic habits. They commonly travelled home to Italy on the Angolan slave ships to Brazil and then on the Dutch sugar ships to Holland. Religious pragmatism in Luanda was so marked, and financial skills so scarce, that Portugal was even willing to auction off the 'tax farm' on Angola's slaves to a Jewish settler who clandestinely served as the rabbi in the secret Luanda synagogue. Pragmatism, like prejudice, was as much a feature of religious life in seventeenth-century Angola as it was in the twentieth century. And the prejudice, then as later, had as much to do with racial antagonism as with theology.

By the late seventeenth century the Catholic Church in Angola was divided into several sections. The four orders of Jesuits, Carmelites, Franciscans and Capuchins remained small, none of them having more than four ordained monks and a few lay brothers. The majority of the friars were based in Luanda though a hospice still survived in Massangano and one Franciscan lived as far inland as Kasanje. Relations between the orders and the civil authorities were not always harmonious. Neither were relations between the orders and the secular clergy responsible for the parishes. The priests fell under the authority of the Angola's bishop whose see had been transferred from Mbanza Kongo to Luanda in 1674 following the restoration of relations between Portugal and the Vatican in 1668. This restoration had enabled Portugal once more to fill vacant bishoprics in its overseas territories including Angola. The bishop's priests, who served the white population of Angola, were salaried by the state. Two of them lived in Luanda and seven of them were posted to the seven fortresses that had been built during the era of the *conquistadores*. In addition to the priests 16 curates and chaplains were responsible for ministering to black Catholics. These curates received no state stipends but were paid by black worshippers who wanted to have their confessions heard or wanted to receive a Christian burial. The poorly-paid, or unpaid, secular clergy deeply resented the state subsidies given to the prestigious Jesuit college. They protested that while parish clergy almost starved the Jesuits owned 50 large plantations worked by 10 000 slaves. The Jesuits, they claimed, were also large-scale landlords who owned many of the finest city residences. These they rented out to wealthy merchants and town councillors who were beholden to them as tenants. Relations between rich regular clergy and poor secular clergy were not harmonious in seventeenth-century Angola.

Beyond the reach of Luanda, the church of Mbanza Kongo was administered by a team of cathedral canons during Portugal's ecclesiastical interregnum and after the translation of the bishop's seat to Luanda. These canons caused much grief to the colonial authorities because their loyalty was to their king rather than to the Portuguese governor-general. Relations between the colonial city and the royal capital had been exceedingly cool long before a dispute over mineral concessions caused war to break out in 1665. This war led to a Portuguese invasion of the kingdom and the killing of the king at the battle of Ambuila. Thereafter the history of the

Kongo church became both fascinating and complex. The two classic histories of Kongo, by Thornton and by Hilton, provide a wealth of detail on the politics of the cathedral close, on the families which provided the cathedral staff, and on the rivalries that pitted ecclesiastical interests against one another. After the collapse of the kingdom Christianity took a new turn with the emergence of independent prophets who adapted religious practices to local political and religious ends. The most famous visionary was, of course, the prophet Beatrice, leader of the Antonine movement. The whole question of the role of prophets in Angola's history opens up research vistas of enormous scope.

One distinctive feature of the Portuguese colonial church was the establishment of the 'brotherhoods of mercy' that cared for their members or sometimes for neighbours in the wider community. The Luanda misericordia provided an asylum and a hospital which cost 3000 *milreis* a year. One-tenth of the cost of the institution came from state subventions but all the rest had to be raised from alms or through a small tithe which the brothers were permitted to raise on fruit, eggs and hens. When the town of Massangano attempted to establish its own independent almshouse there was an outcry in the capital. The people of Luanda feared that gifts to the city hospital, which catered for retired and invalided colonial soldiers, might dry up if the establishment of a provincial misericordia were to be authorised. The crown agreed to forbid the establishment of an up-country house of mercy.

As was the case with the duties of the clergy, the activities of the brotherhoods were racially segregated in Angola. The Luanda misericordia would not allow its hearse to be used for the funerals of Africans. The blacks of Luanda, referring to themselves as the city's 'negroes' or 'slaves', established their own misericordia, the Fraternity of the Rosary. In 1658 the members applied to the Vatican to have the bishop of Angola and the prefect of the Capuchin mission appointed as their joint patrons and sponsors. They wanted the right to use the alms which they gave to the church for the conduct of their own funerals with their own hearse. Among the 12 signatures appended to this appeal by Angola's black people was that of 'Gonsalo Vandunem'. This was presumably either the black son of Balthasar Van Dunem, the trader who claimed to have come to Angola from the Hanseatic ports of Germany in the 1630s, or else of Balthasar's uncle, João Van Dunem, another Dutch entrepreneur who may have been active in Angola at an even earlier date.

The question one may ask about the old missions of the seventeenth century, as one does of the new missions of the twentieth century, is whether they were 'collaborators' with colonialism or whether they were 'conspirators' harnessed to an anti-imperial alliance. The archives do not give any clear-cut answers. Some of the clergy were dependent on the state for their stipends and were essentially appointed to care for the spiritual welfare of settlers, soldiers and administrators. This was true in the seventeenth century and it became true again in the twentieth century. Other priests, by contrast, were appointed to the task of evangelisation. Their responsibility was to convert Africans to Christianity and they did not consider it part of their task to support Portugal's imperial ambitions. This attitude also prevailed in both the seventeenth and the twentieth centuries. In neither century was Portugal realistically able to fulfil the evangelising responsibilities granted to it under the monopolistic *padroado*. Mission activity was therefore always dominated by 'foreigners' whose attitude to Portuguese political pretensions could be very ambivalent.

In activating the Angolan missions the Vatican could not afford to offend Spain but nevertheless had to make some concessions to Portugal in order to get Carmelites and Capuchins into Angola. In one compromise Portugal agreed that missionaries could be recruited in Spanish Italy and the Spanish Low Countries but not in Spain itself. As always, however, the colonial authorities remained anxious lest the missions fail to put the glory of the Portuguese empire, and the Lusitanianisation of the colonial peoples, at the top of their agendas. The attempted use of missions as the cultural arm of the empire caused suspicion to fall not only on 'foreign' missionaries but on any preachers who bridled at the suggestion that they should instil colonial patriotism as part of their teaching. Acrimonious relations between church and state could affect even the most imperial of mission traditions. In the case of the Jesuits conflict degenerated into farce. In 1659 the Luanda city council had decided that for reasons of hygiene and sanitation it would ban pigs from roaming the city streets foraging for scraps of food. The militia were ordered to kill two dozen offending pigs that had been soiling the streets. The swineherds who looked after the pigs took up arms to protect their valuable livestock and fighting broke out. The pigs, it emerged, belonged to the Jesuits. The Jesuits were outraged that the state should interfere with its wealth-generating enterprise. So angry were the fathers that they excommunicated the governor-general. The matter of two dozen pigs became an international *cause célèbre*. Resolving the Angolan dispute between a Jesuit superior and an imperial proconsul required the assistance not only of the dowager-queen of Portugal but also of the pope in Rome. The Jesuits considered themselves not only to be independent of the empire but above the law as well.

The history of popular religion in the city of Luanda is obviously a subject that needs to be traced back in time to the centuries before the Portuguese Revolution temporarily outlawed the church in 1834. Carnival-type celebrations appear to have played subtle roles in the interaction of people and power in the seventeenth century as they have done in recent times. The processions which celebrated the canonisation of St Ignatius Loyola and of St Francis Xavier, both canonised in 1622, allegedly involved street celebrations in which the people of Luanda mocked their overbearing masters and conquerors. The tradition of carnival soon revived after 1834 and was witnessed by Héli Chatelain, the Swiss amateur folklore specialist who lived in Luanda before establishing his industrial mission on the Angolan plateau. A further bout of church persecution in 1910 again failed to repress the carnival spirit of Luanda. By then, however, Angola had been absorbed into the modern colonial world and an immense diversity of religious experience was being brought into the country by missions with many different theological practices and from many different national origins.

The revival of mission activity in Angola half a century after the 1834 dissolution of the monasteries came in a wide variety of forms. In the far north an independent English Protestant mission, the Livingstone Inland Mission, had been exploring Christianising opportunities in northern Angola in the immediate aftermath of Stanley's descent of the Congo river. The Portuguese promptly responded by sending King Pedro V, whom they had imposed on the Kongo throne in 1860, a rival Catholic mission. This mission was led by António Barroso, the pioneer of the Portuguese Catholic revival in Angola. A Portuguese gunboat was supplied to ferry him and his team to the Congo estuary. Meanwhile to the north of the river a French mission had been established by the Holy Ghost fathers. As far as Britain, Portugal and France were concerned mission activity shadowed political activity in the scramble for Africa. In the case of Angola, however, there was also mission activity unrelated to the scramble. Among the independent missions which gained an important influence over local communities in Angola some came from America and others came from Switzerland, neither of them diplomatic participants in the conquest.

The issue of whether missions should be seen as a part of the colonising process or whether, on the contrary, missionaries were allied to their converts in opposition to the main forces of colonisation is a question that should be deeply explored in the context of Angola's complex late-nineteenth and twentieth-century history. One very specific case-study that would be of interest concerns the Bailundu war of 1902. In this war the Portuguese voices of propaganda automatically blamed the Presbyterian Protestants of the American Board of Commissioners for Foreign Missions (ABCFM) for fomenting discontent. The concept of the foreign scapegoat has a long history in Angola and Portuguese authorities were always reluctant to believe that their policies, or the practices of their settler-citizens, could be the cause of African discontent. In the case of the Bailundu war the encroachment of colonial power to challenge the rights of Bailundu kings, and the encroachment of colonial merchants to challenge the historic position of Bailundu caravan masters, were surely sufficient to trigger a major war of primary resistance. But the colonisers nevertheless sought to lay the blame on 'disloyal' missionaries, foreigners who did not support Portugal's imperial ambitions in the highlands and did not make loyalty to the Portuguese flag one of the central themes of their education.

The Portuguese attack on foreign missionaries appears to have been ill-conceived on two counts. Not only did the Portuguese have only themselves to blame for the fierceness of the resistance to conquest, but the missionaries, far from being *agents provocateurs* who stimulated Bailundu resistance, were actually believers in the colonising agenda. They thought that a *pax Lusitania* would help them in their desire to bring 'civilisation' and Christianity to the interior of Angola. Far from encouraging the Bailundu to take up arms and fight a heroic war of resistance, the missionaries secretly supplied the colonial army with military intelligence. The stores of the mission house may even have helped to save the lives of the Portuguese invaders when the troops ran short of supplies. Mission trade goods which could be bartered for food were discreetly sent to the invading force without the knowledge of the African host community. There is clearly scope for interesting work in the mission archives, in the local archives, in the oral folk memory, and in the records of the Portuguese colonial ministry. The perceptions of local politicians, colonial soldiers and Christian preachers all need to be carefully re-examined.

One of the small rivals to the American mission in Bailundu was the Swiss mission in Kalukembe. The records of the mission can be analysed to study inter-mission competition, conflict and mistrust. They can also be used, however, to analyse more deeply the relations of 'foreign' Protestants with both Portuguese colonising peoples and Angolan colonised peoples. The Swiss mission was intended to be an independent, self-financing, industrial mission supported by its own craft industries, agricultural plantations and merchant activities. It was also intended to rescue slaves who had escaped from the caravans of *serviçães* going to the coast to be 'sold' to the cocoa planters of São Tomé. But the path of the mission was never smooth and compromises had to be made at every turn of the evangelising road. The Portuguese authorities were outraged when the mission was called Lincoln, in honour of the American president who had outlawed slavery in the United States, and denied that any Angolan colonial subject was in danger of being enslaved and in need of being rescued. Worse still the most profitable customers in the mission stores and workshops were the Afrikaner immigrants who had escaped British rule in South Africa to find farmlands where they could practise their accustomed cattle-rearing and crop-raising with the help of black slaves. When these slaves escaped from hard labour and cruel punishment to seek asylum in the Swiss mission, the Afrikaners threatened to withdrawn their custom from the mission stores and workshops. The threat may have been an unreal one since no other workshops were as skilled in the forging of new metal rims for the Boer waggon wheels as the mission craftsmen, but the mission nevertheless had to trim its idealism in order to survive. The Swiss, like the Americans, had been absorbed into the reality of early colonial relationships. The Swiss mission, like the American, survived and eventually built one of the largest mission hospitals in the whole of Angola. Its archives are in Winterthur.

A third Protestant mission that had to come to terms with early colonial reality was the British Baptist mission in the north of Angola. This mission, established soon after the western Congo region had been brought into prominence by the trans-African journey of H. M. Stanley, became caught up, 40 years later, in the great revolt of 1917. After Portuguese Congo had been incorporated into Angola it became a labour recruiting ground not for Portugal's cocoa islands but for its hardwood logging camps in Cabinda and the Mayombe forest. The intensity of the pressure put on northern Angolan peasants to leave their families and farms to undertake forced and dangerous work in the timber industry eventually led to an explosion of despair. The colonial authorities made the instant but irrational judgement that the Protestants were to blame for the revolt.

They immediately arrested the Reverend Bowskill on charges of treasonable disloyalty to the 'legitimate' colonial government. It was true that the mission was very sympathetic to the plight of the labour conscripts, and it is also true that the mission may have doubted whether it was the responsibility of a missionary to instil loyalty to Portugal into the minds of its parishioners, but the Baptists were certainly not opposed to the constitutional status of colonial governments. The Portuguese, on the other hand, had always feared that foreign missions might bring foreign governments in their wake. Only the terms of the Berlin partition of Africa in 1885 forced them to tolerate foreign missionaries at all lest any intolerant attitude should lead the great powers to confiscate the Portuguese colonies in the way that Belgium had confiscated the Congo state from King Leopold in 1908 as punishment for malpractice. There is therefore much work to be done on analysing the Baptist mission records, probably now located in Oxford, and the confidential police records, probably located in the colonial archive in Lisbon, to get a closer picture of how Angolans in the north viewed the Protestants. Were they saviours who did their best under very difficult circumstances, or were they flawed prophets who at the end of the day were only one more link in the net of foreign oppression that closed around Angola in the long-drawn-out transition from nineteenth-century colonial influence to twentieth-century colonial rule?

A fourth Protestant mission that had to find its way during the years of transition to colonialism was the Methodist mission. Methodists came into much closer contact with the old colonial tradition since they established themselves in the Kwanza regions which had been overrun by the *conquistadores* of the seventeenth century and later established a church in Luanda city itself. Angolan Methodism was of the American variety, with a hierarchy headed by a bishop. Members of the Methodist church associated with the old creole aristocracy of the city, with the new mestizo middle class fathered by white bureaucrats and shopkeepers, and with the 'assimilated' petty bourgeoisie of black Africans who had gained sufficient Portuguese culture to be incorporated into the lower ranks of colonial society. But city Methodists were not fully trusted either by the old black Catholics or by the new white Republicans and found themselves wavering between a conservative desire for incorporation into modern colonial society and a radical political agenda that prided itself on its African identity. Furthermore Methodism retained a strong provincial dimension in the old proto-colonial provinces of northern Kwanza and among peoples associated with the old trading town of Ambaka and the new trading town of Malange. It must be assumed that there will be extensive references to Methodism in Angola's provincial archives as well as in the mission records.

The taxonomy of Protestant mission traditions does not stop with the four large and lasting mission churches. In the east the Plymouth Brethren appear to have spread into Angola from the British and Belgian territories of the upper Congo and Zambezi basins and to have reached Bihé. Bold moves into the heart of Central Africa enabled them to outdistance both the India mission and the China mission in seeking funds from British Brethren in support of their work. The Plymouth Brethren were less concerned to educate and 'modernise' their congregations and believed that converting them to Christianity was the essential priority. The Brethren did not struggle to teach their converts Portuguese but used their own English language and even flew their own British flag over their mission houses. (Samuels, *Education in Angola*). Another small British evangelical mission was created in the north of Angola and survived until 1961 when it was abruptly dissolved on the outbreak of the colonial war. The dissolution of the mission did not end Christian worship among the converts, however, and they formed the autonomous *Igreja Evangélica Reformada de Angola* which survived the troubles, the invasions, and the civil war and later allied itself with one of the Swiss Protestant churches (Benedict Schubert, *Der Krieg und die Kirchen*). A third small tradition that needs to be explored is the spread of Lutheran mission influence from the German territory south of the Cunene into the Ovambo territories of the far south of Angola. Portuguese fear of a German conquest of the south persisted until the First World War, as graphically portrayed in Pepetela's great saga, *Yaka*.

The Catholic response to the proliferation of Protestant mission stations throughout Angola began as a patriotic demand that Angola's Portuguese colonial identity should be protected from the influx of foreigners associated with rival empires and neighbouring colonies. But Portugal, having dissolved its monasteries in 1834, had a very weak religious tradition. There were not enough priests, nuns and brothers to cater for the home needs of the Portuguese parishes let alone to send personnel to the settler parishes of the colonies or to staff mission churches for Africans. The restoration of the Catholic church in Angola, and the succession to the Capuchin tradition that had been terminated in 1834, fell to the order of the Holy Ghost, many of whose priest were French and German. Fortunately some of the records of this Catholic revival, like some of the records of the Capuchin missions, have been published and provide historians with a useful starting point for a new generation of questions (António Brásio, *Spiritana Monumenta Historica, Angola*, vols 1–5, Pittsburg, 1966–71).

One of the more interesting ironies of church history in Angola concerns the relationship between the church and the New State and its colonial policies as laid out in 1930. Salazar had gained power by supporting the Catholic wing of the Portuguese army in opposition to the Masonic wing of the army, but once in power he was determined that the state and not the church should be dominant in the colonies. It took him 10 years to hammer out a compromise with the Vatican and sign a concordat in 1940. But the Catholic Church under the New State was still primarily concerned with the religious well-being of Portuguese settlers. The evangelisation of Angolans therefore remained largely in the hands of foreigners, albeit under strict rules governing the use of the Portuguese language. The Catholic missions continued to be staffed by Frenchmen, by Italians, by Spaniards, by Alsatians, while the Protestant missions were still Swiss, American, British and Canadian. All of them must have their own libraries, parish magazines, administrative records, letter-books, account ledgers, and family memoirs that will enable historians better to understand Angola during the half-century from the fall of the Republic in 1910 to the outbreak of war in 1961.

During the colonial war of 1961 to 1974 the Protestant churches and the independent churches that had grown from them went through very difficult times. The story is well told by Benedict Schubert in his new book *Der Krieg und die Kirchen*, so far only available in German but clearly indicating the areas for new research, both archival and oral, which the history of Angola in the second half of the twentieth century might follow. After the rebellion in 1961 the possession of a Bible was deemed by the colonial security forces to be proof of disloyalty to the colonial state. Bibles belonging to members of the North Angola mission were destroyed, and in Luanda stones were thrown at the headquarters of the Methodist mission. South of the Kwanza Protestant churches suffered from restrictions to their work although there was no rebellion for which they could be blamed. The independent churches such as the Tokoist church proclaimed their loyalty to the colonial order but were nevertheless viewed with suspicion and even persecuted. Two independent churches that arose out of small missions may prove to be particularly interesting to historians. In the north the independent *Igreja Evangélica Reformada de Angola* grew from the small mission that was closed down in 1961. In the south the *Igreja Evangélica do Suloeste de Angola* grew out of the independent Swiss mission which survived the outbreak of war in 1961 and later adapted to the changing circumstances of independence and of civil war. The Catholic church was far from immune from the conflicts of loyalty that were created by the independence struggle and even Portuguese Catholics who supported the ideals of a civilising mission could be critical of the methods of a semi-totalitarian state. When the time comes from Angolans to explore the history of their liberation it will be necessary to look into the church archives of all the religious traditions as well as into the archives of the many strands of military, police and security services that were responsible for monitoring religious belief and altering religious practice.

Despite the church persecutions carried out during the last, ultra-colonial, phase of Portuguese rule, and despite the suspicious attitude to religion of the semi-Marxist nationalist government that followed, the churches in Angola did not find co-operation with one another at all easy. Each church evolved its own pragmatic accommodation with power in the late colonial and postcolonial periods as they had done in the proto-colonial and early colonial periods. The largest and most nationally integrated of the churches was the Catholic church, which moved from being the 'official' church of the colonial state to being the most influential church of the national state. It will be an interesting project to study the attitude towards the Catholic church of the MPLA government as it evolved from hostility to co-operation and eventually invited the pope to visit Angola and celebrate mass in a football stadium filled with government supporters. The Protestant churches, in the meantime, retained much more regional bases and their attempts at creating ecumenical conferences ran into entrenched theological differences. But the legacies of the local, partially ethnic, Protestant traditions remained strong and need careful analysis by contemporary historians of Angolan society. The received wisdom suggests that Baptists adapted more readily to the market principle than Methodists and that Methodists were more comfortable in the service of the state than Presbyterians. Such generalisations form the starting point for new research on the class aspirations of Angola's local elites along the lines long pioneered by Christine Messiant. They also lead to the need for new work on the churches themselves, and their infant umbrella organisations, as conducted primarily by Benedict Schubert.

The present author is peculiarly ignorant of church history. But he is convinced that for the next generation of historians of Angola there will be many interesting questions to ask. Why did Angola attract so many different groups of missionaries over such a long period? How did the contrast between the many Catholic orders of the sixteenth and seventeenth centuries affect the people of Angola? What were the consequences of the conflict between the Portuguese crown and the Vatican for church life in Angola? How was Christianity modified in African communities which had no regular contact with visiting priests? Who is going to analyse the role of religious prophets in Angola? How did the Catholics of Angola experience the dissolution of the monasteries in 1834? How important were women missionaries in the Christianisation of Angola and what role did women play in the local congregations? What was the importance of education in the mission tradition and how did the scholarly level of missionaries vary from one order or society to another? What was the impact of the self-sustaining 'industrial' missions on the technological practice and economic output of farming villages? When did professionalised medicine become one of the tools of Christianisation and with what consequences for the physical and mental health of converted peoples? How important was the national affiliation of priests and preachers in the mission field? In what ways did the Portuguese divorce of church and state in 1910 affect the colonial situation in Angola? How different was the experience of Christianity in the zones of white settlement, in the coastal towns, and in the 'lands at the end of the earth'? How are the ambiguities of the relations between the Salazarian New State and the Roman Catholic Church perceived a generation later? To what extent was the staff of each mission and church Africanised with local personnel? How far can political ideologies be traced back to mission values in Angolan society? What effects did mission traditions have on the postcolonial humanitarian organisations that flooded into Angola in the 1980s and 1990s? How important was mission affiliation to the identities of the competing elites that tried to control the post-civil-war politics in Angola? And where does one find answers to any of these questions?

8 Joseph Miller's *Way of Death*

One of the most important books ever published on the history of the Atlantic is Joseph C. Miller's Way of Death. *It is sub-titled* Merchant Capitalism and the Angolan Slave Trade 1730–1830. *It represents the imaginative culmination of a long career devoted to the study of the slave trade. It also represents far and away the best work available for the understanding of eighteenth-century Angola, based as it is on extensive field and archival work undertaken in the region in the late 1960s. The book simultaneously opens up new avenues of Portuguese economic history not previously perceived by traditional scholars. This chapter first appeared as a review article in* Past and Present *(no. 131, May 1991) and is reprinted with the permission of the Past and Present Society (175 Banbury Road, Oxford) who hold the world copyright.*

Perhaps the most fundamental turning-point in the later colonial history of the South Atlantic was the Portuguese discovery of gold in the hinterland of Rio de Janeiro at the very end of the seventeenth century. Over the next 30 years Brazilian gold altered the structure of the Portuguese domestic and imperial economies, accelerated the economic modernisation of Portugal's industrial patrons in Britain, increased the demand for slave labour in the Portuguese-frequented parts of Africa, and determined the ownership of a significant section of the world's colonial shipping. This broad canvas has been richly painted in a monumental new book by Joseph C. Miller, sombrely entitled *Way of Death: Merchant Capitalism and the Angolan Slave Trade, 1730–1830.*[1] Each huge, densely argued section of the work consists of a set of richly illuminating chapters, concerning in turn Africa, the Atlantic and Brazil, as well as Portugal itself. The section on Portugal, coming as it does at the end, is in danger of being overlooked, yet it represents some of the best work yet attempted on the economic history of Portugal in the eighteenth century, a century rather neglected by historians who have been mesmerised by sixteenth-century imperial economic history to the detriment of the equally interesting transformations of later periods.

The swift and easy rise of the Brazilian bullion trade had a depressing effect, both on the broad agricultural economy of Portugal and on its narrow industrial base. It was not until after gold-mining had significantly declined, and Portuguese affairs had been taken over by a semi-enlightened modern despot, the future marquis of Pombal, that some attempt was made both to make agriculture more market-sensitive and to develop import-substitution industries to compensate for the loss of foreign exchange in Brazilian bullion. Before that, during the rise of bullion production, Portuguese towns were fed with imported corn and clothed with foreign woollens. Portuguese merchants, however, found their position in the Brazil trade usurped by powerful English factors and their agents. These British entrepreneurs and shippers were so influential that when the Napoleonic armies reached the gates of Lisbon in 1807 Britain forcibly evacuated the Portuguese court and part of the aristocracy and compelled them to move to Rio de Janeiro, in the process opening up Brazil to the British. During this heyday of British influence, Portugal's own merchants in Lisbon were forced to seek alternative niches in the traffic of the South Atlantic.

The one colonial market in which competition was not initially strong enough to eclipse Portuguese shipping and investment was Angola. There the colonial state could favour the sale of over-priced and protected commodities from Portugal, or of imports from the scattered remnants of Portugal's old empire in Indonesia (Timor), India (Goa) and China (Macau). Angola was also a market for rough wine which even the British with their unquenchable thirsts would not import in unlimited quantities. Miller describes Angola as a commercial dumping-ground for Portuguese imperial products not competitive in the world market. His argument is that the Angola–Brazil slave trade was a particularly risky and not always very profitable business, but one which offered struggling marginal traders on the Lisbon waterfront at least some prospect of converting their winnings into bullion or other prized Brazilian produce. French and British competition in the Brazil slave trade was restricted by low profits until late in the eighteenth century, and these powers were fully stretched selling slaves from western Africa to the profitable sugar and cotton industries of Saint Domingue or Georgia.

The success of the Lisbon merchants in getting a slice (albeit a marginal one) of the Brazil trade owed much to their ingenuity in devising a 'slave bridge' across the South Atlantic on which they personally avoided bearing the highest risks. In the African ports they outmanoeuvred their creolised 'Luso-African' trade partners and rivals of mixed cultural ancestry by manipulating their connections with the crown and its miniature imperial bureaucracy. Although their accumulation of capital was limited by the standards of the great traders on the Rio–Lisbon–London routes, they were nevertheless able to offer competitive credit terms to their suppliers. Above all they concentrated their energies on selling goods in Africa, and not on buying slaves which they themselves would own. Instead of being paid in the most perishable of all commodities, humans, they arranged to be paid in credit notes. Far from seeing the loss of slaves as a risk, these merchants of death saw high slave mortality as being to their advantage. The more rapidly slaves died, the sooner fresh ones would be needed, thus further extending the market for their shoddy seconds and off-cuts.

Credit was the driving force of the South Atlantic system. In Africa the Lisbon trade goods were given out on credit to the slave catchers and brokers recruited among exiled deserters and criminals who had been shipped from Europe or Asia to the Angolan ports. In Brazil the agricultural estates were in debt to such an extent that even when plantation profits were poor, the planters had no option but to go on buying slaves and producing sugar to pay off old borrowings. Although the system, with its inexorable pressure, was simple, the management of colonial credit was constantly changing, and involved two broad strands of Lisbon merchants. The new 'Europeanists' sold British-financed manufactures, while the old 'nationalists' mainly sold Mediterranean and Asian produce.

The rivalry of the two groups of Angola traders reflected many contrasts in Portuguese society. The 'nationalists' were primarily concerned with the selling of surplus goods, including traditional Asian cotton textiles, which could not be sold in safer or more profitable markets. The 'Europeanists' were more concerned with ensuring that Brazil had enough slaves to maintain production in both minerals and tropical crops. The two groups had different outlets for the Brazilian commodities in which they received ultimate payment. Gold and raw cotton went primarily to Britain via the great British waterside trading factory at Lisbon. The factory traders were linked to the pro-British faction in Portuguese politics. The rival 'French faction' at court was more closely linked to the old crown-dominated colonial system. They preferred payment in silver obtained illicitly from Peru via the River Plate. Silver sold at a premium in India and, before the rise of the British cotton industry, paid for the Portuguese empire's finished cotton goods from Asia. In addition to silver, traders connected with the French faction welcomed payment in sugar, which continued to be sold to Mediterranean kingdoms with no tropical colonies of their own.

Although the contrasts between the two broad tendencies of the merchant bourgeoisie were clear, there was nevertheless much self-interested collaboration. Both sets of traders needed to keep the price of commodities in Africa high and could not afford to compete to the point of undermining the overall advantage of the European buyer over the African seller. At the Lisbon end of the trade, merchants of the British tendency sold some of their sugar to merchants with Mediterranean outlets, while Asia-orientated traders sold their silks and some Indian cottons to brokers with South American outlets. Both sets of traders received payment in bills of exchange which could be cashed in Lisbon before the underpinning commodities had been shipped to the north, sometimes even before the related slaves had arrived in Brazil. Lisbon merchants also manipulated their government connections so that they could rely on friendly royal courts to favour their cause in any litigation over credit with defaulting Angolan traders.

Not all those involved in Angolan trade belonged to the established 'bourgeois' networks of well-connected merchants affiliated to the two political and commercial traditions. In addition some opportunity-seeking merchant adventurers mounted occasional expeditions to Angola. They were sharply condemned by the 're-spectable' trading houses, and castigated as gun-runners and smugglers. In particular they bought slaves from embezzlers who had accepted credit from the Lisbon trading houses at Luanda, but then sold their slaves in other ports rather than return to Luanda to pay off their debts. Such 'outlaws' offended against the smooth running of 'orderly' slave trading.

One major advantage which the regular Lisbon traders enjoyed was the opportunity to bid for the tax contract associated with the slave trade in Angola. In Spain the better-known though rather different *asiento* slave-trading licence was prized by foreigners as much for the opportunities it provided to smuggle non-perishable goods into the Spanish empire as for the right to transport highly perishable slave cargoes. In Portugal the advantage of bidding for the 'tax farm' was that it gave the holder primacy in calling in debts. It also conferred a crown monopoly in the Luanda ivory trade, and a small profit margin in the collecting of crown taxes.

The temporary benefits which the six-year contract conferred encouraged the contractor to flood the market with goods while he
held the advantage. This caused such inflation in the local textile
currencies that they had to be replaced by standards of value based
on Asian textiles. Each contractor also invaded the Luanda money
market with unsecured commercial bills. These were of somewhat
limited trustworthiness, and were unpopular.

Until the middle of the eighteenth century the tax contractors
were able to play off rival interests against each other: metropolitan
and colonial; commercial and bureaucratic; African and expatriate; Rio de Janeiro and Pernambuco. They illegitimately dominated
the outport of Benguela in south Angola, and at Luanda itself gained
a loading preference in the queues of ships awaiting slave cargoes.
The contractors charged full taxes on all slaves except unweaned
children, and not merely on the dwindling proportion of able-bodied
adult males who technically were the unit of evaluation. Contractors also contravened the legislation on the 'tight-packing' of ships
to get more slaves, and particularly slaves in which they had an
interest, away to Brazil. This overcrowding became one of the most
visible of the contractors' abuses, however, and was one of the excuses
used to attack the system when a new era of 'free trade' began to
permeate Portuguese commercial thinking with the rise of Pombal
in the 1750s.

The marquis of Pombal has tended to feature in received history
as a tyrant in domestic affairs and a xenophobe with a passionate
hostility to Britain in foreign affairs. In fact he was a moderniser
who was well read in the British school of eighteenth-century political economy. He was also a pragmatist in his nationalist sentiments,
and did not take on challenges he could not meet. His grand de-
sign for economic reform did not target British capital in Brazil or
Asian capital in India, but began with the small domestic enterprise of the Portuguese themselves in Angola. Africa, he thought,
might become a market for the infant industries through which he
hoped to modernise Portugal. To gain access, the old-style slave
contractors needed to be dislodged from their quasi-monopolistic
'abuses'. Pombal's plans coincided with a changing Portuguese attitude
to African and Luso-African long-distance traders in the interior
of Africa. A new racism portrayed them as opponents rather than
partners. This hostility was accentuated when the British and French
began to extend their slave trading southwards towards Angola.
Pombal timed his intervention carefully. While Britain and France

were temporarily distracted by the Seven Years War, from 1756 to 1763, he tried to restructure the slave trade with the help of his brother, whom he appointed minister for colonies. The new 'capitalists' were introduced into the South Atlantic as chartered trading companies.

Pombal's initiatives had limited and unexpected consequences. His Pernambuco company gained a small segment of the Lisbon-based slave trade, but left the merchants of Bahia a free hand in the West African trade, and allowed the unchartered traders of Rio de Janeiro to extend their stake in Angola, partly to satisfy their own needs and partly to trade with the Spanish colonies. Rio used smaller ships than Lisbon, but packed them tighter and depended more on the return profit on slaves than on the outward profit on rum. Neither Lisbon nor Rio reached the shipbuilding standards applied to the British West India trade, however, and gradually Britain encroached on the Angolan slaving grounds. As the Luso-Africans were squeezed by Portuguese and Brazilian competition, so they expanded their overland networks to reach the northern ports of Central Africa and the new supplies of European trade commodities, thus squeezing the Portuguese share of the South Atlantic trade. Only after the late eighteenth century did Portugal recover its primacy as a slaving power, and by then Britain had moved from competition to suppression.

If one quarter of Miller's work is a detailed innovative insight into the political economy of the Portuguese empire in the eighteenth century, another represents a major new work on the history of Africa. Indeed this is probably the most important regional history ever written on any part of eighteenth-century Africa, and as such it will attract powerful acclaim in the specialist journals of African studies. The explanation for the dramatic breakthrough is first of all archival. There is a richer collection of documentary evidence relating to Angola than to any other part of eighteenth-century tropical Africa. But the availability of raw evidence is not enough to explain the transformation of historiography. Indeed the Portuguese documentation has long been known and used by chroniclers, editors, colonial historians and even some African historians. Miller, however, has transformed the landscape by the breadth of his synthesis of ideas and evidence. He is already known to Africanists as the man who, in the footsteps of Jan Vansina, revolutionised the interpretation of oral material in the understanding of African history.[2] He now treads in the steps of that other American-based

giant of African history, Philip Curtin, by showing how much more
can be done than hitherto with written evidence.[3]

A major question which has to be asked about Angola is how
important to its history was the trade in slaves. The danger of capture and sale was a very real threat which engendered an extensive
folklore of fear among all the peoples of West Central Africa.
Terrified victims believed that European cannibals provisioned their
ships with salted human flesh boiled up in cauldrons. They also
assumed that European cooking oil was rendered human fat; that
Portuguese red wine was made of African blood; and that the brains
of dead slaves were turned into little grey cheeses. Worse still,
Europeans were thought to burn the bones of slaves and grind them
into the lethal gunpowder which spewed flames of destruction along
the trade paths. It is not surprising that each year many of the 10
million people who lived under the shadow of the Central African
slave trade died of fear as well as of wounds, exhaustion and malnutrition as they were marched away across rock and sand, thorn
and marsh. The actual risk of capture may have been no greater
than the risk of being injured in a modern motor accident, but the
fear of enslavement was profound and all-pervasive. Everyone lost
a friend or relative during his or her lifetime, and each year more
than 0.25 per cent of the population was enslaved.

The economic logic of selling slaves to foreigners in exchange
for the 'bric-a-brac cast off from industrialising Europe'[4] was rooted
in a social system in which people were even more explicitly understood to be 'capital' than they were in Europe. Political power in
Angola was firmly based on the capacity to control people and the
material resources that people represented through procreation,
through production and through exchange. Warlords were able to
increase their 'human capital' by protecting asylum-seekers in their
fortresses, and priest-kings could dominate farmers with the prom-
ise of prayers for rain. People could then be exchanged for material
goods, and material goods exchanged for people, according to the
economic logic of the circumstances. In a slave-using society the
accumulation of human capital was no longer exclusively dependent on the fertility of women, and capital reserves were no longer
held predominantly in perishable agricultural produce.

When a slave-using society came into contact with a slave-trading
society a pricing mechanism had to be established for the conversion of people into goods, and vice versa. When the market was
dominated by the seller of slaves, the unit of human measurement

gradually dwindled from a healthy adult male to any human being, regardless of age, size, sex or health. Inflation also brought 'sweeteners' known as 'dashes' and a steady rise in the availability of credit. But the most difficult aspect of the pricing mechanism for European buyers was the fine grading of the 'assortment' required to make each slave purchase. Europeans

> accepted but seldom grasped why they could buy slaves only for complex, seemingly arbitrary, and unalterably specific assortments of wares hard to assemble and impossible to keep in balance in that remote corner of the world economy. The Europeans saw minor African increases or decreases in price as incomprehensible substitutions of one good for another, perhaps of no significant difference in money cost price but evidently critically distinguished in terms of the uses to which Africans put them. Slave sellers could not be persuaded to substitute one pattern for another and would walk hundreds of kilometers to obtain an item available on one part of the coast but not along portions of it much closer to home.[5]

Slave salesmen climbing that ladder of prestige and social obligation first and foremost bought textiles, alcohol and weapons. Textiles, amounting to half the trade, were needed for warmth in the cool highlands and for boastful displays of aesthetic taste in the hot lowlands. The most costly materials were French linens and Italian silks, but the most extensively available cloths were Portuguese and British imitations of Asian cottons. One-fifth of all imports were spirits and wines landed on the coast in half-ton vats and supplemented with a few kegs of Dutch gin and French brandy.[6] Consumer demand rose so rapidly that even the most successful African traders, who had already built up their power over people, were constantly under pressure to sell slave dependents to buy yet more prestige goods. Powerful trading princes also needed constantly to enhance their arsenals of modern weapons. Miller estimates that by the late eighteenth century the annual global price being paid for 30 000 slaves included 60 000 guns.[7] These guns, and the necessary gunpowder, amounted to about 10 per cent of the sale price. The working life of a trade gun was short, perhaps no more than a year, so that even with such large-scale imports of firearms it is unlikely that more than one man in 100 possessed a gun in the trading zone. Musketeers continued to constitute small elite units among the large regiments of spear-throwers and bowmen.

The complexity of the overland routes along which slaves were driven reflected the relative purchasing power of the various sectors of the coast at various times. The documentary evidence for the changing pattern of routes used is astonishingly detailed. Miller is able to plot the markets and paths on maps of great complexity and accuracy. Not for him the 'Afric' maps where o'er the downs are elephants for want of towns'. To any reader familiar with the region, or with the existing literature, the descriptions make compulsive reading. Each familiar name is brought to life as more detail is revealed than hitherto of its commercial and diplomatic associations. The great broker kingdom of Kasanje, whose history Miller himself has previously done so much to illuminate, is set in the context of its full range of slave-trading partners for 500 miles around.[8] In each of these communities politicians engaged in a constant programme of choosing which of their people to keep and which to sell forward. New male captives were the most likely to be sold and young females the most likely to be retained. All client and subject people had to be conscious of the risk entailed in the captive element in their ancestry. Their patrons took 'foreign' origins into their calculations when deciding whom to keep and whom to sell when in need of goods or capital. Miller likens the whole process to a living organism 'in which the central markets functioned as hearts pumping trade goods out through arterial caravan routes and through the capillaries of trading diaspora and *pombeiro* peddlers'.[9] The corresponding veins brought back slaves to nourish the African body politic.

Ever since Philip Curtin blew the whistle on the overlapping generations of historians who accepted each others' slave-trade statistics with lazy naïvety,[10] serious attempts have been made to quantify the magnitude of the trade along each segment of the African coast. The task is bedevilled by every kind of handicap, but Miller is not deterred, as Figure 8.1 demonstrates. He concludes interestingly that although the total number of exported people rose to a crescendo in the late eighteenth century,

> the true rate of population loss – that is the proportion taken from the changing areas afflicted at any one time – may well have remained relatively constant over the entire course of the trade, with a tendency to increase temporarily with drought and just before and as the slaving frontier made its eastward lurches.[11]

Figure 8.1   Approximate annual exports of slaves from Western
Central Africa

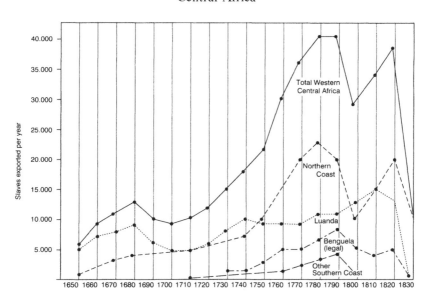

Source: Figure 7.1 from Joseph C. Miller, *Way of Death: Merchant Capitalism and the Angolan Slave Trade, 1730–1830* (London and Madison, Wis., 1988), p. 233.

The economic cost of moving the slaving frontier eastwards was enormous. Each advance tied up more capital and meant longer postponement of profits on the rising credit awarded at the coast. It was a shortage of working capital, as much as a lack of military capacity, which delayed each stage of frontier expansion. If seizure for debt was a prime source of captives, then goods had to be available to create indebtedness. Not only was more capital needed to spread the net, but more risks were incurred from mortality as the time-lapse between the dispatch of goods and the return of slaves lengthened. In the process old raiding states became new broker-kingdoms with modified strategies. Kasanje changed from being primarily a seller of captured slaves travelling westwards, to being primarily a seller of European goods going east to the new slave frontiers.

One feature of slaving society in Angola which was of long-term importance to the colony, and made it distinct from many other trading zones on the Atlantic, was the presence of the creole 'Luso-African' community. The Luso-Africans were hybrid by culture, if not by race, and acted as serious competitors in the trade to both the Portuguese and Brazilian colonists and merchants and the African entrepreneurs. In the early eighteenth century Luso-Africans owned the slaves they bought in the interior and retained ownership during the middle passage, being paid only for those slaves safely landed in Brazil. Gradually they surrendered the risks and profits of the sea-borne leg of the trade to Brazilian shippers, and concentrated on selling their slaves on the African shore rather than the transatlantic one. In the transition the Portuguese continued to avoid owning slaves whenever possible and kept their assets in manufactures, colonial commodities, bills of exchange and good, heavy coin.

The contrast between immigrants and Luso-Africans was severe. Immigrants were social marginals who settled on the beaches of the lower town and were anxious to make a quick profit in Africa and escape before malaria fatally caught up with them. Luso-Africans were the high society which lived in elegance in the upper town, and nurtured their status as well as their business interests. The connection between the two was mediated through marriage as immigrants sought socially desirable local wives. The sexual lusts of immigrants could be violently satisfied with an unlimited choice of expensive but nubile captives to whom violation was but one more feature of the everlasting horror of slavery. Marriage, on the other hand, provided far-reaching networks of commercial association. By providing brides for merchants the creole families increased their degree of genetic whiteness to enhance the honorary white status that went with the ownership of wealth.

In between the two intricate analyses of Africa and of Portugal Miller has inserted two equally compelling studies of slave transport across the Atlantic and of slave utilization in Brazil.[12] The 'floating tombs'[13] which carried the slaves varied in size, in ownership, in destination and in health record, but always the middle passage was frightening, smelly and dangerous. Some cargoes successfully rebelled and ran the ship ashore to escape; others were so tightly shackled that they only rarely got a wash or exercise, or even a breath of fresh sea air. Conditions in the slave pens at Luanda were not much better, and food there was minimal and clothing non-existent.

One of the conclusions Miller draws in relation to Brazil is the relatively small proportion of shipping that was engaged in slaving, only about 10 per cent of the tonnage committed to the European routes.[14] Shipping along the Brazilian coast was also much more important than that on the South Atlantic route. Aficionados of slave-trade studies will no doubt enjoy these sections of Miller's work as much as historians of Portugal and Africa will enjoy the others. They will also recognise the comprehensiveness of the reading which Miller has devoured during his 10-year marathon, and which enabled him to compile his slave-trade bibliographies. Each chapter can be welcomed for the freshness of new insight into the eighteenth-century industry of slaving which he has so comprehensively epitomised as the *Way of Death*.

9 The Coffee Barons of Cazengo

This chapter is based on several months of exploration conducted in 1973 in the previously little-used nineteenth-century archives then housed in the colonial museum at Luanda. At the time when the research was undertaken Angola was the world's fourth largest producer of coffee. It was therefore interesting to find detailed evidence concerning the origins of colonial land appropriation policies and labour recruitment practices which were later to dominate the economic history of the twentieth century. The work was previously published in 1978 in the Journal of African History *(Cambridge University Press). A version of this paper was discussed at the conference on Southern African History held at the National University of Lesotho in August 1977.*

In 1844 Angola exported three tons of coffee.[1] A century and a quarter later annual production regularly surpassed 200 000 tons worth nearly £100 million.[2] Portugal's long-neglected Cinderella colony had reached fourth place in the world coffee league.

When a history of Angola's coffee comes to be written it will be in two periods. During the nineteenth century slave trading was gradually phased out, between 1836 and 1910, and experiments in alternative tropical exploitation were undertaken. Nineteenth-century Angola tried sugar, rum, tobacco, vines, coal-mining, whale-fishing, copper-prospecting, and wheat-farming. Nothing seemed to work except coffee, and production rose unsteadily to about 11 000 tons a year in the mid-1890s. Then the bubble burst. The million-ton world market was left to Brazilian domination.

In the second, twentieth-century, cycle Angolan coffee took nearly 40 years to struggle back to the level achieved in the 1890s.[3] Thereafter production took off and no other export could match it, not even the diamonds of the rich north-eastern concessions of de Beers' Diamang. For the first time Portuguese emigrants went voluntarily to Angola. The convict colony image faded. A new generation of immigrant back-woods traders became coffee farmers and plantation managers. The pattern bore striking resemblances to the colonial initiatives of the nineteenth century. In the twentieth century the alienation of land and the impressment of labour became so intense that in March 1961 Africa's largest-ever colonial uprising occurred. The 13-year war of liberation which began in the cotton fields and spread to the city slums, exploded in the Angolan coffee belt.

Once the colonial war had begun, Portugal took a renewed interest in Angola's development potential. Immigration rose to 10 000 Portuguese a year, and coffee production resumed its growth. The government tried, with increasing economic urgency, to diversify out of the dominant plantation sector. German firms were encouraged to prospect for iron; British teams surveyed ambitious programmes of Europeanised ranching; foreign investors built up import-substitution industries to defray the costs of war. But, despite all the new-found colonial vigour of Portugal, and the revolutionary capitalist break from petty economic nationalism, coffee remained obstinately dominant.[4]

In the late 1950s small quantities of mineral oil were found along the northern littoral of mainland Angola, and in the mid-1960s larger off-shore wells were opened in the Cabinda enclave. Oil production began slowly, but in 1973 the price structure of the industry was revolutionised and overnight oil became marginally more valuable than coffee. Then in the following year, 1974, the Portuguese regime collapsed in Europe and Angola was sucked into the 1975 foreign and civil wars. The country was split apart with the plantation lands of the north sundered from the plantation labour of the south. The coffee industry was devastated. Oil remained Angola's only marketable asset. In its first year of office the MPLA government derived 80 per cent of its revenue from the Gulf Oil Corporation. King coffee was dead.

The purpose of this essay is to take a preliminary look at the origins of the Angolan coffee industry. The fascination is not merely that coffee became such an all-pervasive influence in Angola's colonial history. The small sub-colony of Cazengo, in which it all started, has a written archive which goes back to the mid-nineteenth century. The possibility therefore exists of analysing a proto-colonial African society of the last century in a depth and a detail matched in few areas of Africa. This paper is merely a short descriptive account of the coffee barons of Cazengo written as the by-product of an experimental archival exploration. But Cazengo is not unique. Archives also exist for many other inland districts of Angola such as Golungo Alto and Ambaca, and the rising generation of scholars will be able to explore historical avenues yet unthought of.[5]

96

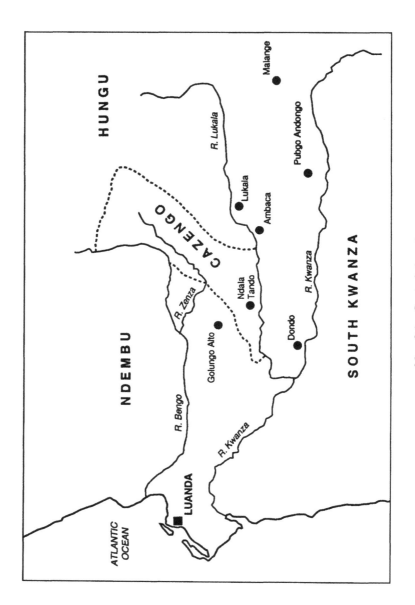

Map 9.1   Central Angola

During the Atlantic period of Angola's history, the district of Cazengo was of little importance. The main slaving routes from Luanda to the interior passed north and south of the wooded hills which stretch throughout its length. When the external slave trade was officially outlawed in 1836, and the Portuguese colony began to seek new sources of revenue, the green and fertile hills of Cazengo appeared attractive. The surrounding land was either poor, or deficient in rainfall, or had been exhausted by excessive burning and shifting cultivation. Moreover, the lowland population had been depleted by warfare, by slaving, and by flight from taxation and labour service. The hills, on the other hand, formed a lush enclave well-peopled by maize and banana farmers. Gradually this enclave was converted into a micro-colony which pioneered Angola's post-Atlantic agricultural economy. In the process it suffered all the conflicts and strains of colonial experimentation.

The potential wealth of Cazengo was initially based on its suitability for coffee growing. From the late 1830s both African and European farmers began planting coffee as a cash crop. The problems they encountered over land-ownership, credit and investment, labour recruiting, coffee marketing, price fluctuations, internal security, external security, and above all transport, were the problems which have affected coffee growers until today. The Cazengo district records do not enable one to examine these themes in a very systematic way, but they do shed spasmodic light on aspects of early Portuguese colonialism. Occasionally a district commander would write a worthwhile report, but more usually one has to rely indirectly on record books, correspondence, law suits, or registered wills, to understand how the planting economy worked. The district office did compile statistics, but with more armchair enthusiasm than accuracy of observation.

In the middle of the nineteenth century Cazengo was governed by 17 African chiefs whom the Portuguese considered to be their vassals. In view of this claimed suzerainty, the Governor-General of Angola took upon himself the right to allocate land, which did not appear to be in immediate use, to foreign land-seekers. Although the first settlers arrived in the 1830s, the earliest surviving register of a *carta de sesmaria* concerns a plot in the chiefdom of Undo-Angombe granted to Candido Augusto Fortunato da Costa in June, 1850.[6] The grant was permanent and inheritable provided cultivation was begun within five years. Taxation was to be based on the yield rather than on the land itself. The *sesmaria* holder was forbidden to interfere with the previously cultivated plots of any third party. Since the land was supposed to be vacant, this odd provision may indicate that islands of African farm land had been encircled by the concession. The creation of enclaves of this kind, which are shown on later concession maps, presumably had the effect of driving the shifting farmer out on the next occasion when he needed to rotate his plot. By 1852 14 coffee growers had registered their titles in Cazengo. Two of them were African chiefs, and the remainder were probably, though not certainly, foreign immigrants from Brazil or Portugal. Chiefs played an invidious role in this scramble, not only as claimants, but also as witnesses who guaranteed that land was 'vacant'. In 1856 António Julio d'Almeida Lima, one of the most infamous of the coffee barons, got 11 such witnesses to measure his *sesmaria* of 1500 fathoms from the king's highway.[7]

The long business of taking up a *sesmaria* granted by the colonial government was not the only means of acquiring land in Cazengo. In his will dated 1855, Joaquim Pinto said that in addition to his *sesmaria*, worked by 25 slaves, he also had a farm bought from a 'free black woman'.[8] This possibility of private land purchase opened the way to a whole set of disputes over land. Such sales had theoretically to be registered at the district office. Once this practice was expected, it was but a short step to declare that unregistered land was vacant. In 1876 a major dispute arose over such a case. Chief Kakulu Kamwinza (Cacullo Camuinza) was informed that one of the estates to which he laid claim had not been registered, and that the district administrator had therefore sold it to a third party. Vehement protests led to the chief's arrest, escape, and capture by 50 soldiers. He was sent under heavy guard to Luanda with a request that he be kept there indefinitely for the sake of peace, since he had severe (and probably justified) grievances against nearly all the Cazengo planters and traders.[9] Clearly the business of land allocation had passed from official grants, through private sale to outright expropriation. Occasionally the district administrator, fearful of an uprising that he had not the force to contain, defended the interests of the black peasants. On the whole, however, the trend was the other way and small farmers were pushed out. So, in due course, were the chiefs. By the end of the century only seven of the original chiefs of Cazengo district were still recognised, and they had precious little influence. By 1910 it was reported that there were no longer any African chiefdoms in Cazengo district.

In looking at the rise of the coffee-planting economy, it would be helpful to measure the amount of capital that was invested in coffee. Pereira Cardozo, one of the first planters to come from Brazil, claimed that his costs had only been a fraction of the 100-odd million *reis* (£22 000) which an estate of 70 000 trees would have cost him in Brazil in the 1840s.[10] Details are unfortunately rarely given. The major source of investment was certainly profits from retail trading. Backwoods traders were the forerunners of Portuguese expansion on all the frontiers of the old slaving colony. They set up shop with very slender resources and bought African-produced commodities. In Cazengo they bought coffee from African growers. The system of credit which they offered was usually ill-defined, but coffee trees and land were the essential security. This meant that at each crisis caused by drought or crop failure the trader took over the land from the producer. The spasmodic bankrupting of small African producers and the consolidation of landed estates by white immigrant traders remained a central feature of the economy of the Angolan coffee zones at least until 1961. Another source of capital used to plant coffee may have been tax revenue. Early district officers seem to have paid a flat-rate tax to the government for their district and kept the balance of all taxation raised for their own purposes, such as land speculation. Later tax officials received fixed percentages of what they actually collected. There were, however, disincentives to investing local capital in Angola. One was the mobility of administrative personnel and the extremely short tours of duty which became normal in inland districts. Even the planter Fortunato da Costa, who rose to be lieutenant of the Cazengo carrier and police service (*companhia movel*), and later district administrator, was transferred to Pungo Andongo after only eight years in the district.[11] Later administrators were often in office only for a few months. The final ambition of many whites in Angola was not to build up their local investments, but to acquire capital which could be transferred to Brazil. For this reason the trading of African coffee remained important even to settlers who owned their own estates.

In order to encourage the growth and diversification of the colonial economy, the Banco Nacional Ultramarino (BNU) was created in Lisbon in 1864. The directors of the Luanda branch rapidly identified Cazengo as one of the few places where an agricultural economy might develop at a time when 90 per cent of Angola and Benguela's exports came from foreign trade, mainly in ivory and wax bought from the neighbouring kingdoms. The bank invested in coffee by advancing mortgages, accepting payment in kind, and campaigning vigorously against the 'short-sighted' proposal to abolish slavery. When the crisis of 1871 came, and the rains failed for five years in succession, the bank was forced to acquire and administer estates whose mortgage repayments became hopelessly overdue. For 20 years it was the largest landowner in Cazengo. Its limited success was partly achieved by exemption from taxation. In 1902 the Bank's lands, now managed by the Cazengo Agricultural Company, were valued at £300 000, but since coffee had by then fallen sharply in price, the investment was a burden of dubious real value.[12]

The supply of labour was, and remained, a much more vital issue among Cazengo coffee farmers than the supply of capital. Large numbers of workers were needed for weeding, pruning, and above all picking. The coffee industry therefore fitted into a policy of reconverting Angolan labour to Angolan purposes after a 300-year policy of exporting it. Labour could be acquired either by hiring or conscripting a local work force, or else by capturing slaves elsewhere in Angola and bringing them to the coffee estates. The first policy did not work well, since the indigenous people of Cazengo were quite competent at growing their own coffee and not at all anxious to work for settlers. If they were pressed too hard by a policy of conscription, they would emigrate to new coffee lands in the Ndembu and Hungu territories, which were beyond the range of Portuguese control. Slavery therefore seemed to be the answer. The old slaving-houses in Angola were, however, curiously reluctant to encourage local industry. In the 1840s the slavers believed that if they could weather the abolitionist storm, things would eventually return to 'normal' and the outbreak of a European war would lead to the withdrawal of the British cruisers. When Dona Ana Joaquina, a formidable mestizo lady whose assets included several trans-Atlantic slaving vessels, decided to invest capital and slaves in establishing a local sugar industry, she was treated by other slavers as a renegade.[13] In Cazengo the earliest slaves were probably captured in nearby districts rather than expensively bought from the long-distance traders. Such labour was not satisfactory, and could easily escape back home. Some planters hankered after the Brazilian system where coffee could be grown by immigrant peasants from the more impoverished parts of Europe.[14] The only European labour which did reach Cazengo was a small number of trusty convicts who were released to traders or planters willing to offer certain guarantees. Most of these *degredados* had been sentenced to life banishment for homicide, but a few had fixed terms of disgrace after convictions for robbery or rebellion.[15]

The labour situation in Cazengo was not made easier by the succession of labour laws which gradually restricted and finally abolished local slavery. In practice, however, Cazengo remained a slave-owning society, and abuses which became familiar on twentieth-century plantations existed also in the nineteenth century. Labour continued to be bought, sold, and maltreated when labourers were no longer called slaves but *libertos*, *serviçais*, or *contratados*. Even slaves who could afford to buy their freedom were sometimes denied the privilege if owners preferred to sell to a third party. Free labour from the local villages was also under a considerable degree of compulsory pressure. In 1895 Alfredo Augusto dos Santos Cardoso compiled a careful survey of the district. The 131 villages were occupied by 7115 free blacks of whom 55 per cent were women. Of these 850 lived on estates and although free were required to work on the plantations for a wage. The slave population was 3798, again with a small majority of women. They worked on 28 plantations owned or managed by 96 expatriates, of whom two were British employees of Norton Carnegie & Co., owners of the 300-slave Monte Bello estate.[16]

The 1890s boom in coffee prices brought particular pressures on labour. Out of 6000 *serviçal* contracts formally recorded in Cazengo between 1887 and 1904, 1170 were registered in the year 1893 and another 1200 in adjacent years.[17] Slaves came from many districts and were normally bought for two or three pieces of chintz. Efforts to prevent escapes – such as the great break-out of 1894 – were severe. On the Prototypo model plantation, one Bernardo was beaten on the palms of his hands and the soles of his feet for being absent without leave; he subsequently died in the municipal stocks. Plantation *serviçais* were less likely than government or military slaves to obtain their right to retirement after about five or eight years. For their 12-hour day they received a wage of six pence (120 *reis*) in kind paid at the manager's valuation in the manager's own shop. Short yards and high prices were usual.[18]

By the 1900s there were a number of ways in which *serviçais* sought to lessen the burden of their servitude. They could offer themselves to the Cazengo Company, where conditions were alleged to be more relaxed and more remunerative.[19] This caused particular grievance to the planters, who complained that the company had the unfair advantage of being exempt from taxation. A second escape route involved signing up as a *serviçal* of Dom André Francisco Fernandes Torres, the Ndembu Kabuku. The adminis-trator complained to central government that allowing the Kabuku's employees exemption from military or plantation service was a bad precedent which caused many 'deserters' and 'slackers' to sit on his estates doing nothing and 'demoralising law-abiding natives'.[20] The third escape from service much favoured by soldiers and carriers was to become a 'Vili'. Originally the Cazengo Vili were eighteenth-century immigrants from Loango, on the north Congo coast. They set themselves up as iron smiths and supplied colonial Angola with hoes in exchange for tax and service exemption. Cazengo settler society was intensely hostile to the Vili communities of the Zenza valley but even in 1906 they did not have the police capacity to challenge their independence.[21]

The nineteenth-century economy of Cazengo, like all colonial economies dependent on a single primary commodity, was subject to severe fluctuations which greatly disturbed the peace. The price of coffee rose from £18 per ton in 1869 to £50 in 1873. It then fell back to £10 in the 1880s but rose once again briefly to £50 in 1893. When prices were high, European planters began extending their estates at the expense of their neighbours. When prices were low African planters boycotted the local European trading community in order to carry their coffee to Dondo town in search of greater profits. In 1892 tensions rose as the price of coffee rose. António Fernandes de Freitas, a notoriously violent man, found himself besieged by an army of black smallholders. The DC reported that 'the cause of these conflicts is the just complaint of the small proprietors whose plots are being snatched by large planters who fail to understand that they themselves are the true instigators of public disorder'.[22] Despite this allocation of blame, 50 troops were called in by telegraph to protect the estates. The fracas caused endless disputes over who was to bear the cost of calling in the regular army, since the local force had no guns in working order. The principal victim of the attack was wanted on eight criminal charges and saw no reason to begin co-operating with the administration now, especially since his own men had bloodily routed the attackers before the army arrived.[23]

The African solutions to rising tension and violent competition were to take flight or to take legal action or to seek more power-ful divine intervention. Legal action was often not effective. A 'native petition' to the Governor-General dated 10 September 1895 illustrated how a chief and the DC had colluded in defrauding 10 Cazengo residents of their coffee estates. These were acquired by a cobbler and a barber from Europe.[24] The court records do not contain enough details of witchcraft accusations to examine fully the role of witches in Cazengo society. They do appear to be particularly troublesome when some people are becoming conspicuously more prosperous than others. Since many Cazengo Africans adopted European names, it is difficult to tell when the victims (or practitioners) of witchcraft were African and when they were European.

The official European solution to rising unrest was to strengthen the military power in the district. Armed enforcement of economic policy had been the fundamental feature of Portuguese activity in Central Africa at least since 1575. There appear to have been four different types of soldier in Angola in the second half of the nineteenth century. Career soldiers from Portugal made up the local administration and were sent out from Luanda for short tours of duty. They were frequently moved about and their average stay in Cazengo declined to not much more than seven months. Interim district administrators were chosen from among planters, clerks or military officers at different periods.[25] The next military group were the first-line troops. These were long-term, paid soldiers, some white and some black, and the majority, at least, seem to have been convicts. The main legal penalty for severe crime in Cazengo was deportation to Luanda and enrolment in the army there. No first-line troops were stationed in Cazengo, but 20 men of the second battalion of gunners were on call from Dondo. The introduction of the telegraph greatly facilitated their main function, which was the recapture of runaway slaves. The third army was the troops of the mobile companies, a kind of escort police and carrier service.[26] Cazengo had two such companies, each with a theoretical strength of about 172 men. In practice the numbers were sometimes down to 30 or so with a majority sick or otherwise absent. The *moveis* troops were not paid, and seem in effect to have been government slaves. They must have worked on the land to provide their own keep when not on active duty. Recruitment was apparently arbitrary, but plantation employees were exempt, although chief Kabuku had great difficulty in proving that he legally owned the *serviçais* on his sugar estates. Many recruits served for life, but others succeeded in getting their release after a number of years. The fourth military category was the *guerra preta*, who seem to have been recruited and used in exactly the same way as the mobile companies.

Cazengo had two companies, nominally of 172 men each, from 1862.[27] In times of labour crisis soldiers were allocated to private employers as labourers. This was particularly true in 1906 when the estates were facing severe competition for workers from the railway contractors at the same time that sleeping sickness was causing its worst ravages.[28]

One of the alleged benefits of colonial rule was the introduction into Africa of mechanised transport systems which freed manpower resources previously invested in carrying, and fostered the growth of new cash-crop economies. Such improvements in Cazengo were slow to materialise. One desperate DC pointed out that the roads were unsuitable for ox-carts, that pack-horses died of disease, that human porters were very hard to capture, and could not the district government be supplied with a few camels.[29] In practice human carriers remained the basis of transport. At first, the 17 African chiefs were responsible for supplying them, but as these chiefs were eliminated, it became the duty of divisional commanders within the district. The system caused endless conflicts. Farmers could not afford to leave their land to undertake poorly paid caravan trips, and if they did so they attempted to recover their loss through petty pilferage. Great planters tried to increase their fortunes by the wholesale hijacking of other planters' caravans. The ferry over the Lukala caused delay and expense and for some time was profitably run by chief Kabuku before the government tried to take it over and put it out to tender. The Cazengo coffee men, unlike those of neighbouring Golungo, who head-loaded all the way to the coast, used the Kwanza river from Dondo for their transport. From the 1870s a steamer service was introduced and run by the National Bank. Each optimistic annual report on the benefits that could be expected from such a service only emphasised that these benefits had so far been outweighed by irritations over delay and inconvenience. Before long planters and bankers began spasmodically campaigning for a railway to link Cazengo and the sea.

The story of the Portuguese Royal Trans-Africa Railway Company must be one of the most farcical pieces of tragi-comedy in the history of Africa. Its progress from Luanda to Malange via Cazengo can be followed through a pile of pamphlets, reports and parliamentary debates in which each claim and each counter-claim is more preposterous or more defamatory than the last. At the height of the campaign influential pressure groups were suggesting that once the railway was built the customs revenue from the moribund port of Luanda would soon equal that from Lisbon itself.[30] The politicians were fired with enthusiasm but the investors were not; the government had to guarantee the profits before a tender could be obtained. The result was a jerry-built line which consumed a large part of Angola's meagre resources, bankrupted its treasury, and wiped out all enthusiasm for further investment. Even the coffee planters were soon disillusioned by high rail costs, delays, and pilferage, caused by a shortage of railway stock. Since the company's profits were guaranteed by the state, they wasted as little money as possible on actually running a train service. António Ennes caused apoplectic rage to the directors by writing ironically about cheap and efficient porters trotting smilingly along the almost disused track.[31] In practice coffee-growers turned to motor lorries as soon as they became available.

The archival information about the people who lived in the colonial enclave in Cazengo is pretty unreliable. The voters' register for 1889 includes 1273 persons who were deemed to satisfy a franchise (presumably of property rather than income) of 100 *milreis* (£22). Of these 43 were eligible for municipal office and had property ranging from 400 to 3000 *milreis* (£88–£666). The richest of them were 18 traders, but not all traders were rich. Also eligible were nine planters, several estate administrators, two lawyers, and an army officer. Of the 1200-odd voters who could not stand for office, all but 80 listed their profession as farmer, with a notional property of 100 *milreis*. The rest practised a range of trades and professions from book-keeper to barber.[32] Other electoral registers include many more voters than this and so the picture cannot be considered completely reliable. The register gives no details of race. The racial composition of the population can be gained from some census returns, but these are even less reliable than voter's registers, where at least names are recorded. The population counts for 1876 and 1877 agree in putting the European population of Cazengo at a little over 100, but differ between 15 000 and 30 000 in their guess as to the nominally Christian African population.[33] Neither community seems to have had much regard for formal education, and the school registers usually show only about two dozen Africans and one or two mulattoes even when the school was functioning. The number of 'pagan' villagers who lived in association with the Christian community was even more difficult to count. In fact one suspects that the count was probably doctored to make the amount of tax levied in any particular year look reasonable.

The energies of the people of Cazengo were much devoted to interminable feuding over trivial economic or political matters which were considered of extreme social importance at the time. In a society devoid of European women great prestige was attached to the ownership of black common-law wives. They provided a potent source of conflict in a small and tense society. In 1888 a convict named Falcão went so far as to telegraph the governor-general when he failed to recover his estranged woman because she was related to the mistress of the judicial delegate.[34] Such disputes led to kidnapping, murder, and fights between armed gangs of slaves. For Cazengo women the position of housekeeper could be prestigious and profitable. In 1882 the Goanese doctor made a will leaving about £200 to his legitimate children in Goa and the balance of his estate, houses and monies from patients to one Dona Maria.[35] Since many of the women concerned were technically slaves, any transfer required a cash assessment. Valuations of between £4 and £6 in the 1850s depended on numbers of children.[36] In 1893 such cases were still brought to court and one disputed sale of a loyal slave mistress with child involved a sum of £13, equivalent to three sacks of coffee or a heifer.[37]

Matters of much greater intrinsic interest than domestic strife are less well documented in the Cazengo archives. Only rather sketchy references have been found, for instance, to the major Angolan crisis which arose in the summer of 1917. An uprising against planters in the new coffee region of South Kwanza spread as far afield as Pungo Andongo, the old seventeenth-century Mbundu capital.[38] The white population of Cazengo became convinced that 'educated natives' were plotting to have them murdered in their beds. In a pre-emptive strike they caught and beat several potential African leaders. Although 'peace had been restored' by October, one victim succeeded in publishing his version of events while in Luanda gaol accused of fomenting the alleged uprising. He was António d'Assis Junior, an employee of the law courts, who spent his energies advising fellow Africans never to surrender their lands or allow themselves to be bought out cheaply when threatened with suits over rights of tenure. The administrator described Assis as a 'cunning knave'.[39] White planters, unaccustomed to this kind of opposition, tried to bribe him, but when this failed they invented the great 'native plot'. He was eventually banished to a remote part of the new territories in the south-east.[40]

The question which now emerges is how important were Cazengo's coffee barons. On the world scale they meant nothing. The Portuguese may have hoped for a new Brazil, and year by year their National Overseas Bank reported optimistically on the future prospects and current disasters. But even in 1893 the Bank's 500 tons and the colony's 10 000 or so looked puny. Brazil had reached 360 000 tons a decade earlier. And 3000 slaves in Cazengo had to be compared to 300 000 in Brazil.

On the African scene Cazengo ranked higher. Production rose more or less in parallel with São Tomé to reach about 2000 tons a year each in the 1870s. But when Angola later diversified into sugar cane,[41] São Tomé switched to cocoa, which was a more successful venture. Several thousand *de facto* slaves were shipped annually from Angola to São Tomé. When, after 1910, some of these were repatriated as a result of an international outcry, the depressed farmers of Cazengo tried to pick up the returnees. Indentured labour originating from as far away as Luba and Lunda, they said, was drifting about the Benguela ports 'losing the work habit' when it might be employed in Cazengo.[42] Angola was still producing between 4000 and 6000 tons of coffee in the decade from 1905 to 1915.

On the domestic Angolan scene coffee once reached a point where it accounted for half of the colony's exports. In the longer term, however, it ranked much lower. And the plantation sector was always small compared to the peasant sector. A set of Luanda customs returns for the period 1864–74 gives the following break-down of central Angola's average exports of £170 000 a year:

Beeswax	£52 000
Coffee	£46 000
Palm produce	£28 000
Groundnut produce	£26 000
Cotton	£7 000
Ivory	£7 000

During this time, declared coffee exports rose from 370 tons to 2400 tons and in 1873 earned £120 000 in export value, and £5000 of the year's £8000 customs revenue. By that year rubber, the new commodity of the late nineteenth century, had begun to feature at £30 000 per annum.

Despite the apparent insignificance of Angola's nineteenth-century coffee industry there are three good reasons why it should be examined. Firstly, and most obviously, the attempt to create an American-style plantation industry in Africa is intrinsically interesting even though it failed woefully owing to deficiencies of labour, transport, management, security and price-stability as chronicled above. The rival island system of São Tomé was able, for some years at least, to do rather better. But the whole episode is one which fits neatly into the mainstream of nineteenth-century African history. Throughout the length of the Atlantic seaboard African societies were adjusting to the demise of the slave trade and reconverting labour for use on African as opposed to American land. The West African palm trade – which only marginally affected Angola – was of course the prime example of this reconversion. More remote but parallel repercussions are to be found in the rise of such inland plantation economies as those of the Hausa cotton and indigo growers.[43] Cazengo is another example, albeit a small one, of the search for economic alternatives to Atlantic slaving.

The second reason why further academic effort, including oral research, should be invested here is that it could produce a fully rounded socioeconomic study of the proto-colonial communities of the Angolan interior. Wider aspects of collaboration and resistance by African peoples undergoing colonisation will emerge. Of particular interest will be a comparative study of the Ambaquistas, who were in some ways agents of Portuguese advance, and the Ndembu who were the most successful opponents of that advance. The Ambaquistas had few immediate dealings with Cazengo itself, if the archives are to be believed, as their trade routes did not pass through the coffee zone. The study of this group will need the records of the Ambaca and Lucala district, and also those of the market towns of Malange and Dondo. As for the Ndembu, they were clearly significant for Cazengo since they provided a close haven of refuge for chiefs driven into exile and for subjects escaping from labour and military conscription. The Ndembu area did not, however, provide an immediate military threat to Cazengo as the adjacent district of Golungo Alto guaranteed the colony's northern security. The Golungo Alto records will presumably therefore yield more rewarding information than the Cazengo ones on external relations.[44] For the other side of the picture the royal correspondence of some Ndembu chiefs may still be extant after it was removed from its custodian by a Portuguese anthropologist some years ago.

Finally, a third reason for initiating a study of Cazengo lies in its place in the revived Angolan coffee industry. The Cazengo Company, whose records future research may unearth, survived the

Portuguese Republic, and survived the world depression, to thrive once more on the high prices of the 1960s. In 1961 guerrilla warfare was renewed in the Ndembu forest and raged as fiercely in the 1960s as it had in the 1870s or 1916. The new coffee barons erected elaborate barbed wire fences, recruited a new *guerra preta* to protect their contract labourers, and prospered mightily. Most interesting of all, however, was the revival of the peasant sector. In the 1950s small producers had been squeezed at least as hard as they had been in the 1890s. In the early 1970s, however, those who survived began to receive unaccustomed encouragement from a colonial government driven to an expensive stalemate by 10 years of war. The army generals argued that a prosperous elite of black coffee-farmers might undermine the militant nationalist cause. Despite strident settler protest, the descendants of the old Cazengo peasants received lavish funds to set up marketing co-operatives. This revival of black initiative did not, however, save colonial Angola from collapse. On the contrary it set coffee-growers against urban workers in a fierce ideological struggle for the postcolonial heritage. City politics won the day, but city politicians later encountered enormous difficulties in mobilising emergency brigades of underemployed town youth to bring in the coffee harvest.[45]

10 Britain and the Ultimatum of 1890

This chapter is the author's only foray into diplomatic history and was written on the occasion of the centenary of the 1890 confrontation between Portugal and Britain over the colonial seizure of the Zambezi heartlands. The episode reverberated long and loud in Portuguese history but not in British history. One of the key figures, however, was Cecil Rhodes, who subsequently became an imperial folk-hero in Britain and an archetypal villain in Portugal. The original paper was presented to a centenary conference on the ultimatum in the Faculty of Letters of the Classical University at Lisbon in 1990 and was subsequently published in the Portuguese colonial studies review Studia *in 1996.*

In a recent History of Central Africa, published in 1983, no reference is explicitly made to the British Ultimatum sent to Portugal in 1890. And yet the Ultimatum might be seen as the key diplomatic event determining the course of colonialism in the southeastern quadrant of Central Africa. The neglect of the subject might indicate that when modern capitalism spread into Africa, after 1867, it was of minor importance to note which of the European nations was nominally in control of the ground. Capital knew no frontiers and money crossed the political boundaries of Europe without let or hindrance. The impact of finance on Central Africa was determined by the share-ownership of the 'chartered companies' which carved the region up between themselves. The share portfolios were spread among French, Belgian, German, Portuguese and British investors whose transactions were measured in gold rather than in the controlled currency of any circumscribed nation-state. And yet in 1890 the British government, for all its extreme reluctance to embroil itself in foreign – let alone colonial – affairs, found it expedient to advise Portugal that Portuguese claims to territory in the Zambezi basin would not be accepted.

The matter of the Ultimatum may have been of minor import to Britain, there is no reference to it in Hobsbawm's *Industry and Empire*, and it may have made little difference to the peoples of Zambezia as they succumbed to the rule of private-enterprise chartered colonisers, but to Portugal the Ultimatum brought profound shock. It challenged the mystique of Portugal as an imperial power and undermined the credibility of the bourgeois monarchy of the Saxe-Coburgs at Lisbon. It also destroyed the Portuguese vision of England as the irritating but essentially benevolent godparent of the nation. It is a serious question to ask how the Ultimatum should be re-interpreted outside the confines of Portuguese domestic history, particularly in Africa, but also in Britain. In attempting such an evaluation it is necessary to look at the career of Cecil Rhodes and at the relationship of crime, investment and diplomacy in the history of South Africa at the time of the Witwatersrand gold rush and of its prolongation into the high veld of Zimbabwe. It is also necessary to measure the emotional heritage of Livingstone in the pious politics of Victorian England, and more especially Scotland. Both Rhodes and Livingstone stamped their names on the unknown map which Portugal aspired to tint in pink.

The disappearance of the Ultimatum from the main stream of British diplomatic history is curious. When Kenneth Bourne published his work on *The Foreign Policy of Victorian England 1830–1902* (Oxford University Press) it contained no reference to the Ultimatum of 11 January 1890 which Britain sent to Portugal. An episode of Anglo-Portuguese relations which features prominently in the Portuguese version of Victorian foreign policy did not even warrant a single line in the British analysis of the same period as perceived in 1970. Two generations earlier however, in 1923, A. W. Ward and G. P. Gouch did deal with the subject when they published the *Cambridge History of British Foreign Policy 1866–1919*. Although bearing the imprint of a famous university press, the text bears the unmistakable tone of a patriotic chauvinism that belongs to a now long forgotten age. The Ultimatum is mentioned, though its significance to Britain is minimised:

> the British Government came into conflict with Portugal. Though warned by Lord Salisbury in August 1887 – when her cartographers were busy annexing territory wholesale in that region by the simple expedient of recolouring the official maps – that the British Government could not 'recognise Portuguese sovereignty in territories not occupied by her in sufficient strength to enable her to maintain order, protect foreigners, and control the natives', Portugal had, in the meantime, persisted in advancing all sorts of unsubstantial claims to sovereignty in the Zambezi region. Not

only had her Government declared that river to be the north-
western boundary of the Portuguese sphere of influence in East
Africa; but it had attempted to close the river against all but
Portuguese vessels, and had advanced exclusive rights over the
valley of Lake Nyasa, and even over Mashonaland. Portuguese
troops and mercenaries, under the notorious Colonel Serpa Pinto,
even invaded territory which had been formally placed under British
Protection and settled by British subjects; and, when requested
to recall them, their Government refused. Portugal claimed, in
effect, a solid belt of territory stretching across the Continent
and so isolating the British Colonies in the south.

   Lord Salisbury, now again at the Foreign Office, resolutely con-
tested these immoderate pretensions as lacking any practical basis
and supported solely by what he sarcastically called 'archaeological arguments'. Before the Portuguese Government came to
reason, however, it was necessary to threaten the suspension of
diplomatic relations (Jan 10th, 1890) *and to despatch to Lisbon a
mild ultimatum.* [My emphasis]. In the end, the attack on the
freedom of the Zambezi was abandoned, while by the Anglo-
Portuguese Convention of June 11th, 1891, the spheres of influence
of the two Powers in East Africa and the Zambezi basin were
delimited in such wise that, while Portugal received a portion of
the territory in dispute, Nyasaland and Mashonaland remained
British. (pp. 212–13)

The strident tone adopted by the author of the passage, William
Harbutt Dawson, and accepted by the distinguished Cambridge
editors, reveals something of the temperature which still informed
British – as well as Portuguese – imperial debates and attitudes
33 years after the event. The description of the ultimatum as
'mild' can be interpreted in two ways. Either it can be seen as
suggesting that Lord Salisbury adopted a limited response to a severe
provocation. Or it can be seen as reflecting the author's assessment
of the relative unimportance of the event, a part of the normal
course of diplomatic relations between Britain and Portugal. Lord
Salisbury's policy towards Portugal might thus be interpreted as a
continuation of the arrogant attitude of Lord Palmerston, who
thought of Portugal as a semi-barbarous nation in occasional need
of sound chastisement (W. H. C. Smith, *Anglo-Portuguese Relations
1851–1861*, title page).

   The Ultimatum, however, was neither mild nor was it an

absentminded reflex action by an autocratic and aristocratic British prime minister. On the contrary, it involved a significant shift in British imperial and diplomatic history. The long-standing reluctance of Britain to become embroiled in African disputes was being challenged. The Ultimatum of 1890 was the first step which carried British commitment in Africa down the road to war. One key protagonist of intervention was Cecil Rhodes, who profoundly influenced British imperial attitudes before his political fall in 1896. However, the war of British expansion in Africa, when it came, was not against Portugal but against the Transvaal. The Transvaal's 'Second War of Liberation', known to Britons as the Anglo-Boer War of 1899–1902, was (with the possible exception of the Crimean War) the costliest war in which Britain engaged between Waterloo and the Great War of 1914. The idea that Africa was worth fighting for would have astonished the reluctant imperialists of both political parties in Britain in the 1880s. Yet Salisbury opened the way to British expansion by sending an Ultimatum to Portugal as early as 1890. The consequence was a Portuguese withdrawal not only from territory in which claims to British sovereignty had been made, but also – the misleading assertions of the *Cambridge History* not withstanding – from territory which might in future be claimed by Britain.

The reluctance of the British government to become involved in colonial adventures was more firmly associated with the Liberals than with the Conservatives, but Lord Salisbury nevertheless had to tread carefully when advocating the potentially costly and controversial creation of a British empire stretching northward from South Africa into the Zambezi heartlands of Central Africa. His agent in so doing was a minor diplomat called Harry Johnson whom he appointed in 1889 to be British consul in Mozambique. The prime minister had previously discreetly encouraged Johnson to write an anonymous article in *The Times* of 22 August 1888, 'Great Britain's Policy in Africa, by an African Explorer', which laid out a grand strategy of imperial aggrandisement.

> From this western shore of Lake Nyasa, along the course of the Loangwa River, through a country rich in gold, tin and iron, we may eventually extend our rule over the relatively short distance which at present separates our recently acquired protectorate over the middle Zambezi from the British settlements on Lake Nyasa. Thus, if our Government only grants some measure of support

to the British agencies, commercial and evangelical, which have obtained such a footing in the Lake region, our possessions in South Africa may be linked some day to our sphere of influence in Eastern Africa and the Egyptian Sudan by a continuous band of British domination. The day will come, let us hope, when the African Lakes Company will shake hands with the British East Africa Company on the northern shores of Tanganyika; and Emin Pasha will rule in England's name and for the interests of civilization on the Albert Nyanza and the White Nile. (Cited in Roland Oliver, *Sir Harry Johnson and the Scramble for Africa* [London, 1957] p. 143.)

So while Portugal was advocating the 'Rose Coloured Map' to link Mozambique to Angola through the Zambezi basin, Lord Salisbury was quietly flying in the face of anti-colonial British public opinion and of Treasury opposition to imperial expenditure by encouraging the idea of a 'Cape to Cairo' route which would lay claim to the self-same Zambezi heartlands. The two dreams were incompatible. Salisbury was aware of this when he appointed Johnson to what was going to be a highly sensitive diplomatic posting. Conflict was already apparent in 1888 when the Portuguese customs posts in Mozambique delayed supplies of arms to the British on Lake Nyasa while entrusting one of their own exploring heroes, Serpa Pinto, with a scientific and diplomatic mission to the same lake. Johnson's secret instructions were to 'proceed up the Zambezi and report on the extent of Portuguese rule in the vicinity of that river', preferably without telling the British Colonial Office more than was necessary about his activity, which was directed from the Foreign Office (Oliver, p. 146).

Before setting out for Mozambique to try to stake a British claim to territories which would link South Africa with East Africa, Johnson was sent on an extraordinary mission to Lisbon to sound out the Portuguese government on its Central Africa policy. He went to great pains to gain favour in Lisbon and admired 'the sky, the public gardens, the local opera, the novels, the wines, the recent realistic fiction, the colonial administration, the language, the history, the army, navy and police, and anything else Lusitanian on which my opinion is asked'. He went on to say 'I also paint Lord Salisbury as a raging lion where his least little tiny bit of British interest is concerned'. Such a diplomatic approach apparently met with success. Barros Gomes, the foreign minister, agreed to abandon the claim to a Portuguese transcontinental colony and instead allow Britain to have a corridor running north and south. In exchange, however, Johnson allowed Portugal to lay claim to the Shire Highlands, to Blantyre and to part of the west shore of Lake Nyasa. In his report he argued that South African interests would feel much more harmed by being hemmed in below the Zambezi by a transcontinental Portuguese colony than by losing some of the Nyasa territories of the African Lakes Company or the Church of Scotland Mission. He recognised, however, that British politicians might feel much more attachment to a British company and a British mission than to the South African 'Road to the North'. His admiration of all things Portuguese, moreover, was less fulsome when defending the need for absolute British control of that road. Guarantees of transit rights, he claimed, were inadequate when they could be 'hampered and restricted by a jealous, spiteful, little power like Portugal' (Oliver, pp. 148–9).

Lord Salisbury was quite unwilling to make a concession of the Shire Highlands and the lake-shore in order to secure the road to the north that Johnson had won. To refuse the terms might create serious anger in Portugal. To accept them would create even more serious anger in Scotland. The highlands of what was later to become Nyasaland were associated with the evangelising activities of Scotland's greatest hero, David Livingstone. To sacrifice any such hallowed ground to a foreign power, indeed a Catholic power, would have been politically foolish. Salisbury, as Oliver put it, 'knew very well that he would rather face the wrath of Portugal than that of Scotland' (p. 150). He went further and encouraged the popular protest in Scotland to be made public. A memorial drawing attention to the danger of losing the land of Dr Livingstone to the Portuguese was signed by no less than 11 000 ministers and elders of the Church of Scotland. The protest was sent to the Foreign Office and received with satisfaction by Salisbury. He wanted to prove to the Portuguese government that he, like they, had to contend with strong sentiments of public opinion. Johnson's attempt at grand international diplomacy on behalf of Lord Salisbury thus failed and he reverted to being a mere Foreign Office consul about to sail to Africa for a minor posting in Mozambique. Before leaving London, however, he attended a dinner party at which he happened to meet a little-known colonial entrepreneur and mineral speculator, Cecil Rhodes. Cecil Rhodes' vision of the 'Road to the North' began in Cape Town. From there he moved his interests to

Kimberley and from small business beginnings he climbed the financial ladder until he monopolised the South African diamond industry. When the Witwatersrand gold-fields were discovered in 1886 Rhodes was slow to stake his claims and although a major manipulator of gold shares he never gained the dominant position that he had obtained in diamonds. To compensate for this partial failure he hoped that a 'Second Witwatersrand' might be found further north, on the gold-reefs that lay between the Limpopo and Zambezi rivers. His imperial vision for extending South Africa towards the far north was similar to, but not identical with, Johnson's idea of a British highway from the Cape to Cairo. Indeed, Rhodes adopted Johnson's slogan and made it his own. To further his northern ambition Rhodes went into colonial politics and was elected a member of the local parliament of the Cape of Good Hope. Although he was of British origin he formed an effective working alliance with the Afrikaner politicians of the Cape. He also bought shares in the local press and developed newspaper contacts in Britain to further his imperial ambitions. By 1889, when he met Johnson, Rhodes was still little known in Britain and Salisbury may not even have heard of him. He was a minor colonial figure suspected by British imperialists of being in the pocket of the 'Boers'. He was still far from being Britain's arch-imperialist.

Rhodes vision of empire was one which saw a federation of autonomous imperial nations. He thought that the Home Rule movement in Ireland might lead to a suitable model for South Africa and contributed no less than £10 000 to the Irish cause, incidentally buying the support of many Irish votes in the British parliament. What he did not want was direct British involvement in the imperial nations. The London government was liable to be too sympathetic to African rights in southern Africa. It was also liable to listen to the powerful mission lobby which opposed some of the more aggressive land alienation and mineral prospecting by settlers and miners who were the key to the Rhodes policies. Rhodes, therefore, was an imperialist who wanted to spread the power of white settlers, but not an imperialist who wanted to spread the power of the imperial government.

Rhodes found that controlling the road to the north was difficult. If he attempted to put it under the influence of the Cape settlers there would be a protest from the missionaries who, in the footsteps of Livingstone, used it as their highway to the north and protected the Christianised villages on the borders of the Kalahari desert. On the other hand there was a disadvantage in bringing British colonial control in too, since Britain would defend the rights of Africans over and above the rights of settlers and prospectors. In the end the first step was taken by Britain when in 1884 it overcame its reluctance to intervene and incurred the considerable expense of sending an invading force of 4000 men into the Tswana territory. It did so not especially to further Rhodes' cause but to stop Germany from closing a potential road to the north by linking Namibia (German South-West Africa) with the independent Afrikaner republic of the Transvaal. Even a Liberal prime minister, Gladstone, recognised a sort of 'Monroe Doctrine' for Africa, which said that other European powers should not intrude on Britain's broad though ill-defined 'sphere of influence'.

Opening up the north under the controlling eye of Britain was not to Rhodes' liking. He aspired to spread his influence beyond the corridor which Britain had secured between German and Afrikaner territory by planning a private empire on the Zambezi. His first intermediate objective was to reach the Ndebele kingdom ruled by King Lobengula. Beyond that he aspired to control the high, healthy and fertile lands of the Shona people where prospectors had been reporting the existence of old medieval gold workings. This is where he ran into rival aspirations emanating from Portugal. To overcome Portuguese claims he planned to obtain a treaty with Lobengula and then to argue that the Shona territories were dependencies of the Ndebele kingdom. Obtaining control of Lobengula's kingdom, however, presented a difficult challenge.

The steps by which Rhodes gained influence over the Ndebele kingdom were carefully calculated. First of all he persuaded John Moffat, son of a famous missionary, to obtain from Lobengula a kind of 'negative treaty' which did not give his kingdom to Britain or South Africa, but did exclude the rival claimants from Germany, Portugal, and the Transvaal. This treaty, which was subsequently used to justify British influence which it did not in fact obtain, was signed on 11 February 1888. Rhodes' second step was to send Charles Rudd to Lobengula's court to obtain a concession of the mineral rights in the kingdom. This concession also did not grant sovereignty but was treated as though it had granted more than the words intended. In exchange for money and weapons that included 500 Martini–Henry breech-loading rifles and 50 000 rounds of ammunition Lobengula granted Rhodes' envoys:

The complete and exclusive charge over all metals and minerals situated and contained in my kingdoms, principalities and dominions, together with full power to do all things that they may deem necessary to win and procure the same ... to take all necessary and lawful steps to exclude from my kingdom, principalities and dominions, all persons seeking land, metals, minerals or mining rights therein. (Cited in John Flint, *Cecil Rhodes* [London edition, 1976] p. 107.)

The Rudd concession was signed on 30 October 1888 and sealed with the royal elephant seal while two missionaries witnessed the document. It gave Rhodes a mining monopoly but no sovereignty. His third step, therefore, was to obtain a royal charter from the British government that would enable him to claim administrative rights over his proposed private empire in the north. Rival business interests with greater weight in England than a colonial outsider were also bidding for a charter to gain administrative rights over the Zambezi territories. Rhodes succeeded in joining forces with them in a manner which secretly ensured that they would gain for themselves the profits of the mineral concession but not bear the costs of the colonial administration which was to be set up. The mineral rights Rudd had won were vested in a central search association owned by Rhodes and those whose favour he needed to obtain. It was widely but incorrectly assumed that the mineral rights would be vested in the future British South Africa Company which was to bear the chartered responsibilities of administration. This arrangement was unknown to both the British government and the investing public.

The third stage of Rhodes' empire building occurred on 29 October 1889 when a charter was finally issued to his new British South Africa Company in the name of Queen Victoria. There were several reasons why Lord Salisbury had granted such powers to Rhodes. Rhodes promised to build a railway to the north which would join on to the British government's Bechuanaland railway and so improve its profits. Rhodes' private empire would carry the cost of bringing a 'British' presence into Central Africa in a way that Salisbury could never have persuaded the British parliament to accept. The company spread its influence across the Zambezi and into what was to be Northern Rhodesia (now Zambia) where rival interests of King Leopold of the Congo and Germany threatened to advance. The charter had no northern border only a southern (British) one and an eastern (Portuguese) one. Furthermore Rhodes was an ally of the Cape Afrikaners and so his advance into Central Africa did not elicit hostility from President Kruger of the Transvaal in the way that a British annexation would have done. Granting a charter to Rhodes thus advanced Salisbury's interests without creating serious hostility or expense. Even more strikingly Cecil Rhodes gave Harry Johnson £2000 of his own money to further British treaty-making in Nyasaland. He also won the support of Flora Shaw, the colonial correspondent of *The Times* and of W. T. Stead, the editor of the more sensationalist *Pall Mall Gazette*. His final coup was to recruit two dukes to the board of the proposed chartered company to allay the fears of the English ruling class (Flint, ch. 6).

Rhodes gained a charter to administer his affairs in Central Africa, but he did not gain sovereignty. Lobengula was too clever a politician to give way to Rhodes' pressure for further concessions. Rhodes therefore decided in December 1889 that Lobengula would have to be overthrown by force. He commissioned a force of several hundred men to kidnap and if necessary murder the king of the Ndebele. The coup failed, but unlike Rhodes' attempted coup against the Transvaal in 1895 it did not lead to his own downfall. On the contrary, six months later Rhodes became prime minister of the Cape Colony. Thus the one government that might have exercised some limiting influence on the colonising activities of the British South Africa Company was actually headed by the company's own ruler. For five years Rhodes dominated southern Africa. It was only when he tried to overthrow the government of the Transvaal that he fell from power. By then, however, he had suffered several disappointments in his northern empire. Not least, he had lost his hope of gaining Nyasaland which went to the British Government and its agent, Harry Johnson, who had been Rhodes' friend.

Harry Johnson, on behalf of Lord Salisbury, reached Mozambique on a British gunboat, the *Stork*, in July 1889 and set off at once to sign British treaties with chiefs in the future Nyasaland. These treaties, on a printed form, gave an undertaking not to cede any territory to another European power without the permission of the British government. The chiefs who signed them had had 10 or 15 years of experience of English and Scottish missionaries who had become their advisers. This activity brought Johnson into confrontation with Serpa Pinto, who was engaged in gaining Portuguese domination over the southern highlands. It was this rivalry which – unbeknown to Johnson who was travelling in the far north – led Salisbury to take firm action in protecting British interests. The account of the event is well portrayed in Roland Oliver's biography of Johnson:

> [Johnson] reached Mozambique on January 30th, 1890, and five days later received a telegram from the Foreign Office informing him that the Portuguese Government had in consequence of representations engaged not to settle any territorial questions by acts of force, and to instruct the authorities in Mozambique to withdraw their troops from the Shire and Makololo districts.
>
> Lord Salisbury had already acted with vigour [...] there had been information of three Portuguese gunboats being sent to the Zambezi, and also of the embarkation of troops at Goa for Mozambique. Energetic protests had immediately been lodged at Lisbon, culminating in an ultimatum delivered on January 2nd and another on the 11th. The Portuguese ministry had first yielded and then resigned. Salisbury's outward attitude after his coup was one of inflexible contempt. 'Since there is no shame in the surrender of impotence', he told his parliamentary critics, 'the weaker of two widely unequal powers enters upon a dispute with the stronger consciously immune from ultimate catastrophe and proportionately reckless'. In private, however, no one knew better how far-reaching might be the effect on his relations with other powers, and the still imprecisely known activities of Johnson in the rear of both German East Africa and the Congo State became temporarily a source of real anxiety. Johnson had achieved a certain international notoriety as the target of Portuguese Anglophobia – he had been described in the Lisbon papers as a 'slippery individual, mellifluous and insinuating' (Oliver, pp. 169–70)

Johnson had been working for two masters in Nyasaland, publicly for Salisbury and privately for Rhodes. Salisbury had been mainly anxious that Johnson might tread on German toes and worried less about his effect on Portugal, though in the end both borders were settled to the satisfaction of the British Government and Johnson became the effective ruler of British Central Africa. Rhodes on the other hand was acutely dissatisfied with the rewards he had obtained by helping to finance Johnson. His aspiration had been an opening to the Indian Ocean. His protest to Johnson was strong:

I cannot congratulate you on [. . .] the Portuguese treaty. It is a disgraceful treaty and I will have nothing to do with it. You have given away the whole west, including half the Barotse just ceded to me, and the whole of Manicaland and Gazaland, and we have got nothing which we had not already got. I can only express my opinion that you ought to be thoroughly ashamed of your work, but in spite of your desertion I shall go on fighting, and I have not the slightest intention of giving way to the Portuguese. [. . .] I am now occupying Manica, and I do not think even you and the Portuguese combined will turn me out. The least I can ask you to do is to repair the mischief you have done by getting the Portuguese treaty dropped (Oliver, pp. 176–8).

Rhodes and Johnson met again in February 1891 and made an agreement which was acceptable to the British Government and to the British South Africa Company. Nyasaland was to become a British Protectorate under the Foreign Office and the remainder of the north Zambezi territories were to become part of the territory of the chartered company. Johnson was to rule over both. Rhodes meanwhile, having failed to persuade Lord Salisbury to drive the Portuguese out of Mozambique as he had vainly hoped, set about consolidating his influence in Portuguese East Africa by a combination of military, financial and diplomatic manoeuvres of his own.

In 1889 to 1891 Portugal found its aspirations in the Zambezi basin squeezed between two distinct strands of British imperial aspiration. On the north side London imperialism defended the vocal mission lobby and the financial interests of the city and its stock market. On the south side Cape Town imperialism defended the future ambitions of settlers and prospectors. An alliance of the two imperialisms was a formidable challenge to Portugal. Rivalry between London and Cape Town, although it resurfaced with great bitterness, could not be manipulated by Portugal with sufficient force to retain or recover any of its three prize objectives, the Nyasa highlands, the Shona goldfields or the pink road to Angola. Portuguese penetration was halted at the old market town of Zombo though the British imperial lobby regretted surrendering even that piece of territory. South Africa went on to colonise the Shona south and drove its African subjects to the great rebellion of 1896. Britain colonised the Nyasa north and suffered from the uprising of indignant protest which broke out in 1915.

11 Colonialism in Angola: Kinyama's Experience

This story is not history but is fiction based on historical circumstances. It was not intended for publication, but was given as a lecture at the University of Cape Town in 1977 in an attempt to illuminate, for the benefit of South Africans, the colonial situation in which their army had become embroiled. The lecture's subsequent publication by the Historical Society of Nigeria in the journal Tarikh *in 1980 led to its use for training undergraduates in the United States. This inspired not merely its inclusion in this collection, but the very idea of publishing a collection at all. Kinyama, it must nonetheless be emphasised, remains a fictional peasant. He was created out of the author's imagination even if the traumatic experiences attributed to his life, and to his family, closely mirror real events in Portuguese colonial Africa in the last decades of empire.*

Kinyama was a 36-year-old farmer who lived in a valley in southern Angola, on the northern slopes of the Benguela Highlands. By 1956 he was not rich for a man of his age, but he was comfortably off. He had three acres of hoe gardens. He also had 15 acres of fallow land which he was able to use while worked-out land was resting. He had three cows, and this made him one of the more prosperous middle peasants in the valley. His farming, like all farming, was a risky business but not as risky as that of people who lived in the poorer and drier and less fertile parts of Angola. Despite his comfortable farming circumstances, Kinyama nevertheless constantly felt that his prosperity was being threatened. Slowly, very slowly, the colonial system which the Portuguese were building in Angola had begun to encroach on the valley in new ways over the past five years.

The first way in which Kinyama had begun to feel the authority of the 'New State', which Salazar had founded 20 years earlier, was in the more systematic levying of taxes. Instead of using maize to feed his family Kinyama now had to sell it in order to pay tribute to a newly-appointed District Officer. Instead of being able to use his maize to buy consumer goods, Kinyama found that maize had become a sort of tax-crop to pay new or revived hut dues.

Colonial taxes fell heavily upon a southern peasant growing three acres of maize.

When Kinyama tried to sell his maize he found only one trader in the valley to buy it. This was a Portuguese immigrant who had arrived in 1951 and had a monopoly. He could fix his own price for buying maize since there was no other trader nearby. Thus Kinyama had no bargaining power: he was a prisoner of a limited trading system. When he needed to pay taxes in cash he could only sell maize to the valley trader. The trader knew his plight and lowered the price.

In 1956 Kinyama's maize money was not enough to pay his taxes and he was declared a tax defaulter. The District Officer ordered that Kinyama, a respected farmer of the valley, should be beaten. He was taken into the closed courtyard behind the District Office where he was to receive 25 strokes. The beating was carried out with the *palmatória*, a wooden paddle drilled with holes. He was beaten on the palms of his hands. Although Kinyama was a grown man, the beating was carried out by a young cousin of his own family who worked in the office. The resultant loss of family status and prestige was as painful as the colonial style of physical punishment.

A week after his ordeal Kinyama decided that the only way in which his family could recover from their financial difficulty was by sending his brother away to work on the coffee plantations of North Kwanza. The decision was a distressing one. The farm could not afford to lose the services of one of its best labourers. There seemed, however, no other way in which the colonial taxes could be raised. The trader offered Kinyama credit against the money his brother would earn if he signed a coffee worker's contract. With this credit he would be able to pay his taxes. The interest to be charged until his brother returned was to be 30 per cent.

The coffee industry in Angola had begun 100 years earlier and many peasants from the valley had worked in it. The town of Ndala Tando meant 'the place where the smoke rises', the name given to it by Bailundu coffee harvesters who arrived from the Southern plateau and had never seen a town before. When Kinyama's brother reached the coffee estates in 1956, he found problems in earning money there, for the estate-owner would not pay his workers in cash but gave them tokens instead. These tokens could only be used in a store which the plantation owner ran himself, so although Kinyama's brother was able to buy some over-priced cloth for his work on the plantation, he was not able to raise money to take back to the valley.

Gradually Kinyama succeeded in reorganising the work on his farm to compensate for having to send his brother to the North. A few months later, however, a new calamity struck the valley. A government labour recruiter came to the District Office and said that he required a levy of 40 men immediately.[1] Forty men were rounded up and put on the back of a lorry. Kinyama was one of those who were caught. This represented a total disaster for his family and for his farm. At that point, however, Kinyama gained reprieve: he managed to speak to the African recruiting assistant and offered to find a substitute who would go on the lorry if he himself could be released. The assistant agreed, and Kinyama, with a heavy heart, offered his eldest son. Kinyama's son was only 16 and did not know where he would be staying. Kinyama never did discover where his son was taken by the recruiter. In fact he went to the fisheries in the desert of Porto Alexandre in the far south of Angola. It was a remote and harsh country and the labour contracts were for two years. Living conditions in the low barracks of mud were crowded and very uncomfortable. Four months before he was due to return home, Kinyama's son caught pneumonia. He died a week before his eighteenth birthday.

Early in 1957 a policeman was appointed to serve in the valley. He brought with him the Portuguese tradition of hostility and antagonism between police and people. In Portugal a policeman was somebody to be feared.[2] The one who arrived in the valley came from a peasant family of 17 children in the remote and depressed Tras-os-Montes district of Northern Portugal. He had been able to attend school for three years as a child and had rudimentary skills in literacy. In Africa everything he saw was new, incomprehensible and terrifying. He spent his time shouting at the frightening black people around him. Soon after his arrival, the new policeman sent a message to Kinyama saying that his daughter was required to work in the policehouse laundry. Kinyama's daughter was 14. She did much of the hoeing on Kinyama's farm and the loss of even a child's labour was a serious blow. Kinyama only hoped that she would be able to earn a cash wage as the policeman's laundress.

Within months disaster struck Kinyama's family yet again. His daughter was violated by her new employer. The family were profoundly shocked to discover not only that their daughter was carrying a child, but that it was the child of a policeman. Even more shockingly it was the child of a white man. Kinyama was distraught, but there was no redress. The Portuguese prided themselves, regardless of the brutality involved, on the way in which their young soldiers and officials raped the black women of their colonies. They hoped to create a mixed population which would entrench the culture and language of Lusitania in Africa.[3]

In June 1957 Kinyama's uncle arrived home in the valley from the port of Lobito. The uncle had been more successful than many inland migrants to the colonial towns. He had gained a training as a motor mechanic. After 15 years, however, he suddenly found himself thrown out of his job. He was displaced by a new, white immigrant from Portugal. The immigrant was less well qualified and much less experienced. But in the towns of Angola by the 1950s the colour bar was gradually reaching downwards. Jobs for skilled and semi-skilled people were being taken away from Africans and given to the new Europeans and Cape Verdeans.[4] When Kinyama's uncle returned to the valley there were no mechanical jobs for him. He was unemployable as a wage-earner. Kinyama knew well that in the next season his uncle would be picked up by the sisal recruiter. He would become embittered as he moved from a relatively well-paid city job to cutting sisal, an unrewarding, prickly and unskilled drudgery. Like increasing numbers of Angolans he had been squeezed off even the narrow ladder of colonial opportunity which had existed before the 1950s.

In 1958 alarming rumours began to spread through the valley. The government in Lisbon proposed to settle white peasants from Portugal in Kinyama's valley. When they eventually arrived there were 24 families. The government built them brick houses, gave them free tools and seeds. Each new white peasant gained the shared use of a plough and the loan of an ox to draw it. These Portuguese farmers were free from all tax burdens. But most catastrophic of all, one of them was given Kinyama's maize farm. And another was given three of Kinyama's fallow acres which he had planned to use in the following seasons.[5]

The blow to Kinyama was severe in the extreme: his best land had been seized and he and his family had to move out of the valley and up onto the hillside. Overnight they were compelled to break new, stony ground. Instead of having a reasonably viable small maize farm, they were starting from scratch on the edge of the wilderness.

In 1959, shortly after the beginning of the rainy season, Kinyama's wife fell ill. There was no clinic in the valley; there was not even a shop which sold simple medicine. The nearest hospital to which Kinyama could send his wife was a Spanish hospital run by priests. This hospital was 250 miles away.[6] Kinyama assembled all his savings but still he could not raise the price of a bus ticket to the Spanish hospital. His wife got worse, so he decided to sell the fourth-hand bicycle he had bought only the year before. Despite her sickness his wife had to travel alone on the bus. She carried with her, Kinyama hoped, enough food to keep herself during her stay in hospital. It was five weeks before she was able to return home and three months before she was well enough once again to take her full part in running the farm.

Late in January 1961 rumours of fighting on the north side of the Kwanza began to reach Kinyama. The war in Angola did not begin in the highlands. At first it did not greatly affect the Ovimbundu farmers of Kinyama's valley. The war began further north in the lands of the Kimbundu. Among the Kimbundu the encroachment of the colonial economy had occurred earlier than in the south and its effects had been more severe. As far back as 1945 Kimbundu peasants had been protesting vigorously against a policy of compulsory cotton-growing. District Officers had written to Lisbon explaining that families were starving because people were required to use much of their time and much of their land growing cotton for the government. The government replied sternly that such famine only occurred in the imagination of an idle, black colonial population. Compulsory cotton growing was to be pursued vigorously.[7] The consequence was a reluctant, and long-delayed, but violent revolt of despair. Cotton warehouses were burnt down in 1961 and cotton buyers were driven out. The colonial government reacted with speed and violence. An air force was brought to Angola to bomb the villages. Many Kimbundu fled to the new independent republic of Congo-Léopoldville (later renamed Zaïre) across the river border.

Kinyama did not feel that the cotton war had anything to do with him. His farmer's caution led him to keep quiet. Although his life was precarious, and becoming more so, he had not yet suffered real famine in the family.

In February 1961, a few days after the cotton war began, news began to reach the valley of a second uprising in Angola. This took place in Luanda, the capital city. The frustrations of city people, experienced several years before by Kinyama's uncle, the mechanic in Lobito, were becoming less and less bearable. They rose in revolt and attacked the city gaol to free their imprisoned leaders. The white folk, many of them new to Africa, panicked. Young men bought guns and invaded the black township, attacking anyone they thought might be responsible for the uprising. Many were killed, especially those who had been to school and who had begun to adopt European ways. None of Kinyama's family had ever gone as far as Luanda to seek jobs or schooling but others from the valley began to return as refugees. They sought ways of re-entering farming after the failure of opportunity in a capital increasingly dominated by white immigrants. To most of the peasants in the valley, however, events of the city seemed very remote and unreal.

In the middle of March 1961 a third phase of the Angolan revolution touched the people of the highlands more closely. The great coffee rebellion broke out in the north of Angola. In this rebellion it was not only white planters who were killed by Angolans who had lost their lands, but many of the black plantation workers too. The latter were seen as collaborators – albeit forced ones – who enabled the planters to seize land from the former black peasant coffee-growers. Many of these black conscripts had continued to come, as in former times, from the Ovimbundu Highlands, so an acute sense of fear seized the valley. But still no southern uprising occurred. It was not clear to the Ovimbundu how they should react to this third outbreak of war in Angola. Since several people from Kinyama's valley became victims of the nationalist uprising they found it difficult to identify with the aims of the rebels.

Kinyama took no part in the wars of 1961. In 1962, however, the war came to affect his family in a most personal and painful way. Back in 1958 a rare and unexpected ray of hope had come into the life of Kinyama. A Presbyterian catechist had passed through the valley and offered to find a place in school for his middle son, then aged 12. The school was 200 miles away in Huambo, known as New Lisbon. Kinyama had not been able to afford 30 escudos for a bus fare to school and his son had to walk all the way. It took 11 days, and he never came home for holidays. Kinyama's son did well at school. It looked at last as though the fortunes of the family were to change. One person from the valley was gaining an education, and would be able to seek a job with a high income. This, however, was not to be. In 1961, when the fighting began, Kinyama's son was in the fourth form. A year later the PIDE police came to the school. They took away 25 children. One of them was Kinyama's son. Kinyama continued for several years to hope that he might return from some prison camp. But he was never heard of again.[8]

Although none of the highland peoples had become involved in the war, the colonial army was nevertheless occasionally in evidence. Late one afternoon towards the end of 1967 Kinyama was up on the hillside looking for one of his goats. A jeep drove into the valley and sped towards his house. In it there were three young white soldiers and one black one. As they drove past the farm a soldier fired his gun at one of Kinyama's cows. The cow was killed instantly. In that moment Kinyama lost 30 per cent of all his wealth. The young lads drove away laughing at what they saw as an amusing incident. But for Kinyama it was a major disaster. There was no way in which he could even begin to seek justice or redress. In a few short years Kinyama's relatively comfortable peasant life had come to be threatened by the increasing encroachment of a colonial society. He was almost ready to leave the valley and become a freedom fighter. Almost, but still not quite.

Very early in the war colonial authority in Angola had become afraid that war might become more widespread. Already it was more than Portugal could handle, despite large-scale help from Western allies in the North Atlantic Treaty Organisation. To forestall further uprisings the Portuguese, in the late 1960s, decided to follow a new policy in the as yet unaffected areas. One June day in 1968 a new army official arrived in Kinyama's valley. He called together Kinyama and the other heads of valley households and announced that from now on they would have to live in a government village. Each family would leave its farm and build a village house beside the road. Everyone in the village would be required to stay indoors at night. Farmers would be allowed to work their fields, but would walk to them each morning and return from them each night. A tarred road would be built to speed the military patrols.

The policy of forced villagisation, also adopted by Americans in Vietnam and by Rhodesians in Zimbabwe, greatly increased the difficulties of farming in the valley. Kinyama, his aunt, his wife and his two youngest children, had to walk for one and a half hours each morning to reach their fields. And at harvest time their bags of maize and beans had to be carried for one and a half hours back to the government village in which they were compelled to live. The government called it a security village but to Kinyama it sometimes felt almost like a concentration camp.

Two years after Kinyama had completed his huts in the security village, a great storm hit the valley. It swept through, destroying crops, tearing the roofs off houses and Kinyama lost nearly all his standing maize. He now had to find money for enough thatch to repair all four of his huts. He went to the trader, who said that he would be quite willing to sell Kinyama four sacks of maize on credit. He would also be willing to advance him 300 Escudos (£4) credit in cash to buy thatch. But in exchange Kinyama would have to sign a six-month labour contract to work on a new European ranch recently opened up in the highlands. Kinyama had no choice. He needed the maize and he needed the thatch. So he signed the contract and two weeks later went south to work for six months on a cattle ranch. But it meant leaving his farm with only women to work it. His wife, his aunt and his two small children managed to farm alone. Although compulsory recruitment of labour by the District Officer had officially come to a stop, the valley trader had become even more powerful than before as a recruiter of contract labour. The trader received a generous fee from white employers, sometimes exceeding the wage of the worker he recruited. In the new security villages the need for credit compelled even heads of households to become migrant labourers.

By 1971, when Kinyama returned from his contract, Angola had been at war for 10 years. Kinyama had survived and was still farming on the edges of the valley. But he was now over 50 and ever since 1956 his condition of life had seemed to decline. He had been forced to sign a labour contract; he was still required to use a part of his crop to pay taxes; his eldest and second sons were now presumed dead; he could not return to his old farm on the flat, although it had long been abandoned by its white occupier who had gone to the city to become a taxi driver.⁹ Kinyama finally overcame his farmer's caution. Carefully, furtively, he made contact with other members of the valley community who were ready to join the nationalist cause and take up arms against colonial oppression.

Kinyama was obviously too old to leave the valley and walk the many miles needed to join the freedom fighters. But as a well-known and respected community elder, he was ideally placed to recruit younger men who had decided to break with their colonial way of life. In 1971 young Angolans were being recruited into the colonial army in increasing numbers. Those who wanted to escape from fighting against their own people secretly visited Kinyama's house at night despite the curfew regulations. A local party cell was informally set up. The idea of freedom from colonial rule and the ways of achieving it were discussed. Local subversion was planned.

While Kinyama was beginning to organise and mobilise the people of the valley into novel political activity, the Portuguese army, on the other side of the war, was beginning to alter its tactics of dragooning and villagising the highland peasants. Senior military officers were becoming increasingly aware that they could not win a shooting war. They would have to try political methods of recovering initiative in the colony.

New ideas about how to create a satisfied and loyal colonial population had already been developed not in Angola, but in Guinea Bissau, then known as Portuguese Guinea. There General Spinola, the Portuguese Governor and Army Commander, changed his policy from one of direct military confrontation to one of political wooing. He argued theoretically that only by providing economic betterment could colonial subjects be persuaded to abandon national independence as their aim. In practice Spinola's policy seldom went much beyond verbal promises of a better Guinea (*Guiné melhor*), and failed to undermine significantly the nationalist movement. When such ideas and promises were introduced into Angola, however, they naturally met with much fierce white resistance. The traders objected most vehemently, for it was they who made the largest profit margins from buying peasant crops cheaply and selling them at town prices. Despite the anger of the traders, however, the army won its point. Early in the 1970s a policy of positive rural development was approved for Angola.

On the morning of 12 May 1972 Kinyama received a white visitor. It was the first time that a white man had ever come to his house. The white man was not a Portuguese but a German. He had been appointed as a rural development adviser. His interpreter explained to Kinyama that the government had decided to give back to him his three acres of flat valley land. It had also decided to allow him to grow a new cash crop on this land. The crop was to be the delicate *arabica* coffee of the highlands. Kinyama knew nothing about growing coffee, although his uncle had worked on the great lowland plantations of the coarser *robusta* coffee in the north. No one in the highlands had ever tried growing his own coffee. The development officer assured Kinyama that rural education officers would teach him how to plant coffee trees, how to weed them, care for them, and prune them. In a few years' time he could expect to harvest a crop of coffee worth many times more than his old crop of maize.

For the next year fortune began to smile on Kinyama as it had never smiled before. He received government credit to improve his returned farm. The government brought transport to carry state-supplied fertilisers to his fields. The farmers of the valley were encouraged to set up a co-operative. Instead of selling produce to the one white monopolist trader, they would be allowed to sell it at better prices to wholesalers in the city. The co-operative would be allowed to buy a lorry instead of relying on white trucking firms. The whole colonial economy, which had increasingly oppressed Kinyama and the people of the valley, seemed to have been set in reverse motion. Kinyama's dreams and expectations had never been higher. The twin ideas of political freedom and economic betterment had both reached the valley.

Kinyama, like many people in different parts of Angola, was caught in a trap between two sets of expectation. The liberation movement offered visions of a new society in which the interests of a peasant would become those of the government. The development officer offered a counter-programme in which some peasants – Kinyama included – would escape from subsistence to become successful farmers, and even agricultural businessmen. In its search for survival the colonial government was creating confusion, despair and divisions within Angola. Kinyama, in his slow and careful way, was still keeping all his options open.

The prospect dangled before Kinyama of developing a prosperous family business in the highlands was actually a false one. The coffee experiment absorbed an unreasonable amount of finance from the government and could never be expected to return real profits. More seriously the Angolan highlands were becoming agriculturally exhausted by this time. The best maize lands had been worked out and the fallow periods were becoming too short. The cost of colonial government, the cost of transferring wealth from the African countryside to the European towns, and the cost of paying for the colonial war, were impoverishing the majority of Ovimbundu. The coffee scheme and the co-operative movement could only buy a little more time for the Portuguese and that at great expense. Time, however, was not on their side: suddenly, on 25 April 1974, the Portuguese Government in Lisbon was overthrown in a military *coup d'état*.[10]

The collapse of the Portuguese Government was felt in Angola. Over the next 17 months the political parties began to mobilise their supporters and the colonial army gradually withdrew its troops. Kinyama, meanwhile, kept on farming. He still had 15 goats to pasture on the hillside. He kept his two surviving cows in the valley. He hid his corn seed in an old hut far from the village. He made charcoal in the woods on the hilltops. And he waited for independence. But independence was deferred in Angola. November 1975 did not bring peace and freedom but new invaders. In the South the invaders came from South Africa.[11] They entered Kinyama's valley in armoured cars early on the morning of 15 November, four days after the last Portuguese colonial flag had been lowered. One of the cars opened fire on the village. Kinyama's house was hit. His wife lost an arm. The children were terrified. Kinyama died instantly.

Angola had to go through a long and painful new war before independence was achieved. Many more innocent peasants died, like Kinyama, in the sorry aftermath of Portuguese colonialism.

12 Youth and War in Angola

This chapter was presented in absentia to a Paris conference entitled Les Jeunes en Afrique *and subsequently published in 1992 by Harmattan in the two stout volumes of transactions. The year 1992 was Angola's first – and last – year of peace since the great rebellions of 1961. A whole generation had grown to adulthood knowing nothing but the insecurities of war in which boy-soldiers were conscripted as colonial auxiliaries while girl-children lived in constant fear of the brutal lust of expeditionary regiments from overseas. Some youth escaped the colonial nexus to join the irregular forces of the nationalists and lived for years in the lands at the end of the earth, or in foreign exile, before returning to war-torn cities in search of a new life.*

On 4 February 1961 the young people of the city of Luanda experienced terror. Some of them, led by their elders, had hot-headedly tried to storm the prison in order to liberate leaders of the incipient nationalist movement in the city. They had failed and the white population launched a revenge vendetta of extreme virulence. The police allowed expatriates and settlers to have weapons and to enter the suburbs and slums in search of potential nationalist sympathisers. An informal white militia led a savage vendetta. The blacks they most feared were those who had received some Portuguese colonial schooling. They were the ones most likely to deprive illiterate white immigrants from the backlands of Portugal, or the slums of Lisbon, of access to the racist colonial eldorado they had come to seek, riding on the crest of the coffee boom. Adolescents were dragged from their beds and murdered in the streets. Some managed to flee and become boy-soldiers in the hilly fastness of the Ndembu forest, the 'First Military Region' of the Popular Front. All of Angola's youth lived the next 30 years under the shadow of war, colonial war, factional war, liberation war, civil war, foreign war, city war, war in the wilderness at the ends of the world. No child grew up in Angola without risking a daily encounter with violence, police violence, gang violence, domestic violence, conscripted

133

violence, exiled violence, the violence of permanent fear permeating a whole society and a whole generation.

The experience of Angolan youths who joined the liberation movements in exile is perhaps most vividly portrayed in fiction rather than in the fragmentary hidden historical records or in the propaganda leaflets put out by foreign support groups. Pepetela's novel *Mayombe* speaks of the boredom, the waiting, the timelessness, the hopelessness, the loneliness, the remoteness, of all those youths who lived in guerrilla camps far from any city lights. Occasionally they were spurred to military action and elation or fear obliterated other sentiments. For much of the time their preoccupation was how would they next get hold of a cigarette, what would the next meal be, who would give them credit for a drink, but above all when would they next have an opportunity to momentarily banish their endless misery in the arms of a woman. The perceptions of sex as the soldier's panacea was not unique to the Angolan youths who signed up with the liberation guerrillas. It was also a central experience of those who were conscripted to fight against them in the colonial regiments.

Sexual exploitation had always been a strong feature of Portuguese colonialism and in his memoirs General Delgado recorded how senior government officials visiting Angola expected their hosts to provide them with African girls so young and inexperienced that they were unlikely to infect their abusers with disease. In one extreme case a black novice nun was forced to act as hostess. Armies were less discriminating in their sexual demands and the female youth of Angola was the constant victim of rape, pregnancy and disease. White youths who fathered unknown mestizo children were almost commended for furthering the colonising cause, but their illegitimate offspring were frequently the victims of double prejudice, being rejected by both black and white communities and subject to such violent atrocities as are portrayed in Bridgeland's biography of Savimbi. The legacy of war left a generation of psychologically warped male youths who saw women as objects to be competed for and won, and of deprived female youths whose careers were dragged down by premature and indiscrimate child-bearing. Only a few young women learnt to use their sexuality as a weapon in the struggle for influence over the adult men who monopolised power.

The most difficult ideological experience of African youth was the pressure to join the colonial army. Initially the army was mainly an expeditionary one brought out from Portugal and reinforced by white youths whose parents worked in Angola as settlers or more commonly as expatriates. But as war-weariness grew in Portugal, and increasing numbers of conscript-age youths fled to France, the colonial authorities adopted a policy of 'localising' or Africanising the colonial army. Some young blacks joined for want of a better job with regular pay. Some committed themselves even further and become informers to the security services and the 'secret' political police. Others were conscripted against their will. Many were used in the most dangerous tasks, walking along dirt roads in front of a convoy, for instance, so that a boy-soldier rather than an expensive vehicle would be blown up by a hidden mine.

In the colonial wars of Mozambique and Zimbabwe it was relatively easy for those who had fought on the colonial side to 'purge' their 'treason' and accept incorporation into the new national forces of independence, sometimes after a period of detention in a so-called 're-education' camp. In Angola the situation was much more difficult. No single nationalist faction won the liberation struggle and the young men who had military experience in the colonial army were courted by no less than three sub-nationalist armed forces, those of the MPLA, the FNLA, and the UNITA. Ideological confusion and the absence of a clear identity was further confounded. Angolan youth sought other loyalties than those towards the state which was so severely fractured.

One of the lasting legacies of the Portuguese presence in Angola was the love of football. Salazar's variant of fascism, like Mussolini's original model, effectively diverted the attention of many youths away from politics and into football competitions. Youths in the post-independence years of austerity in Angola queued up to rent pages of the Portuguese sporting press from bars. They also supported their own teams, and football was one of the key factors of national integration. The horizons of youths were lifted beyond their own backyard as they followed the fortunes of their teams into alien ethnic territory. They even encountered foreigners through football and were astonished to discover that while Portuguese was the universal agent of national unification in Angola, foreign football teams did not speak English or French but Bemba or Lingala. A football club, however, could become a vehicle for deep internal ideological debate as well as a means of furthering the national solidarity that governments tried to encourage. Such was the case with the attempted *coup d'état* of 1977.

The abortive coup of 1977 was a young person's revolt which broke out after the shattering of illusions and expectations aroused by independence. The leader, Nito Alves, was no longer a young man, though he was much younger than the grey-heads who dominated the cabinet. He still held fast, however, to the uncompromising ideals of youth and to the visions which 15 years in the *maquis* resistance of the First Military Zone had engendered. He was contemptuous of the soft luxury life-style which returnees accustomed to city exile fell into when they inherited the villas and yachts of the departing colonials. He set out to defend the *sans-culottes*, the youth of the slums to whom independence had brought no eldorado. Under the guise of supporting the Sambizanga football club, and with the help of ultra-radical outside supporters, he mobilised political discussion groups which studied the ideology of Mao Zedong and, more quixotically, of Enver Hoxa, the ruler of Albania and the last of Europe's unreformed Stalinists. When the time came to strike a blow for the young and underprivileged, however, the army quavered and the Cuban expeditionary force moved with alacrity to protect those of its political masters who had not been killed in the first flush of rebellion. The government recovered its equilibrium and – like its colonial predecessor in 1961 – blamed the young and made them pay for their temerity with their lives.

It was not ideology alone that sparked off the young men's coup of 1977. The city youths feared that the government was going to conscript them in a campaign of rural work programmes. In particular the government had been bankrupted by the decline of coffee production. The great estates were abandoned by their owners in the white stampede of July 1975 and a crop which had once made Angola the fourth largest coffee-producer in the world was no longer being harvested. Unemployed or under-employed city youths seemed to be the obvious answer to the need for labour to bring the estates back into production. By the young supporters of the Sambizanga football club were townsmen to the tips of their toes and the though of being sent to the wild, unknown, hostile, snake-infested bush filled them with terror. They risked their lives in rebellion rather than risk loosing their place in the city.

One alternative to football as a form of social control has traditionally been the church. In Angola the church was always seen with ambivalence. The republicans of 1910 virtually outlawed Catholicism at home but recognised that it had its uses in the colonies as a means of awing the subject masses. The authoritarians of 1933 slowly restored their relations with the Vatican and even tolerated the Protestant churches, though they were always half convinced that Protestants were the prime source of nationalist agitation. The nationalists of 1961 added Marx and Mao to the firmament but preferred to think of themselves as the heroes to be hero worshipped. The traditional church structures nevertheless remained an important focus for youth and provided one of the most deeply rooted sources of identity in Angola.

The 'old *assimilados*' of Luanda, descendants of the great creole families of the nineteenth century, sent their children to Catholic schools in the main, and invited white members of the colonial elite to become their godparents. The Catholic church was also the social focus of the mestizo community of Luanda which grew out of the white immigration of the republican era of 1910 and beyond. The children of white bachelor fathers were often accepted into favoured schools in spite of the fact their mothers were black and unwedded. The new mestizos and the old *assimilados* formed a sort of elitist creole alliance in the city in the last colonial years. A few of their number, however, broke away from the Catholic tradition to become Methodist. This brought them into contact with the black, lower-middle-class, layer of 'new *assimilados*'. Unlike creoles whose parents punished them for speaking African vernaculars, the new *assimilados* only spoke Portuguese in school, preferring Kimbundu in the playground or at home. This social preference for an African identity brought the new *assimilado* youth into closer contact with the upper working class. It also gave them a spiritual home in the Sunday schools of the Methodist church rather than the more strictly Portuguese-orientated Catholic church.

Outside of the Catholic and Methodist networks of the city, two other Sunday-school networks were of fundamental importance in establishing the social ties which bound Angolan children to their contemporaries and determined their political affiliation when they reached political and military age. In the south the network was Congregationalist, with close ties to the traditional aristocracy of the old Ovimbundu kingdoms of the plateau. The children of the south were unable to find affinity with the creole children of the city, even when sharing their war-time exile. They were also unable to find a common cause with the children of the north who attend Baptist schools both inside Angola and in the huge communities of Kikongo-speaking Angolans which had grown up in Zaire from the beginning of the twentieth century and been reinforced by a wave of 100 000 refugees in 1961.

Far and away the largest exile community of Angolans was the Kikongo-speaking community. By the time the colonial war ended in 1975 half of the community were children under the age of 15 who had been born in exile. Their language of wider communication was French, their church affiliation was Baptist and the survival strategy of their parents had been to move into the business world. The children of the 'Zairotas' went back to Angola with no experience of Angolan education or of the bureaucratic ladders of opportunity which the creoles and other assimilated persons had learnt to master. The returnees came with a profound suspicion of youths whom they had not met in school or chapel. They came as apprentice peddlers and taxi touts rather than clerks and office-boys. They did not recognise the youths they met on arrival as fellow nationalists because they had served in different armies during the liberation struggle.

Independence did not bring an end to conscription and the military way of life for most young Angolans. On the contrary the wars of South African and Zairean intervention led to even greater mobilisation than that practiced by the colonial authorities. Girls as well as boys were brought under military discipline. Children in fatigues were found at every street corner reading whatever pulp fiction they could lay hands on to while away the time. The positive feature of conscription was that it enhanced literacy, increased the use of Portuguese as a national language, and brought people from different regions of a huge country together even more effectively than the following of football clubs. On the other hand the years of conscription seemed to drag on without end and desertion came to be seen as the only form of demobilisation. A youth sub-culture developed in which communities protected children who threw away their uniforms and melted into the urban landscape, hidden from the ever more intrusive forces of the police.

If city conscripts were bored and under-employed, front-line children were the victims of war whether in uniform or not. The 'civil war' and the 'war of destabilisation' which followed the initial interventions of 1975 spread slowly to most of the countryside. Each army laid mines in the paths of its 'enemies', who often turned out to be innocent children going out to the fields early in the morning to scare the birds from the crops. Some children were threatened not merely as casual by-standers, but as porters over the long thorny trails of eastern Angola. Child labour may have been an old tradition on the farms but it became a tradition in the hard-pressed irregular forces of insurgency as well. Lucky children were the ones that escaped to a slightly less uncertain future in the not always well tolerated refugee camps across the impoverished borders of Zambia and Zaïre.

The uncertainty of war and the suddenness of death was captured in one of the most vivid war diaries of the late twentieth century, Richard Kapuscinki's *One Day of Life*. He travelled with the young heroes of the Popular Movement as they sought to repel invaders and hold the capital. In the culminating hour of the independence struggle, midnight on 11 November 1975, three foreign armies were within range of Luanda as the last Portuguese forces left the colony under cover of darkness. The victorious army came from Cuba and that too was composed of youths, anxious and far from home. By the time the Cuban intervention ended 15 years later some 300 000 young Cubans had had experience of war service in Africa. Many went home maimed and diseased to a less than heroic welcome in their impoverished Caribbean island.

One of the less military features of organised youth activity in Angola related to an attempt by the state to revive the tradition of street festivals and carnivals in the city, and if possible in the provincial towns as well. The government decided that it would celebrate annually in March the 1976 expulsion of the first South African invasion. The format adopted for the celebration was that of the old Lenten carnival. Each section of the urban community prepared its youth for a competitive display of elegance and virtuosity. Market women dressed up their granddaughters in the finest cloths that their trading profits could buy. Members of the seamen's union used their opportunities for overseas travel to buy exotic finery that would enhance their public prestige. The fishermen were among the wealthiest working-class citizens of Luanda and expected that their young people would put on the best display of competitive dancing. The less wealthy patched-and-made-good in order that their young people could also establish one of the several hundred Luanda dance troops that took part in the preliminary elimination trials for the Carnival of Victory.

The final competition and parade of the Luanda carnival contained several messages. One was the simple message of a country that had been invaded celebrating its victory and the recovery of independence. But a second was that of the exuberant youth of the city displaying its power and vitality before the soberly suited gentlemen of the party central committee. Their placards might protest at the survival of privilege and wealth behind high walls guarded by dogs while the mass went hungry. But another message was the rivalry between the different boroughs of the city, each with very distinct urban traditions of their owns. Those who lost status in the eyes of the carnival judges were violently dismayed and had to propitiate their gods with rich libations of foreign spirits and illicit rum. The kings and queens of the carnival were under great pressure to win.

Dancing was no substitute for employment for the youth of Angola. In his Orwellian satire of post-colonial society, *O Cão e os Calús*, Pepetela describes the life of a lad-about-town kicking a pebble along the waterfront. He meets his aunt: 'Why aren't you in school?' 'I have finished school Auntie', 'Then why aren't you at work?' 'There is no work Auntie'. His aunt is clearly and irredeemable bourgeois. He on the other hand is a truly liberated revolutionary who despises property. He therefore goes into a beach-bar and spends some of his mother's errand money on a beer and a plate of rice for the stray Alsatian dog through whose eyes the scene is portrayed. The dog then goes on to play with the children of the bureaucrat in their suburban garden, but fails to stop the street urchins from climbing the wall to steal mangoes. The dog has no sense of the sanctity of property and no gratitude for the meals he is given. He goes on to become the guard and companion of a pretty mestizo bar girl who earns her living by comforting lonely overseas aid workers in exchange for foreign luxuries. The dog finally becomes a hero when he reveals himself to be an unemployed stray who used to work for the 'fascist' police and uses his old skills to sniff out a terrorist bomb in a children's playground. The experience of Angola's youth always came back to the war.

The fiction of Pepetela not only illuminated the exile of the freedom fighters and the hypocrisy of the bureaucrats but also the racial ironies of the colonial and liberation periods. His great family saga, *Yaka*, culminates in the final collapse of colonialism when the youngest generation in the family adopts different stances. Race is not the ultimate determinant. Some of the most radical youths in 1975 were in fact white, while some of those who managed to flee to Portugal for safety were mestizo or black. One of the supporters of the apparently black youth movement behind Nito Alves was of a young woman of Indian racial origin. Liberation, like colonialism, may have had its racial tendencies but they were not absolute.

The normal experience of youth is education. In the Angolan wars education suffered. Radical new ideas could not be converted into adequate supplies of textbooks and so children either had no books or continued to cling to old colonial ideas and school methods. The seeds of the conservatism that were such a striking feature of a régime with a stridently revolutionary rhetoric were found on the school benches. The alternative to continuity was the importing of overseas aid teachers from the German Democratic Republic or Vietnam, but such teachers had to struggle to learn Portuguese and then found that there were no African materials they could use for teaching purposes and so fell back on abstract stereotypes in their teaching. Rather than converting education from Portuguese to African values they instilled theoretical constructs into their struggling pupils. Meanwhile the war conscripted the teacher-trainers who would otherwise have taught a new generation of Angolan teachers. The youth of Angola seemed likely to suffer from yet another generation of educational deprivation as a result of the war. Even the educational elite in the university faculties was deprived of teachers, books, periodicals and scientific materials by the overwhelming economic demands of the ministry of defence.

13 The Twenty-Seventh of May

On 27 May 1977 the newly-independent Popular Republic of Angola was shaken to its foundations by an unexpected, though abortive, coup d'état. This preliminary history of that coup was written less than a year after the event and was presented to a conference on Angola which the author convened at the School of Oriental and African Studies in London. It sheds light on post-colonial politics in Angola, on the social stratification of Luanda city, and on the role of the Cuban expeditionary force which landed in Africa in late 1975 and helped to keep the supporters of Agostinho Neto in power. The article was originally published in 1978 in African Affairs, *the Journal of the Royal African Society and is reprinted by permission of Oxford University Press.*

The attempted *coup d'état* in Luanda on 27 May 1977 came as a surprise to many outsiders. The evidence about it published subsequently shows that it should not have done. High-level confrontation within the Central Committee of the MPLA had been building up at least since the previous October. But it was not in the city that MPLA expected to experience its major difficulties. In this respect the pattern of politics in Angola after the Portuguese cease-fire was markedly different from that of Mozambique. In Mozambique Frelimo was a rural-based movement and its greatest initial problems were those of accommodating to the realities of the industrial cities with entrenched economic systems and economic expectations that were widely at variance with those of the long-standing party recruits. It was not surprising therefore that Mozambique experienced one or two patches of turbulence in the capital during the transition. In Angola, by contrast, MPLA did have city experience – in Luanda, Benguela, Malange – and its difficulties, highlighted by the war of intervention, were to accommodate to the rural populations of the north and of the plateau. The search for this accommodation still goes on. Meanwhile, however, the 27 May illustrated how deeply the war stresses had bitten into the MPLA's own urban constituencies, previously taken so much for granted.

The official history of the attempted May coup, produced in July 1977, ranges over most of the problems which Angola inherited from its protracted and painful birthpangs. The central theme, however, is the struggle to create a coherent and credible ideological creed which could act as a focus of loyalty, of dynamism and of comfort during the inevitably long period of material austerity, institutional inadequacy and foreign insecurity. Throughout 1975 and 1976 political debate seems to have thrived in Angola. Ideas were intensively debated in Action Committees, in the so-called Amilcar Cabral committees, in Trade Union committees, in Women's Movement committees, in 'Henda' committees, in Youth committees. This vitality of debate was mainly seen as a strength within the MPLA. But gradually the need was felt to curb some of the freedom of rhetoric and establish a more unitary ideological driving force. In the parlance, the 'liberation movement' was moving towards the creation of a 'party' with a 'correct' political line. The 'Amilcar Cabral' committees seem to have been among the first to have been accused of schismatism and to have been suppressed. Nito Alves was accused of having used them as a 'trampoline' and then helped in their eradication. Other committees were subsequently accused of deviationism. Gradually the debate seems to have been polarised into two major tendencies, the official one of President Neto and the unofficial one of Nito Alves. This divide was recognised as early as October 1976 when the third plenary session of the MPLA Central Committee set up a commission of enquiry to investigate factionalism within the Movement. After much strain, anxiety and delay the commission's report was finally presented to the Central Committee on 20 and 21 May 1977. It stated that:

> Factionalism presents itself in an apparently revolutionary cloak but really aims to divide the MPLA and consequently deflect the People from the true objectives of the current stage of struggle which is national reconstruction and defence of national integrity against imperialism.[1]

The resolution went on to state that factionalism was led by Nito Alves and José van Dúnem, who would consequently be stripped of their membership of the Central Committee forthwith.

The stage was set for a *coup d'état* which unrolled with incredible slowness, callous brutality and farcical incompetence over the next six days. The question remains: how did Nito Alves come to be seen as either the source of all evil, or alternatively the fountainhead

of all hope, in the 12 months following the withdrawal of the South
African army from Angola? The answers, although in many cases
contradictory, do shed some light on the political process in a sparse,
poor and weak country under siege.

The first question concerns the nationalist credentials of the coup
leaders. Nito Alves rose to his positions of authority in the first
military region of Angola. This region, in the rugged forest hills
north-east of the capital, fought its own war against Portugal almost
in isolation. The leaders of the region were not well integrated
into the cosmopolitan set who had lived in Algiers or Paris, who
had studied in earlier times in Portuguese universities, and who
mixed confidently with Africa's leaders in Zambia and Tanzania.
Nito Alves has been frequently described as a racist within a
nationalist movement that prided itself on its complete absence of
racial consciousness or animosity. But although he used racial rhetoric
at times in his fervent speeches to the shanty towns, racism does
not seem to be the essence of his separateness. His position was
more that of a military captain who felt uncomfortable in the more
suave cultural environment of the broad political leadership. At
the same time his companions-at-arms provided him with a distinctive political base strong enough to get him elected to the
Movement's Central Committee. His most powerful ally from the
first military region was probably Ernesto Gomes da Silva, who
used the *nom-de-guerre* Bakalof, and whose arrest, announced on
23 November 1977, marked the last capture of a major coup leader.[2]
Bakalof was also a close collaborator of José van Dúnem, who gained
him the post of chief political commissar in the army when the
former holder was killed in Cabinda.

José van Dúnem had his own launching pad into politics. He
was a 'prison graduate' of the Saint Nicholas camp. His leadership
of this group was enough to get him elected on to the MPLA Central Committee at the same time as Nito Alves at the September
1974 meeting held in Zambia. The Saint Nicholas group were subsequently accused of planning their capture of the Angolan revolution
over three years. Even in prison, their detractors claimed, they were
a closed elitist group who could not transcend their petty bourgeois preconceptions and mix with prisoners of the truly exploited
colonial classes. They formed the backbone of the Luanda regional
committee. In November 1974, as negotiations with Portugal were
in train, this Luanda power nucleus tried to buy time for itself by
delaying the transfer of the Movement's leadership from the East

to the capital. In alliance with Nito Alves, the van Dúnem group were clearly a significant power. They too were accused of misusing the concepts of scientific socialism and of advocating crude racism.

The coup was seen in May 1977 as an uprising of the *musseques* slums of Luanda. The subsequent MPLA report on it makes it out to have been a much wider phenomenon, with strong provincial cells. Nito Alves, in his capacity of Minister of Internal Administration, had close contacts with all the provincial administrators. At first it was planned that the rising should take place in Malange, and only when those plans dissolved did the leaders realise that the capital must be seized first in any successful takeover. In addition to Malange the provincial commissioners of Benguela, North Kwanza and South Kwanza were alleged to be implicated in the Nito plot. These four areas are the four core centres of traditional MPLA strength. The anxieties which led to the split in the Movement obviously went to its very heart, or so the report prepared for the Political Bureau thought.

The greatest problem which Angola faced during the year after the Civil War was the problem of agricultural production and food distribution. In West Africa it was said that military coups occurred when the government failed to maintain an adequate supply of St Louis lump sugar. In Angola the whole food distribution network failed. It failed at three levels, in production, in transport, and in retailing. Marketable agricultural produce was grown in colonial Angola both on white agro-industrial plantations and on African plots where the main tax-crop was maize. The plantation sector depended heavily on the transfer of labour from south to north. When the 1975 war tore the country in two, the integration of northern land and southern labour under Portuguese capital and management was destroyed. Expatriate management withdrew to Europe, and Ovimbunda labour retreated to the kith-and-kin shelter at the Congregationalist highlands. Since then one of the major campaigns of the MPLA has been to mobilise underemployed urban workers as agricultural brigades for the estate sector. Failure to recruit enough workers, or to get them into the required rural areas, was laid at the door of Nito Alves' Luanda committees. This administrative inadequacy was, however, demonstrated in all too many areas, for instance in channelling the enthusiasm of youth into the mass literacy campaigns that were designed for the city.

African surplus agricultural production was heavily linked to high levels of colonial taxation. Even if the 1975 war had not severely disrupted large parts of the country, there would have been strong demands for the curtailment of the heavy tax burden which produced maize for the towns. Between them, the freedom of independence and the disruption of war caused the shortfall of foodstuffs available in the towns to become severe. Foreign exchange needed for producer goods had to be spent on emergency supplies. The debate over long-term and short-term priorities, over consumer satisfaction and basic development, was at the heart of the MPLA's political anguish. In the Nito split each side accused the other of political opportunism.

Production, land and labour were not the only reasons why food shortages became so severe as to almost unseat the government. The second war of liberation severely disrupted the whole communications network and transport system. The Benguela rail only operated on limited sectors, dozens if not hundreds of road bridges were demolished, civilian transport planes were flown out of the country and repainted in Zaïrean livery, Portuguese lorries were driven out by refugees or destroyed in scorched-earth bitterness. Even where food crops were grown, there were few opportunities to carry them to market, particularly to the remote Luanda market.

In addition to failures of production and transport there were difficulties of distribution. Angola's colonial society was built on a countrywide network of small white shop and inn keepers. Even in Luanda retailing – down to the meanest level of bread and cigarette salesmanship – was a white preserve in both black and white quarters. The rebuilding of an identical African lower middle class of petty traders could have been undertaken given a little time, but that was not within the government's social strategy. Instead the ideal was a state-run system of people's shops. Adequately trained entrepreneurs and administrators were, however, in acutely short supply. So the capital lacked either an adequate network of responsive capitalist outlets or a social control of retailing to match the needs of a newly liberated people who had waited 13 years of their golden tomorrow.

The scapegoat needed to carry the blame for the disintegration of essential economic services was found in Aires Machado, known as 'Minerva', the Minister for Internal Trade. A whole thesis of economic sabotage was erected around the ministry complete with a named Portuguese destabilisation agent at the centre of the web. The minister was alleged to be seen by the Nitistas as a man loyal to their ideals of the revolution who refused all the pragmatic compromises of the cabinet. To his colleagues he became responsible for deliberately creating shortages in order to foster enough discontent to facilitate the overthrow of the government. Improbable though the conspiracy theory may be, the reality of the food crisis must certainly be accepted as a fundamental cause of the political fission and an attempted *coup d'état*. The exposure of the plot did not, however, solve the problem of the food supplies. Six months later Angola had to airlift 30 000 bags of maize from Zambia for emergency feeding.

One of the greatest of Angola's post-independence difficulties was the shortage of trained and experienced leaders, organisers and administrators. By African standards Angola had become a closely governed country in the 1970s. The withdrawal of 90 per cent of the white settlers and expatriates between July and November 1975 left many essential services – transport, harbours, currency, customs, police, revenue, local government, health – chronically short-staffed. The expatriates available after independence fell into two highly remunerated categories: those who remained to earn a living as disinterested technocrats, and those who were in a committed position during the factional struggle. The latter had less room for pragmatic adaptation to shifting circumstances than the indigenous nationalists. Nito Alves was accused of surrounding himself with foreign political ideologists for whom doctrinal purity was the only source of legitimacy on the Angolan scene. One might perhaps be reminded of the Tanzanophiles at the court of Nyerere who sometimes found themselves in the uncomfortable position of thinking that they understood the president's mind better than he did himself.

One of the prime leaders of the expatriate group was Cita Vales. She came to Angola in mid-1975 almost unnoticed, and possibly as part of a tide of Portuguese youth who wanted to experience free Angola at a time when their own revolution was beginning to pall. Cita Vales had experience in the union of communist students and her dynamic organising abilities were immediately put to use in organising a think-tank to assemble and correlate basic information and policy options. She seems to have worked in the organisation of political mobilisation. Through it a constellation of young Portuguese militants had been set to spreading the ideas of Nito Alves through the schools of Angola. At first their texts were allegedly based on Enver Hoxa of Albania, but in 1975 they switched to the writings of Mao, and Nito Alves lectured widely on Chinese-style class analysis in Angola. Cita Vales turned these groups on to Lenin. The debate was now open within the MPLA about the true and the false interpretations of common political ideas.

The major centres of intellectual anti-leadership discussion seem to have been in the civil service. But it was not only in the civil service that overenthusiasm for the cause led to disenchantment. The press apparently played an important role in building the Nito wing of the MPLA. In the capital the *Diário de Luanda* was alleged to be pro-Nito and the provincial papers of Lubango, Lobito, and Malange disseminated his ideas. Local radio stations and the prestigious Kudibanguela programme from Luanda began to question the wisdom of party and government decisions and to build up the local importance of the popular ward committees. The radio gradually became the focus for the revolt, no doubt helped by the stirring memories of 25 April when the Portuguese radio played a song about freedom to set the tanks rolling in Lisbon.

Trade unionism in Angola has always seemed to be one of the cornerstones of the MPLA. Once in office, however, the MPLA, like many African governments, expected the unions to switch from opposition to the colonial state to collaboration with the national state. The national confederation of workers in Angola failed to co-ordinate its policies with the government's national goals. It was promptly accused of factionalist deviation, of subverting the party action committees and of prejudicing planning and production targets. Unions opposed the formation of MPLA cells on shop floors claiming an exclusive right to organise industrial labour. Syndical commissions sought autonomy from the party and individual union leaders in places as far apart as Lunda, in the north-east, and Benguela, in the south-west, were accused of disrupting both industry and agriculture.

Other features of national life, less important than the trade unions, were brought into the great debate. The role of sport in African politics is a subject worth developing for instance. In colonial Angola football was Salazar's white alternative to politics and also the black cover for some forms of resistance. In creating the Nito wing of the MPLA sport also was used. Nito became president of the Sambizanga football team and built up its prestige and success. It became a focus of passionate support among the *sans-culottes* of Sambizanga parish. One supporters' group was allegedly trained as a murder squad for the coup. And it was in Sambizanga that the coup really began in the form that Nito Alves had planned it. This was a mass march of demonstrators from the slums into the city.

The event which started the brush fire of disturbances through the slums was a house-to-house search by the army in Sambizanga. It is not stated what the search was for – hoarded food, inflammatory literature, hidden dissidents – but it led to spontaneous and irate meetings of popular assemblies which condemned the MPLA, the army, the DISA security service and the government. Violently worded solidarity with Sambizanga spread to six other slum districts, including the central working-class areas of Rangel, Operário and Prenda. The president of the republic himself was called in to investigate the abuses allegedly committed by army searchers. Before calm was restored, however, the long-delayed meeting of the Central Committee was finally held. It opened on 20 May to discuss dissension within the ranks of the MPLA. 20 May was therefore chosen for the *coup d'état.*

The coup of 20 May was designed to kidnap President Agostinho Neto. It failed for the simple reason that the venue of the Central Committee meeting was changed fifteen minutes before the opening. The conspirators were left high and dry around the Museum building. They were quite unable to shift their activities to the school building on the other side of town. A second and quite different coup was therefore planned for 25 May. This time the army was to lead the offensive and kill half a dozen top leaders who had been most hostile to the Nito group. When 25 May dawned, however, the army did not move. A third coup was therefore planned without the army for 28 May. Before it could take place, however, the revised army version was attempted on 27 May with the support of a leading military man known as 'Immortal Monster' who expected to become minister of defence in the Nito–van Dúnem government. The military details need not detain us. The insurgents of the 9th brigade apparently had 10 armoured vehicles with which they blew open the prison and captured the radio. The government's 15 loyalist vehicles were not actually in town when the coup broke, and were moreover suffering from faulty communications equipment. They nonetheless re-entered the city, retook the radio, and were then joined by four Cuban tanks before obtaining the surrender of the 9th brigade headquarters at 1.30 pm. One hundred prisoners were released but six leaders designated by Nito were smuggled out during the negotiations and shot in a house in Sambizanga.[3]

During the first year of independence Angola went through all the stresses of African nationalism in the most acute possible form.

If one takes a parallel in Ghana, one can watch the 15-year evolution of a central party trying to accommodate the conflicting interests of a society overcharged with the expectations of liberation. Angola underwent the same process in as many months. Some of the common points are simple enough: a trade union movement which sees its role as defending the sectional interests of some wage-earners rather than being the industrial arm of the government; the difficulties of food supply management and severe accusations of hoarding and consumer sabotage; the importance of women's movements whether as market sellers demonstrating in opposition, or as powerfully organised women's sections of the government party where loyalty needs to be watched over; the accusations of elitism, of social distance, of improper wealth, of alienation from the grass roots take on a particular virulence. All statements of both sides are peppered with accusations of disregard for the peasants and workers. The MPLA is accused of 'social-democracy, rightism, social chauvinism, anti-communism, maoism, and anti-sovietism' and retaliates with charges of a similarly catholic range. Both sides are wounded by accusations of living in middle-class ease without understanding the feelings of the poor. Nito is accused of ignoring the 'hundreds of thousands' of people who lost their homes and all their possessions in the war.

The difficult question that arises out of all this vituperation is what was really going on in the minds of the average Luandan or Angolan underneath the rhetorical froth of the leaders. In Luanda the mood had been changing rapidly. The euphoria of the Portuguese collapse – a surprise to most Angolans since the war was won and lost in Mozambique and the key changes took place in Lisbon – was followed by acute spasms of fear at the early build-up of FNLA military power in the city. It was to resist the intrusions of FNLA soldiers into the slums that the popular power structures of the city had been developed. During the second, 'South African', war these committees had been loyal to the MPLA. Disillusion certainly set in afterwards as the costs of reconstruction came to be measured, but the disillusion was not so severe as to cause the masses to abandon their hard learnt caution and follow Nito Alves in a wild and ill-conceived plan for mass unarmed insurrection. The level of their disillusion was such however that the MPLA reverted to building up the rural peasants as the heroes of their 14-year struggle. After the suppression of the coup much play was made of the fact that the urban workers had never been adequately politicized and had not carried a large share of the anti-colonial struggle.

If it is difficult to know what was going on in the minds of the lumpenproletariat upon whom Nito Alves relied to carry out his coup, it is even more difficult to see into the minds of the soldiers whom van Dúnem brought in to the conspiracy. The Angolan army was very different from most post-colonial armies. It was not a long-standing group with a common interest well-rooted in the national bourgeoisie. It was an integrated section of the political movement which combined guerrilla veterans, former colonial troops (mainly but not exclusively black), and young recruits drummed up during the second war of liberation. The coup was not really an army man's coup and distinctive army interests, isolated from the broader political ones, should not be expected. Nevertheless a number of army commanders had been seriously embarrassed by the MPLA defeats of 1975 and their discomfiture was further highlighted by the success of the Cuban expeditionary forces. Some of these military leaders may have been anxious to erase those memories. A much more serious military factor, however, is the fact that in 1977 Angola was still suffering endemic warfare. The role of the army was therefore quite different from some coup countries where the armies not only were not at war, but had never been at war.

The MPLA's own assessment of the causes of the attempted coup make little mention of the fighting in the country. Yet it was significant in five zones. In Cabinda the Gulf Oil Company was happy to have 3000–4000 Cuban soldiers to defend its installations from separatist or foreign attack. Some fighting was certainly going on, as shown for instance by reports of wounded in the mission hospitals of neighbouring Zaïre. The second zone, in North Angola, was apparently quiet at the time with the government administering the roads and towns but adopting a quiescent policy in some rural areas where the FNLA provided rudimentary forms of local organisation. Border activity was apparently minimal, but from February 1977 Angola was anxiously preparing to repel a new Zaïrean invasion code-named Cobra 77. Under these circumstances manpower and resources were needed to keep defence at its peak. This detracted from civilian reconstruction and further aggravated the disenchantment of the peoples of the towns who were relatively safe and far from any actual fighting.

The third war zone was in the east, on the other joint frontier with Zaïre. It was there that the Congo National Liberation Front launched their March 1977 attack on Mobutu from Angola and reached the fringes of the Zaïrean copper belt. However much or little support Angola may have provided to this task force of former Katangan troops, the whole episode diverted even more of Angola's attention away from its true priorities. Fear of a Zaïrean counter-invasion was still strong at the time of the May coup and had not been lessened by the Franco-Moroccan rebuilding of Mobutu's army after its second rout in twelve months. The state of animosity between the two countries was epitomised by Mobutu's premature welcome of the overthrow of Agostinho Neto on 27 May.[4]

The fourth war zone to keep Angola in a state of disarray was the Central Highlands of Benguela where UNITA had so effectively consolidated its political base during 1974. The extent of the fighting in May 1977 may not have been as great as it became later in the year. Basil Davidson, for instance, reported in May that UNITA's forces were fairly restricted in their zones of operation and were dependent on arms left over by the South Africans. Nevertheless, anxiety over insecurity in the centre of the country can but have made the tasks of government more difficult and the appeal of an ultra-radical alternative seductive.

Finally the activities of the fifth war zone in the south are the most complex and shrouded of all. It would be particularly interesting to know how many young recruits, able to organise worker-brigades in the maize lands, were tied down on the Cunene along with SWAPO, UNITA, and South Africa.

All five of the war zones involved foreign interests. Although it would probably be unwise to look for any active foreign participation in the attempted coup, one can certainly look at the range of foreign responses it engendered. The government were naturally chagrined that the plotters had had such close friendly relations with the Soviet Union, and indeed Cita Vales expected the Russian embassy to rescue her after the coup failed. The Cubans must have been highly embarrassed by the whole affair but there is no suggestion that they did not support the government. There is indeed one curious report that when the radio station was captured, the end of the insurrection was accidentally announced in Spanish rather than Portuguese. The desirability of having a disinterested foreign military presence in the country – discovered long ago by such unlikely people as Nkrumah, Nyerere and Mba – was proven yet again, even if the Cuban role was only a safety-net to give courage to loyal units. To those for whom the government had seemed to betray the fruits of freedom, the Cuban presence must have grown increasingly unpalatable.

Western interests in the events of 27 May were naturally coloured by the embarrassment they felt about Angola since late 1975. Zaïre was ready to welcome any change, even one seeking a purer form of Marxism. The South Africans probably concurred. The United States had long been seeking signs of fission between the black population and the mestizo elites. It would certainly have been willing to act as marriage broker between Nito Alves and the old FNLA–UNITA leadership. France was singled out by the Angolan government for particular condemnation among interfering foreign powers. Such a role might well fit France's oil-thirsty and expansive Africa policy and tie in with its close alliances with Zaïre and South Africa, but the evidence to support such a thesis will have to be found.

Such are a few preliminary questions which a historian might start to ask about the events of May 1977 in Angola. One random thought might also occur to such a historian: what parallels may be found between the unfolding Angolan Revolution and the exactly contemporary revolution in Ethiopia? The search for outside help led in both cases to Cuban offers of military and administrative help, offers made out of Cuba's long-term commitment to freeing the third world from big-power domination. In both cases the Soviet Union was resorted to as a supplier to heavy arms in a crisis of military weakness. In both countries the old elites were important to the revolution for their administrative and military leadership and their adoption of radical positions. These new radicals were at the same time suspect for having so comfortably made the transition from the old order. More graphic parallels arise in the twin problems of ideological confrontation and territorial disintegration in the two countries. In Ethiopia the ideological confrontation took place between incipient political parties – EDU, EPRP, AESM – whereas in Angola the stress has been within the broad tendencies of a single party – the Active Revolt, the Eastern Revolt, the Nitista faction. In both countries regional political disaffection has been organised and armed with varying degrees of external support. And in both countries the whole slow social revolution has been accompanied by both actual and threatened foreign intervention. Clearly many of the Angolan events which led to the rather pathetic attempted coup of 27 May have not been solved, yet the prospects of solving them in Angola seem rather better than they do in Ethiopia.

In one respect, however, the Angolan plotters adopted a distressing feature of the Ethiopian revolution: the cold-blooded personal murder of antagonistic leaders. The stakes of violence were thereby raised at a time when they needed to be lowered in the aftermath of the Angolan civil war.

14 Angola Revisited

This portrait of Angola in 1987 was written shortly before great changes came to the region. Within three years South Africa had been militarily defeated in Angola and its army had surrendered power to reforming Afrikaners and nationalist Africans, the Cuban expeditionary force of 30 000 soldiers had returned to the West Indies, and the Soviet Union had collapsed as a global power and rival to the United States. This chapter therefore analyses Angolan society and politics in the last year of powerful political intervention and five years before the outbreak of the country's third, and particularly destructive, civil war. In that war, which raged from 1992–1994, some of the provincial cities mentioned in this chapter were starved and destroyed as war moved from the countryside into the towns. The chapter was first published in the Journal of Southern African Studies *(1988) and is reprinted by permission of Carfax Publishing Ltd, Box 25, Abingdon, OX14 3UE.*

Long ago, in April 1975, I visited Angola in the early days of the Battle for Luanda which pitted three liberation movements against each other in the aftermath of the collapse of Portugal's colonial administration. By July 1975 Agostinho Neto's wing of the MPLA had won the battle for the city and within a year had gone on to win the second war of liberation as well, repelling foreign intruders with Cuban assistance. The next 12 years were devoted to coming to terms with their enemies and winning the peace. The struggle was uphill all the way, as I discovered when I returned to Angola in March 1987. In many way, however, the changes grafted onto Angolan society were less striking than the entrenched continuities which struck a historical visitor familiar with the colonial past.

In most ways Angola did not fit any of the received models of decolonisation. In conventional colonial states the capital city formed the hub of the new nation. In Dakar or Nairobi or Harare, political life, social life and economic life focused on a single capital city. Not so in Angola. Luanda was but one of three poles of opportunity that had attracted colonial subjects throughout the course of the twentieth century. Luanda and its hinterland along the corridor to Malange was unified by a river, by a line-of-rail, by the Kimbundu language, by the Methodist network of schools and chapels, by a sad history of Iberian *conquistadores* and slavers, by the rise of the black creole elite in the nineteenth century. But it was not closely linked to North Angola or South Angola. These regions had their own metropolitan centres in the Belgian colonial city of Leopoldville, now Kinshasa, and the British railhead of Lobito, commanding the Benguela railway to the Copperbelt. It was therefore no accident that Angola, instead of developing a single political bandwagon onto which everyone jumped when the liberation movement began to roll, initially developed three political movements with three urban focal points, three missionary traditions, three vernacular languages and three rival sets of sub-national leaders. The decolonisation model based on a focal city hub therefore did not fit Angola.

The second model of decolonisation which did not fit Angola was that concerning traditional patterns of neo-colonial partnership. In most African countries the 'paleo-colonial' power became the neo-colonial economic patron. Portugal delayed its decolonisation for over a decade in the hope that it could develop a sufficiently powerful European manufacturing and financial base to serve that role when its colonies were given flag independence in the French style. Portugal feared that a premature decolonisation in Angola would let in West Germany and the United States, the main industrial powers without conventional colonies in Africa. In the event the Portuguese attempt to hold on to Angola involved such acute racial confrontation that most settlers and enterprises were compelled to withdraw. The United States, as predicted, became the main economic partner through control of the oil industry which gradually rose to dominate over 90 per cent of the export economy. But the main industrial partner turned out to be East Germany rather than West Germany and it was East Berlin that came to consume all of Angola's surviving coffee exports. More strikingly still, of course, was the arrival of the Soviet Union and the Cuban expeditionary force. The predominantly white Iberian creoles of Cuba provided the ideal partners to the predominantly black Iberian creoles of Angola. They came to call each other 'cousin', to more or less understand each others language, and to supply administrators, teachers, medical staff, scientists, planners, all paid for out of oil revenues from Gulf Oil of Texas and other western multinational corporations. Portugal, meanwhile, kept a very low political profile in Africa and had little neo-colonial power. It was surprising therefore to discover how deeply entrenched the Lusitanian traditions were in Lusophone Africa.

The first striking continuity is, of course, the entrenched position of the Portuguese language. During the liberation struggle Portuguese had been one unifying factor which held the MPLA together. In 1971, when the term 'Portuguese Africa' seemed inappropriate for territories where large sections of the population were in rebellion against Portugal, I coined the term 'Lusophone Africa' which was rapidly adopted by the media and foreign governments though not by the nationalist movements, who refer more cumbersomely to their nations as 'countries of official Portuguese expression'. After independence the political significance of the Portuguese language became even more crucial to Angola than it had been during the long years in the wildnerness at the end of the earth when the MPLA struggled to survive in its exiled havens and peasant-based military regions. Language became a central feature of political rivalry, of ideological confrontation, of regional factionalism, of rural discontent, of class confrontation, and of neo-colonial interference.

One role of language in the political division of Angola concerned the rivalry of the MPLA and the FNLA. The latter commonly used French as its *lingua franca*. The supporters of the now defunct FNLA were primarily northerners many of whom had lived for years in Zaïre. The old generation had gone there to seek economic opportunities during the Belgian colonial hegemony in the region between 1908 and 1960. They had successfully worked their way up through the commercial system to become craftsmen, artisans, traders, and the factotums of a Portuguese petty bourgeoisie which dominated the retail trade of western Zaïre both before and after the Belgian decolonisation. In March 1961 the old migrants in Zaïre were joined by a large influx of refugees as quarter of a million Angolans escaped the colonial slaughter in the Portuguese coffee belt. The new Angolans found opportunities among their ethnic brethren and some became a dynamic merchant class. As they prospered they sent their children to French-language schools and used them to fill the economic niches neglected by Zaïreans who had by now found richer pickings after independence in the state sector of employment. By 1974 half of the 'Angolans' in Zaïre were Zaïrean born so that when they went 'home' to Angola, speaking French rather than Portuguese, they were disdainfully described as the '*Zairotas*'. Despite the social antagonism the exiles returned home in large numbers, initially to their ancestral villages in the north, where the old support structures of localised ethnicity and Protestant chapels were revived, but much more significantly to the

city of Luanda where their long foreign experience of urban living
and commercial practice found broad openings.

A first attempt by the Kinshasa exiles to take over Luanda ended
in armed confrontation and defeat in 1975. The significant military
help provided by President Mobutu of Zaïre, who lent the FNLA
his army, and by Henry Kissinger, who allowed the American secret services to recruit brutal but incompetent mercenaries to assist
the FNLA, were not enough to evict the MPLA at the battle of
Quifandongo on 10 November 1975. Ten years later the peaceful
economic infiltration of Luanda by the Kinshasa exiles was much
more successful. The Angolan economy required all the skills it
could muster and many of these were provided by the northern
returnees. Their position in Luanda was not dissimilar to that they
had held in Kinshasa in the 1960s. In Kinshasa Zaïreans held the
state jobs and the immigrants held the private sector jobs, often
under the high patronage of the state president, who was the greatest
private entrepreneur of them all. In Angola the returnees found
that the state sector was monopolised by the supporters of the MPLA,
but the private sector was vacant and open to them. The private
sector in Angola had been dominated by white migrants from Portugal until 90 per cent of them fled in the panic of 1975. There
were therefore openings for taxi-drivers, shirt-makers, shopkeepers,
bar-tenders, cook-stewards, electricians, plumbers, lorry mechanics,
and every kind of wheeler-dealer. Such were the opportunities that
the Francophone *Zairotas* could not fill them all and other immigrants began to drift into Luanda, drawn by oil-fuelled prosperity.
Artisans came from the Cape Verdes whose drought-afflicted people
had already discovered the road to exile in Portugal but now found
that there were richer pickings in being major-domos in the foreign
embassies of Luanda or in maintaining the air-conditioning systems
of the multinational offices. Further up the scale the Kinshasa
returnees also found competition from a new generation of Portuguese expatriates and even from French master-craftsmen brought
in to work on prestige public contracts when the oil prices were
high. When the oil prices began to dip, however, the white expatriate
began to slip away, unsure of their ability to remit their rich earnings,
the Cape Verdians began to fear the rise of urban violence directed
against their relative economic success, and the Zaïre returnees
expanded their sphere of opportunity more widely than ever in the
city's thriving free-market economy.

For a country with a centrally planned economy Angola has de-

veloped a free-market sector which makes the famed liberalisation
of Chinese and Soviet market opportunities seem relatively tame.
In fact nothing resembles the Angolan urban economy more closely
than the unbridled dynamism of Kinshasa from which so many of
the Angolan returnees had come. Parallel markets sprang up everywhere to supplement the state stores, to retail stolen and smuggled
consumer goods, to resell rationed surpluses for scarce luxuries, to
provide the necessities without which the fat cats of the state bureaucracy would be unable even to attempt to imitate the colonial
living of yesteryear. Unlike China, however, where two official currencies co-exist, one hard and one soft (as indeed they once did in
colonial Angola) modern Luanda lives with a free market and closed
market which use the same currency. The free-market value of the
Kwanza is flexible and responds accurately to world markets, to
the price of oil, to the availability of consumer and commestible
goods. It is worth about 15 Kwanzas to the US cent. In 1987 the
official value was about 50 times free value, or 30 Kwanzas to the
dollar. The effect of this caused stunning distortions in the economy,
unrivalry opportunities for market-orientated entrepreneurs and
unprecedented difficulties for expatriate organisations which were
finally driven to use the black market despite all their moral and
legal scruples. In 1988 the *Observer* correspondent in Luanda found
that a small pig, on sale for an apparent 1000 US dollars, was actually a bargain if you knew your parallel markets properly. State
guests were relieved of embarassment by being given everything in
kind and therefore never dealing with money at all. Everyone else
bought regulation goods with dollars or escudos in hard-currency
state-shops or with rationing coupons in government-employee shops
and then sold the surplus for Kwanzas at 50 times the nominal
government price. The parallel market then supplied such necessities
as eggs, meat, fowl, shoes, torch batteries, Volkswagen parts, Scotch
whisky, fresh fish, frozen Soviet-trawled fish, fruit, ice-cream and
thousands of gallons of Portuguese green wine which never runs
dry even when wheat flour has been unavailable for months on
end. Those who have no access to state shops, and have no authorised residence in the city, live precariously by their wits while
those who operate the free market (and presumably those who
provide them with political and bureaucratic protective cover) do
rather well. At the pinnacle of the free-market system housing is
the scarcest commodity of all and at one time involved favours
which were measured in matchboxes filled with illegally won

diamonds. Official diamond sales were commonly thought to have been 'creamed' of the top ten per cent of gems. Under these circumstances the city has learnt to live with the returnees with their alien French ways but their necessary urban skills. They are mocked because of their clannishness, because they do not speak Portuguese properly, because they are a predominantly male enclave which preys on local women with material gifts, because they were on the wrong side of the battle lines on 10 November 1975 when every true Luandan remembers what he or she was doing while the guns pounded the suburbs. But they are tolerated. Rather different is the attitude to the migrants from the countryside.

Luanda, like all capital cities in Africa, is the great magnet for those with initiative who want to leave the countryside and make more of their lives. The rural immigrants are known in the city as the 'Bantu', a term of unexpected opprobrium applied to those who do not speak Portuguese or adopt the middle-class table manners of the departed colonials. The rural immigrants are, however, the productive backbone of the city. They have dug up the parks and grass verges to plant vegetables, they have turned the sandy suburbs into cassava plantations, they work for the old fishermen hauling their nets and paddling their canoes, they clear the roads after the age-old torrents of sand and mud have flooded the city, they build the still mushrooming shanties where ever more of their kinsfolk seek refuge from the encroaching war in the provinces. Country people come from every part of the country, but especially from the Kimbundu-speaking Luanda corridor along the line of rail to Malange and from the Ovimbundu-speaking highlands where a third of Angola's people are now facing their thirteenth year of civil war. The highland city of Huambo was described as the 'Beirut' of Africa where the government builds by day and the guerrillas destroy by night. Living in a war zone does sharpen the survival strategies, however, and the Ovimbundu who have moved to the capital have re-created a whole new caravan network of long-distance trade similar to the great commercial systems which they pioneered in the eighteenth and nineteenth centuries.

The first step in the rebuilding of the caravan networks was based on road transport. Although bridges were blown and roads mined during the South African war of intervention in 1975 and although much of the national vehicle stock was taken away or destroyed be fleeing colonials at the same time, a transport system was gradually rebuilt and even recruited once again some of the long-distance white driver-entrepreneurs who had been the backbone of colonial cartage when in the 1920 and 1930s they underpriced the government railway and outgunned the African headporters. After independence crops, fish and beer continued to be driven long distances until the civil war began to make many of the long-haul networks unsafe. Lorries began to travel in cumbersome armed convoys which then took weeks rather than days. Even Malange, the Kimbundu twin to Luanda, ceased to be accessible by road and the state president had to put his Mercedes on a military transport plane when visiting his closest provincial capital. Quickly the Ovimbundu merchants began to grasp the opportunities of air-transport to ferry goods to the archipelago of provincial towns where government writ held sway. Luanda developed two air terminals, one officially called February the Fourth, after the date of the great nationalist uprising of 1961, decorously dealt with VIPs and government servants. The other, informally called February the Fifth, was thronged with day-long queues of peddlers trying to jostle, bribe, shout, buy, their way onto the aircraft with great head-loads of retail merchandise. The system thrived on the two-tier currency which meant that a 100 dollar air-ticket legitimately cost the price of a free-market pack of lager and could be validated (unofficially) with a gratuity for the kinsman allocating seat numbers and boarding passes. Boeing jets fly to all parts of Angola carrying a dozen politicians, diplomats, bureaucrats and the odd visiting lecturer in the front two rows and 100 caravaneers and market mammies crowded in behind them until the doors will barely close on their boxes and bundles. In the smaller towns markets are only held on the days when the plane comes in and makeshift stalls mushroom. My own surplus luggage allowance was used by someone to carry back to the city two boxes of apples grown on a state farm that had not yet been returned to a white settler in the southern highlands. This farm was technically still the Fourth of February Production Unit but since the workers had not been paid for 17 months commercial practice diverged from ideological theory. Where farm produce is not available as the return pay load on the planes, artisan craftwork for the world market in Africana is bought from carvers and trophy hunters. The illicit trade in ivory and ivory carvings now runs into large sums and transcends international boundaries.

The air caravans which have replaced the nineteenth-century headporters and twentieth-century Portuguese truckers are not confined to domestic trade. During the second war of liberation Hausa merchants began to fly in from Kano, but they were soon superceded by indigenous Ovimbundu and Zombo entrepreneurs. Angolan textile merchants may not yet rival their Brazzaville neighbours by breaking into the Middle East markets and flying textiles to Kuwait, but they do operate within the African subcontinent and across the south Atlantic. Ultra-cheap soft-currency air fares mean that goods can be profitably bought and sold in Brazil and Brazilians have re-established the old Portuguese specialism of producing alcoholic rotgut for the African market. Meat – possibly diverted from the refrigerated trains that ply between South Africa and the Zaïrean Copperbelt – is flown in from Zambia. Pharmaceuticals, of which Angola is chronically short, are regularly embezzled and diverted to hard currency outlets in Kinshasa. The old border markets of Zombo and Noqui thrive on border traffic and smuggled goods as never before. Beer remains the big long-distance commodity and although apologetic official figures suggest that beer production has dropped since independence, there is little data on the quantities which leave the breweries by the back door to be flown to more lucrative destinations than the state shops of Luanda. So while world media-men concentrate on the political aspirations of Ovimbundu guerrillas who man Savimbi's red-eye missiles, many other Ovimbundu have recreated the world they lost in the colonial war of 1902 and are learning how to live with a divided society split between those who feed on the market and those who feed on the state bureaucracy.

The bureaucratic tradition in Angola is a deeply entrenched one and has been intimately linked with each stage of the country's twentieth-century political evolution. Under the monarchy at the beginning of the century the bureaucracy contained many of the scions of the old creole families who had dominated local recruitment to the army, the teaching profession, and the civil service. The great families, often with roots in the seventeenth century, were received into colonial society, graced the governors' balls and paraded on the great festive occasions such as royal birthdays when floats were presented to the smartly attired colonial elite. In 1910 the old creoles began a long period of decline from which they did not recover until their star rose once again in the 1980s. The first challenge came with the overthrow of the Portuguese monarchy by a conspiracy of liberals, republicans and junior army officers belonging to secret cells of the Carbonaria. Under the republic of 1910 to 1926 the bureaucratic tradition in Angola was reinforced by under-employed white carpet-baggers who came to the colonies in search of state salaries and drove the old creoles out of their accustomed niches in the public service. Racism became a criterion for preferment in the bureaucracy and remained so until the end of the colonial period. At the same time, however, the new whites commonly came without spouses and had to accommodate themselves to African society. Some male immigrants were forced to acknowledge that if they wished to marry African wives they would have to be circumcised and to pay customary bride-wealth to their chosen in-laws. They also found that there was a conflict between their desire to hold government jobs by virtue of their race rather than their often inadequate qualifications, and their desire to see their brown children properly educated and integrated into the state sector of employment. A new creole society, predominantly of mixed race, grew up in the second quarter of the twentieth century which developed a profound animosity to the old black creoles of the nineteenth century. The new creoles were not only an important part of the urban citizenry of Luanda but also evolved in the southern capital of Benguela.

Benguela had been founded in the seventeenth century and in the eighteenth and nineteenth centuries had been a major slaving port. In the twentieth century it had a significant white population. Some of them were traders as portrayed in the brilliant prize-winning novel by Pepetela called *Yaka*. Others were a liberal segment of colonial society which was sent there in semi-exile during the 1940s and 1950s and created both mixed and white families with a distinctive southern creole culture. They formed one strand of the nationalist movement of the mid-twentieth century which was integrated into the MPLA. They also became antagonistic to the brash new rival city of Lobito which grew up at the rail head and attracted large numbers of immigrants from the highlands who were subsequently mobilised by the rival UNITA. Benguela's long tradition of cultural and ideological autonomy from Luanda was reinforced by its independence from and antagonism to the 'fascist' variant of colonial practice as experienced in Angola after 1930.

The effects of Iberian-type fascism on the bureaucratic tradition in Angola were particularly deep and lasting. Colonialism was authoritarian in its stance at the best of times so that the colonies of Britain, France and above all Belgium were run as petty gubernatorial dictatorships on police-state lines. In Angola this authoritarian tradition was reinforced by a residual element of doctrinaire Catholicism. Both the Portuguese Republic and the fascist New State had problems with the Catholic Church in the colonies. At home in the metropolis it was first of all persecuted and later tolerated within carefully limited confines, but in the colonies persecution was muted by the fact that the church was seen as a useful tool with which to tame indigenous subjects and even turn hewers of wood into clerical scribes who would reduce the cost of the bureaucratic superstructures of the state. The combination of colonialism, fascism and Catholicism created a reverence for order and authority which Angola has never succeeded in shrugging off. Indeed the advent of Marx in the liberation pantheon has made the matter worse. Obedience, subservience and resigned acceptance of the all-powerful written order with the red seal have become an ingrained way of life which survived the first war of liberation, the day of independence, the second war of liberation and 13 years of civil war. When this particular VIP found that his pass to attend the Luanda Carnival was stamped with a blue seal when it should have had a red one, his busy and distinguished host did not try to bluster or pull rank but philosophically went back to the relevant bureaucratic strangle point and sat for several hours until an administrator personally known to him arrived with enough influence to use the red seal.

Acceptance of the long march of twentieth-century bureaucratisation has many explanations in Angola. One of them dates back very specifically to 1957 and the introduction into the colony of a 'secret' security police system. This police force was designed to monitor political attitudes, especially the democratic aspirations of white dissidents but subsequently also the nationalist causes espoused by mixed-race and black middle-class activists and their white sympathisers. The police came to be profoundly feared for their lethal methods of torturing their suspects in a manner which had the maximum degree of social and political reverberation in society. When independence came the secret police were the prime target of recrimination in both the metropolis and the colonies, but having lived for a generation with such methods of social control, neither Portugal nor Angola felt safe in abandoning some form of political monitoring of potentially subversive opinions. A political police, with Soviet advisers in place of the Gestapo officers and CIA operatives who had trained successive generations of the Portuguese secret police, therefore survived in Angola and silently ensured that respect for authority was entrenched during and after the heady days of liberation. Since independence was accompanied by foreign and civil wars the case for a more liberal democratic stance was muted and the bureaucracy was able to carry on with astonishingly little change to its work practices.

The survival of an over-staffed bureaucracy in Angola is only partly explained by the needs of an inherited colonial system rooted in Portuguese fascism and serving a new Marxist concept of a centrally planned society and economy. It is also due to the political ability of members of the bureaucracy to defend their positions and salaries. Many of the places in the administration serve no earthly residual function, but to abolish them would be politically inconceivable. The country is acutely short of skilled administrators and clerks, yet to discontinue age-old work practices and shake out labour cannot be contemplated. The preservation of custom and order has some benefits in that those who speak Portuguese, are literate and understand the system know where they are and can feel reasonably secure and confident in their survival strategies at a time of general insecurity and war. The cost, however, in terms of thousands of staff-hours wasted queueing for valueless permits, unnecessary licences, authorisations, chits, booking forms, boarding passes, meal tickets, provincial visas, lodgings registrations, *laisser-passer* stamps is uncalculated and incalculable. One consequence is undoubtedly a great deal of moon-lighting as holders of government posts, with copper-bottom access to housing and state shops, also work in the private sector advising companies, drawing oil salaries, playing the parallel market and ensuring that their standard of living, which surely dropped in the 1980s, still remains far above that of the average Angolan urbanite. In political terms, however, the bureaucratic class has seen its influence being steadily eroded since the heyday of 1976 when the new creoles dominated the MPLA and when the MPLA army – in alliance with the creole expeditionary army from Cuba – defeated the South Africans and temporarily gained control of the whole of Angola.

Army power has risen steadily since independence in Angola and is the main rival to bureaucratic power in the central councils of the ruling party. It is said that the army is the most powerful unifying factor in the country. The only other institution which draws people together so strongly across the regions is football. Football remains a national passion, as it did under the fascist colonial regime which imitated Mussolini by giving people football instead of politics. Individual pages of Portuguese sports newspapers are rented out to avid readers in bars. Foreign teams are invited for championships

and exhibitions, though the Zambian national team caused amaze-
ment in Angola when it was found that they spoke to one another
in an African vernacular rather than a 'civilised' language. But for
all its importance in creating a national identity and enabling people
to meet Angolans from unfamiliar districts, football is still second
to the army as the national institution par excellence. In colonial
times the lorry-loads of young conscripts that careered around the
streets and the army boys who sat at street-corners reading pulp
fiction were 50 per cent Portuguese and 50 per cent Angolans
recruited into the colonial army. Now the most visible conscripts
are all Angolan, and the 30 000 or more Cuban soldiers are less
visible in the cities than ever the Portuguese were. Indeed one of
the transformations of the war is that whereas the Portuguese put
as many blacks as possible into the front line to minimise metropolitan casualties, the Cubans are leading the defence of Angola
on the front line. In the far south Soviet advisers rub shoulders
with the returning settlers in the old colonial hotels and restaurants.

The prolongation of the 'Civil' War against South Africa and
Unita has transformed the balance of political power inside the
MPLA and brought a confrontation between the bureaucratic 'new'
creoles of the twentieth century and the reviving 'old' creoles of
the nineteenth century. The new creoles seemed to have the upper
hand until 1977 when an attempted coup severely jolted their com-
placency. Black, underprivileged *sans-culottes* in Luanda itself, their
cultural stronghold, almost succeeded in turning out the bourgeois
elite that had inherited colonial positions and prestige, including
the fancy housing, the plush bars, the yacht-racing in the harbour,
and a complacent political condecension towards those who lived
on short rations in the slums. The Nito Alves coup was stalled by
the incompetence of its hot-headed leaders, by a split in the army
and by the rapid decision of the Cuban local command to rescue
the president and his surviving men rather than leap into a more
radical unknown future. Thereafter the army had to be much more
carefully cherished by the politicians, as it had been in colonial
times. Confrontations with Zaïre to stop northern interference did
not succeed in toppling Mobutu but on the contrary brought in
right-wing military support from the United States, Morocco and
France to bulwark the hostile northern presence on Angola's frontier. The next rise in the military stakes came from the south when
South Africa, presumably with tacit if not overt approval from the
USA, began to attempt the destabilisation of its uncomfortable left-

wing neighbour. Defence absorbed an increasing proportion of an increasing large budget in Angola. Fortunately for the army oil revenues rose in 1979 to pay for increased military spending and an increased Cuban presence. The result was that the military in the MPLA gained increasing influence and gradually squeezed out the non-military element. By 1987 the government was controlled by a network of a dozen families of the old creole military caste that had dominated the black elite in the nineteenth century. The new president who replaced Agostinho Neto had an official Russian wife, but his significant ethnic and family links were with the great Luanda families, notably the various branches of the Van Dúnem family. The old creoles completed their clean sweep in removing the new creoles when such a fatherly veteran as Lucio Lara was promoted to the honorific position of secretary-general of parliament, and Lopo de Nascimento was sent off to the provinces as commissar for the southern plateau. The army had imperceptibly but firmly ousted the old political elite and taken command of senior decision-making. In an ironic parallel exactly the same thing took place over the same 10-year time-span in South Africa as the militarisation of decision-making began to affect the committees of Botha's cabinet, and the South African army decided whether foreign policy was to aim at front-line destabilisation, which gave wealth, power and prestige to the armed forces, or seek neo-colonial industrial partnerships which would have given more muscle to the rising Afrikaner capitalists of Johannesburg. On both sides of the war the army won, leaving their puppet-masters in both the USA and the USSR with increasingly limited power to intervene in defence of their own geo-political global strategies.

The 'old' creole militariat which captured the political initiative in the 1980s was no more able than the 'new' creole bourgeoisie of the 1970s had been to capture the loyalty of the 'peasants' and 'workers' who had been the nominal heroes of the liberation struggle. In 1977 it had been the urban workers who had rebelled against austerity and the threat of being sent to work in the countryside from which they or their forebears had escaped. In the 1980s it was the peasants who rebelled against both the bureaucratic and the military tradition of politics which neglected their interests. In the 1960s the peasants of Angola had been painfully integrated into the market. Some worked for whites, growing pineapples, sugar, cotton and coffee. Others continued to work their own land, growing the lesser crops such as maize, but were dependent on white shopkeepers for their markets. The earnings were meagre but better than pure subsistence without any access to lump sugar, kerosene and corrugated iron. In the 1980s these peasants were cut off from the market in a process that was even more painful than being drawn into it. The rural rebellion was therefore more virulent than the urban one had been. It also coincided with a renewed attempt – orchestrated in Washington and Pretoria – to destabilise the country. It was not surprising that the army increased its political weight in the country.

A large army, an enormous bureaucracy, and a love of football are three of the colonial legacies in Angola. A fourth is an educational system in urgent need of reform but which is desprived of financial resources, political initiatives, qualified personnel, scholarly books and basic stationary. The most striking aspect of continuity in education is to be seen in the buildings. In colonial times the rector of the University of Luanda camped out in a suite of rooms in a down-town hotel near the waterfront. He was appropriately reached by a tortuous side stair. Thirteen years later his African successor, a medical man with an economist as his deputy, still struggles to keep the ramshackle bits and pieces of surviving higher education together from the same hotel rooms. In Lubango, deep in the southern war zone, the Faculty of Letters is still housed in the annexe of the old grammar school, where change is in the name of the patron over the door rather than the content of the syllabus or the quality of the library. Libraries never featured large in the Portuguese tradition of oral higher education where following in the steps of the Master was more important than initiative and creativity. Learning by rote seems to have survived at all levels of education, but finding the new generation of teachers in the post-colonial period has been an uphill battle. The history section of the Faculty of Education, for instance, hires East German and Vietnamese lecturers who have to learn Portuguese during their period of conscription to Africa before they can teach their own brand of dialectical materialism or European history. One graduate spoke enthusiastically and without apparent irony of his history degree: 'Yes, I studied all history, Mesopotamia, Greece, Egypt, Rome!'. Recent attempts to introduce Africa into the syllabus by one Malian and one Angolan teaching assistant have met with fierce resistance. The Municipal Council does not want undergraduates prying into its archives for material on which to write their BA dissertations, the City Museum keeps its rich library a closely locked secret, the University has a few relevant works in English but none of the students read English, so everyone reverts wearily to abstract historical theory and a mode of teaching that even Portugal and Russia find outdated. The one imaginative spark of historical growth is in the Department of Architecture, where a well-known novelist has been hired to teach social history in a creative and imaginative fashion which would enlighten architects of the first world, trapped as they are in a concern for materials and stresses rather than humans and societies. From this gem it is hoped that a Centre for African Studies, even a Faculty of Social Science, might grow. But the social sciences in Angola are a delicate plant of enormous political sensitivity.

Academic censorship in Angola is exercised by the department of ideological affairs in the central secretariat of the ruling party. The question which exercises both academics and ideological planners is the matter of 'National Identity'. Who are Angolans and how do they feel themselves to be such. Historians, anthropologists, creative writers, political scientists struggle with the problem, but behind semi-closed doors. Research projects and seminars are held in Havana, safely removed from the day-to-day realities of the civil war. Debates about the national question are not brought out into the open yet. Although UNESCO has commissioned a study of the history of Angolan nationalism, Angola's own study remains under wraps at party headquarters. Meanwhile school teachers have no texts which they can use, Cuban lecturers in the training colleges do not have so much as cyclostyled sheets of information about Angola. A provisional text book on history produced at the time of independence barely touched on the modern and contemporary periods and has long since gone out of print. Giving education a higher profile will apparently have to await the end of the war and a reduction in the nervous sensitivities of the collective leadership at the very summit of MPLA government. In the mean time those involved in education suffer from a curious kind of schizophrenia. Half of their commitment is to radically revising the whole interpretation of society along Marxist Leninist lines. The other half is desparately trying to stem the tide of erosion which is undermining education and hold tightly onto everything that has survived the turbulent years of civil war. This conservatism is the more dominant since the pedagogical processes of the old colonial fascism and the new Marxist nationalism have the same doctrinaire thread running through them.

Revisionism is a difficult subject to grasp in even the most apparently straightforward of cases. In Angola I was asked to lecture about Salazar, the old Portuguese dictator. The request seemed absurd, since everyone in Angola lived under his yoke, until I realised that time had passed and a figure of current politics, or so it seemed, had actually died before many students were born. But lecturing about the history of Iberian-type fascism and its colonial outreach turned out to be complicated. The argument that Salazar had imposed heavy burdens on his colonies because of the essential weakness of the mother metropole did not get a good reception. Angolan nationalists had, after all, defeated Salazar, and his crown prince Caetano, and to see him as weak was to belittle their achievement. Worse still the ambitions of most educated Angolans centred on finding a place in the structure of employment, privilege, status and culture which the Portuguese had created and bequeathed to Angola. There is a fine balance between blaming Portugal for the post-colonial evils which befall the country, and holding tight to the certainties with which one has grown up in a neo-colonial world.

Neo-colonialism in Angola is peculiarly complex. At one level it feels like the French style of neo-colonialism. Affluence of an almost obscene luxury survives in small niches as it does in Gabon or the Ivory Coast. People expect services like telephones and water-supplies to work in a way that they rarely did in British or Portuguese colonial Africa, but do in French neo-colonial Africa. The attitudes of Portugal to Angola are changing. The old-guard socialists were soon disillusioned by their failure to create a post-colonial Angola in their own image, and were among the most bitter critics of economic mismanagement and the squandering of oil resources. The new generation of Portuguese 'Thatcherites', led by their York-trained economist and prime minister, are lumbered by no such disappointments in their ideological baggage. They can happily plan a conservative neo-colonial partnership devoid of all sentimental welfare concepts. They stand poised to take over economic management when Cuba and the Soviets decide to leave. An old colonial project such as the prestige hydroelectric scheme on the Kwanza River awaits their return, having been nursed for years by Soviet planners and Brazilian technicians although it bears no relation to the industrial reality of the country and cannot supply remote markets for energy as the Zambezi dams can. Every benevolent and malevolent potential neo-colonial entrepreneur is waiting in the wings to pick up some of the public service contracts which will capture the oil wealth when the war ends. Even more grandiose projects relate to agricultural revival and even renewed white colonisation such as Lonrho is investigating in Mozambique and Mobutu is encouraging in Zaïre. In the meantime the Cuban interlude has provided the Soviet Union with far and away its most successful foray into Africa after the disasters of Egypt, Guinea, Ghana, Zaïre, Somalia, and yet in the long run it was counter-productive because it gave credibility to the South African claim to be the bastion of free-market capitalism in Africa. It also forced the United States to risk a partisan involvement in the civil war in spite of the alienation of the American black vote. By 1987 both the USSR and USA seemed ready to pull out but this would have been damaging to South Africa so the war stakes were dramatically raised by Pretoria with a major white South African invasion. The foreign element in the war grew to match the escalating civil element.

The roots of the Angolan 'Civil' War are in part ideological. In the last years of the colonial war the Portuguese deliberately encouraged the growth of a black capitalist peasantry in the coffee industry. Producer cooperatives were established and given the right to compete with whites in selling coffee at something approaching market prices. The black provincial entrepreneurs, predominantly members of the northern Baptists churches, were supporters of the right-wing FNLA rather than the left-wing, city-orientated MPLA. After independence the rural sector and the entrepreneurs were severely neglected. Peasant incomes dropped, opportunities for marketing farm produce declined, the city fed itself on imported produce paid from oil revenue. The tension between town and country paralleled the ideological tension between entrepreneurial and bureaucratic, between right and left. By the 1980s this tension had become a key feature of the 'civil' war. Guerrilla groups from the south and east could recruit sympathisers in the west and north with whom they had no ethnic affinity but who were distressed at the rapid decline of rural opportunity. The situation closely paralleled the events of Zaïre five years after independence when the dramatic fall in rural standards of living led to the great rural rebellions. But whereas in Zaïre the peasant mob was able to penetrate some of the provincial towns and carry out murderous attacks on townsmen, in Angola the towns were mostly protected and the rural assaults were confined to roads, railways and small government posts. By 1987 the conflict between town and countryside had spread to the entire nation. The United States had opened up at least one of its Zaïre bases to the UNITA guerrilla command thus shortening the communications lines from South Africa and avoiding dependence on the ambivalent government of Zambia. The military situation was now the reverse of the one that had prevailed during the military stalemate of the early 1970s when the Portuguese held the towns and the MPLA caused insecurity in parts of the countryside and along some of the strategic highways. The MPLA now holds the towns but has lost the countryside and the roads. Efforts by South Africa to capture even one small town in the south have been effectively thwarted by a combination of Soviet air cover, Cuban ground troops and the popular militia. The two wars, civil and foreign, continue tragically enmeshed until a negotiated settlement can free the country to find its own destiny of rich potential.

One the face of it Angola is the country which appears to have gone through the most radical transformation of any to be found in Africa during the process of decolonisation. Yet the most striking impression created on a visitor is the continuity from the past rather than the transformation of the present. Independence was gained through a liberation struggle fought on behalf of the 'workers' and 'peasants' yet in the 1970s the workers rebelled against the popular movement's government and in the 1980s the peasants did the same with even greater persistence. The Angolan freedom fighters rebelled against one of the most authoritarian and bureaucratic of all the colonial regimes, yet the successor state remains extremely bureaucratic and relatively authoritarian. The popular movement expected to create a broad-based political system with a mass party, but in practice as been driven by the circumstances of war to concentrate power in ever fewer hands until it looks like an inverted pyramid balancing precariously on a point consisting of a dozen families related to the 'old' black creoles of nineteenth-century fame. The 'civil war' between town and country and the 'foreign war' between Luanda and Pretoria have become intimately enmeshed and can only be ended when power shifts back from the military to the civilians in both Angola and South Africa. Meanwhile entrepreneurs with an instinct for survival have created a dynamic free-market economy in the archipelago of state-controlled cities linked by a new air-borne network of caravans. Businessmen associated with both the colonial FNLA ideology of northern capitalism and the traditional Ovimbundu skills in long-distance marketing thrive once again. Their prime domestic clients are the 'new', sometimes mixed-race, creoles of the twentieth century who captured the old Portuguese bureaucracy and blended painlessly into a Soviet style of ease supported by their creole 'cousins' from Cuba. This private enterprise which feeds the bureaucracy and feeds on the oil revenues from America has begun to reach out to market opportunities abroad, in Kinshasa, Lisbon, Rio de Janeiro and even Paris.

15 Black and White in Angolan Fiction

Angola has been richly served by its writers. Its novelists and poets founded a writers' union and obtained the necessary sponsorship to publish books which were widely read throughout the country. At the very beginning of the twentieth century Assis Junior witnessed the advent of modern colonialism and prudently expressed his social comments in fictional form. In the last quarter of the century fiction became an even more effective critique of politics in the hands of Pepetela, the most powerful of whose novels, A Geração de Utopia, *is not yet available in English. The first half of this chapter is taken from an essay on Assis published in 1990 by the University of Stirling in Gray and Law,* Images of Africa *and the second half from an essay on Pepetela which appeared in the* Southern Africa Review of Books *in 1996.*

In a locked and dusty cupboard of the municipal library at Luanda the colonial regime kept the forbidden books – translations of Kim Il Sung and other subversive ideological writings. Among them lay a long-forgotten novel of Angola by António de Assis Junior which once more saw the light of day after liberation and was published in paperback. It was called *O Segredo da Morta* ('*The Secret of the Dead Woman*'). It was the last-known publication of a black colonial writer before he fled into exile to die, old and fearful, in Lisbon. His family furtively burnt his papers lest the Portuguese imitation of the 'Gestapo' should find them. His children, fearful of persecution, had never even seen the novel secreted away in Luanda Town Hall.

Assis began his career as a political activist and journalist at the dawn of the century. He belonged to the community later known as the 'old *assimilados*', who were descended from a mixture of African and European traders and soldiers who had formed the colonial middle class since the seventeenth century. Some of them, including the black Van Dúnem lineage into which Assis married, were remotely descended from Catholic Netherlanders who elected to stay on in Angola in 1648 when the Dutch Calvinists were driven out of Luanda by Brazilian *conquistadores* led by Salvador Correia de Sá. These Edwardian creoles, with their black skins and their white customs, formed an enclave on the Atlantic coast of Africa which was not dissimilar to the American creole settlement in Liberia, or the French one in Sénégal, or the Anglo-Scottish one on the Gold Coast, or the Afro-Brazilian one in the Bight of Benin. By planting some Mediterranean culture and a few genes in Angola the Portuguese had created a middle class elite in a proto-colonial society. They rather proudly called themselves 'natives' (*nativos*) in haughty contradistinction to the 'aborigines' (*indigenas*). They were notable lawyers, army officers, medical doctors, journalists, property-owners and civil servants.

By 1900 the old *assimilados* of Angola, like those elsewhere from Upper Guinea to the Cape of Good Hope, were beginning to find themselves overwhelmed by a rising tide of formal colonialism and of pseudo-Darwinian racism. Their loyalty to the colonial state, their patriotic adoption of Portuguese norms of behaviour, their fluent command of the language of Camões, meant nothing to a new generation of colonial carpet-baggers arriving in the colonies to seek employment in a bureaucracy which the creoles had made their own. Virulent racist sentiments crept into the newspapers as the newcomers denounced the blacks whose jobs they aspired to capture. The *assimilados* retaliated. In 1901 11 self-taught intellectuals published a collection of anonymous essays of angry righteousness called *A voz de Angola clamando no deserto* ('*The Voice of Angola Crying Out in the Wilderness*'). Their protest had no effect, however, and in 1910 the declaration of the Portuguese Republic made matters worse. The revolution had been unleashed by cells of unlettered *carbonari* in the metropolitan army, and the new government found it expedient to create colonial sinecures for potentially revolutionary cadres of the lower middle class in the home provinces. The creoles were driven yet further back in the social pecking order.

Assis was only 24-years old when the racial diatribes of 1901 broke out and he must have been deeply shaken in his personal identity. He became the last of the torch-bearers in black Angola before the long night of 'fascist' silence descended in 1926. But his informal career as a journalist and attorney was persistently hampered by persecution under the 1910 imperial republic. In 1917 rebellion broke out in the coffee capital of Ndala Tando (later to be known for a few years as Cidade Salazar). As coffee prices rose during the Great War, and as Portugal sank into bankruptcy, white land-seekers moved into Angola and began systematically robbing blacks of their coffee groves. Assis came to their legal defence and published a two-volume analysis of the crisis, only to be accused of fomenting race conflict. The disturbances spread to other coffee zones as stones rained down on the estate farms. A white mob attacked Assis and the government posted him into exile in the wilderness at the farthest end of Angola. Journalism died.

Twelve years later the voice of Assis was heard again. This time he adopted a new format and his commentary, like that of Charles Dickens before him, took the form of a serialised novel in the now stringently censored newspapers. For additional personal safety his social comments were given a historical setting. The question that arises is how far was Assis's reconstruction only an allegorical sidelight on the censored present and how far was it also an accurate description of the historical experience of the previous generation? The historical detail seems tellingly plausible. Where in the archives is it recorded, for instance, that the slave bearers who ran through the woods of pre-colonial Angola wore ankle bells like Russian sleigh ponies? And who else has described the nineteenth-century pilgrims who came to seek intercession at the sixteenth-century shrine of Muxima in times of profound personal or communal crisis?

The Assis novel captures the flavour of the great transformations that afflicted Angola in the second half of the nineteenth century. In the 1860s a paddle-steamer opened the river service on the Kwanza and created a new market-town called Dondo. The heart of the novel is a social history of the town, rife with jealousies, adulteries, thievings, gossiping and endless disputes over inheritance.

Dondo, like Abeokuta in Nigeria or Boma in Zaïre, saw the grafting of Victorian material values onto an African moral culture. In this seething history of change and torment unexpected insights suddenly emerge. Dondo, it turns out, was known as the town of the Jews. After centuries of Portuguese persecution, burning, exile, conversion, here they are bubbling up in nineteenth-century fiction. In the seventeenth-century the royal tax collector responsible for Angolan slave exports had also discreetly been the rabbi of a clandestine synagogue. Did the trade fairs of nineteenth-century Angola have discreet synagogues? A twentieth-century traveller, René Pélissier, found Jewish street names in Dondo unchanged 40 years after Assis wrote his novel. He too wrote a remarkable novel, part myth, part travelogue, part history, part journalism. It is called

Explorar and, in the tradition of Assis, provides penetrating insights that go beyond any academic presentation.

Two fundamental crises affected the life of Dondo at the end of the nineteenth century. The first was the great sleeping-sickness pandemic of the 1890s. Assis described it graphically in his fictional accounts of the great exorcising funeral ceremonies of the Kwanza valley. Perhaps it was here more than anywhere else that he was overtly committing himself to an African rather than a European identity. He had been brought up a creole, proud of his status in the colony. Now he was explaining African custom to an uncomprehending generation of new colonists. More deeply still he was explaining and justifying African custom to his fellow Angolans, who had lost respect for the past and mocked their fellows for their idolatry, their superstition, their unmodern custom. Assis had made the shift to defending an African way of life, and African personality, and showing that it was necessary to preserve it when wholesale disasters such as sleeping sickness struck.

The second great crisis of Dondo was the advance of the railway, that great symbol of modernisation and colonial penetration. Leopold of the Congo had proclaimed that 'to colonise is to transport' and the Royal Trans-africa Railway Company aimed to transport the goods not only of Angola but also of the Congo. In so doing, however, it by-passed Dondo and left the little town on the margins of the colonial economy, at least until the railway itself was superseded by a road that once again passed through Dondo. The train bites deep into the social awareness of colonised peoples. A generation after Assis, Agostinho Neto – doctor, war-leader, state-president and poet – also spoke of the railway as it rolled inland:

> Many lives
> Have drenched the land
> Where the rails lie
> Crushed under the weight of the engine
> And the din of the third class
> Slow absurd and cruel
> The African train.

Not exactly the bard's best verses, but fiction does give steam its due in penetrating Old Africa.

But perhaps the greatest question that the Assis novel presents is how far does he portray the late slave trade with historical accuracy. He describes slave-trading expeditions led by women, for instance, and one wonders if the daughters of the merchant houses did have much greater ambitions than selling bolts of cloth and trays of cooked food on Dondo market. He suggests that they set off with columns of slave-porters and returned months later with herds of bought cattle and coffles of bought people. The circumstantial details are plausible and precise. The paths, the canoe crossings, the river ports, all correspond to the earliest colonial ordinance maps.

But what about the evidence of brigands and highway robbers? One fictional caravan in the novel bought textiles from a fictional merchant called Manuel António Pires. On the first night after setting out for the interior the porters are attacked by a band of robbers in the dark. Their leader supervised the moonlight plunder with a breech-loading rifle while everybody else still carried muzzle-loaders and flint-locks. Manuel António Pires is suspected of looting the textiles that he had so recently sold to the caravan and taking them back to his store to be sold again to the next caravan. When trapped by incriminating evidence he turns murderous. But is it history? The name rings a bell. Documentary research led to the finding of the following paraphrased quotation:

'Do you grow wheat in Angola?' 'Oh yes in Pungo Andongo.' 'Do you grow grapes, or figs or peaches?' 'Oh yes in Pungo Andongo'. 'Do you make butter and cheese?' The uniform answer. But when we arrived here we found that the answers all referred to the activities of one man, Colonel Manuel António Pires. Anyone who has tasted the butter and cheese at the table of Colonel Pires would prefer them to the stale produce of the Irish dairy in general use throughout the province. . . .

Colonel Pires is a good example of what an honest industrious man in this country may become. He came as a servant in a ship and by long course of persevering labour has raised himself to be the richest merchant in Angola. On any emergency he can appear in the field with several hundred armed slaves. The slaves in Colonel Pires' establishment appeared more like free servants than any I had elsewhere seen. Everything was neat and clean, while generally where slaves are the only domestics there is an aspect of slovenliness as if they went on the principle of always doing as little for master as possible. . . .

While enjoying the hospitality of this merchant prince in his commodious residence I visited the banks of the Kwanza with him about once a week for purposes of recreation.

So the historical source is well-informed and not a casual passer-by. How does one then handle the conflict of evidence between the novelist writing in 1929 and the eye-witness writing in 1854, the conflict between the portrait of a well-armed bandit holding the country to ransom, and the pillar of law and order bringing civilisation to the heart of Africa. A serious historian must opt for the contemporary eye-witness, and yet the black novelist seems convincing, detailed and circumstantial. So who is this white traveller, anyway, who writes such a euphoric account of these happy slave servants, this peaceful well-policed haven, this idyllic land flowing with cheese and beeswax? He is of course that paragon of rectitude, the Reverend D. Livingstone, *en route* across pre-colonial Africa to the Victoria Falls. Perhaps it takes a black novelist to get a little closer to the historical truth.

Assis, in trying to debunk the 'myths' of the civilising role of white traders does his background reading with seriousness. He knows the anthropology-cum-fiction of the seventeenth-century friars of the minor religious orders who wrote extensively about Angolan society. He has read the military documentation of the *conquistadores* who struggled to build the first earthen redoubts along the valley towards Dondo in their vain search for seams of silver. He has thought about the history that has brought him to the point he is at, the butt of racial caricatures. But he goes beyond history and turns to psychology, to the explanation of dreams, to the interpretation of the signs of nature, to the role of snakes and beasts and crocodiles. In so doing he finds his own roots. He also finds that he cannot, as one lone Don Quixote, challenge the apparatus of colonialism. He dies at 83 in another world, another age. But his novel was rediscovered.

Angolan fiction was long in abeyance. For a time it seemed that secret policemen did not read poetry and the literature of protest and of historical longing for an authentic past was presented in verse. In 1951 the Movement of the New Intellectuals of Angola organised its first (and last) literary competition. The policemen caught up with them and the winning poem could not be read out. It began:

> We are a people who fought and lost
> Our flag should be black as a moonless night

The poetry circle closed down and many of its members joined a nationalist Movement for the Popular Liberation of Angola which

was a cross between Methodism and Marxism. Poetry went under-
ground, but democrats and nationalists, intellectuals and protesters,
blacks and whites, all continued to write verse, to write the poems
of the dispossessed, the poems of the *bairo operário* where the workers
had no light. They launched an armed struggle within which the
tradition of fiction was reborn. The most striking heir to Assis and
his historical novel and his fictional social commentary came from
a white Angolan freedom-fighter with the MPLA, Artur Pestana,
who wrote under the pseudonym Pepetela.

Alexander Semedo, the fictional 'hero' of Pepetela's historical
saga of colonial Angola (*Yaka*, African Writers Series [Oxford:
Heinemann, 1996]) was born beside a trek wagon on the northern
fringe of the Namib desert in 1890. His father claimed to be a
'political', convicted and transported by royalist Portugal for his
liberal beliefs. Old Oscar and his wife struggled to farm the thirstland
with the help of an elderly female slave, but gradually they gravi-
tated to Benguela, like the regular criminal convicts, and survived
on the margins of bush trading. While dreaming away his dejected
days behind a heavy storehouse counter Oscar taught his son about
the glorious legends of ancient Greece. Young Alexander got little
formal schooling as he scurried through the dusty town like a liz-
ard, recording everything he saw in his mind but sharing his thoughts
only with his carved family fetish, the Yaka with the amber eyes.

Alexander's greatest excitement was welcoming the rubber caravans that came down from the Congo and made the town hum
with business. The drums played all night and the bars were packed
with drinkers. But the boy also witnessed the collapse of the great
Benguela rubber boom, the heartlessness of the shipping agents
who were caught by the crash in prices, the suicidal despair of the
shop-keepers who had hoped to buy their way back to Portugal,
the fierce pride of a Bailundu chief who burnt his whole stock of
rubber rather than be cheated by white men.

The old caravan world of Benguela was dramatically undermined
by the sudden emergence of competition from the Asian rubber
plantations. Then, out of the ocean, came the English in pith helmets and long shorts with a licence to build a transcontinental African
railway. They ignored the proud Portuguese harbour-colony and
built their port at Lobito, a new town of new people who never
did come to understand or empathise with old Benguela. Meanwhile, in the interior, the Bailundu rose in anger as their trading
world collapsed with the disintegration of the caravan economy.

War broke out and missionaries, Catholic and Protestant, were irrationally blamed for fomenting native unrest with their soft humanitarianism. Convicts in town threatened to kill the 'tar-heads'; whites armed themselves to the teeth; and the army, biding its time to avoid another of its historic fiascos, eventually seized Bailundu and paved the way through the highlands for the iron road.

Alexander, meanwhile, played war games with his friends in the woods around Benguela. Occasionally they ambushed a hapless black girl upon whom the gang could prove their prowess without committing the dread sin of touching white womanhood. Alexander caught the colonial lust for black sex while very young, but untypically he remained haunted by the memory of the African boy in his gang who cringed helplessly at the silent pain which mindless rape caused to his ethnic sisters. Despite a residual ambivalence, adolescent sexual experience deeply marked Alexander's adult life. He was easily aroused to temptation by black women even though his mother arranged a 'proper' marriage for him by bringing out to Africa a first-class, European-born, white bride, albeit one who in the motherland was a morally tarnished domestic servant.

The story of the white Africans of Benguela is already known to readers throughout the Portuguese diaspora, but it will now appeal also to South Africans with their several comparable strands of history. Benguela was founded (or more accurately re-founded) by Manuel Cerveira Pereira in 1615, almost 40 years before van Riebeck founded Cape Town further down the coast. Benguela later grew with new immigration during the years of the post-Napoleonic depression at a time when the English were sending white settlers to Grahamstown and the Eastern Cape. In Benguela the 'coloured' Portuguese-speaking mestizos saw their status rise and fall in ways not dissimilar to the fluctuating pattern of acceptance and rejection experienced by their distant neighbours, the Afrikaans-speaking mestizos of the Cape of Good Hope.

Pepetela, the *nom de plume*, and incidentally also the *nom de guerre*, of Artur Pestana, was himself born in Benguela, though not until 1941, 51 years after his fictional character. Pepetela's historical touch, however, is a sure one. The later sections of his saga, like his previous writings, also make use of direct personal experience. In *Mayombe* (now reprinted in English by Heinemann), Pepetela powerfully evoked the bittersweet balance of tedium and fear which he had experienced as a guerrilla in the Angolan war of liberation. The Brazzaville exile of the Angolans in the 1960s had been one long round of cadging cigarettes, waiting for meals, longing for sex, and anticipating violent bouts of terrorist action in which lives were cheaply lost.

Pepetela's career later moved from soldier to politician when he became Angola's minister of education, but his wit remained as sharp and ironical as ever when he surveyed the fruits of independence through the imaginary eyes of a redundant Alsatian dog which had formerly belonged to the colonial secret police. The dog cut through the pretensions of the new political, bureaucratic and business classes of Luanda as it found favour, and food, with idealistic but unemployable verandah boys, materialistic urban home-owners, sophisticated call-girls who thrived on the hard currency of the aid workers, or canny farmers who profiteered from the illicit use of collective farm machinery. Pepetela left the compromising world of politics to lecture in history at Luanda's school of architecture but his literary output continued to flourish. The story of the dog was followed by a darker look at the mix of the traditional and the modern in postcolonial society but neither book was translated into English. Now *Yaka*, the Benguela family saga published in 1984, has appeared in a translation by Marga Holness which does full justice to the author's genius.

Fear, and the violent reaction to fear, were the constant companions of the people of old Benguela. The most powerful, mystical fear during Alexander Semedo's youth was fear of the Germans, the imagined foe of the deep south, the villains who sold guns to the Kwanyama and so brought the destruction of a whole colonial army of patriotic Portuguese and their black militias. To be worsted by 'Germans' was less shameful than being routed by 'savages'. The fear of Germans seized the minds of whites until Germans were seen behind every bush even though, as was wryly observed, fear can make someone mistake even an elephant for a German. The reality of war, as Pepetela described it, was less heroic than the myths and one of his fictional soldiers talked, without pause or punctuation, of the

> diarrhoea from drinking water from the Cunene, that infernal river full of alligators and the rotting meat of animals swept along by the current, diarrhoea that sapped all one's strength, one could barely lift a leg and the soldiers were shitting in the middle of the camp because they were glued to the ground for fear of the bullets of the Cuamatos and there was an unbearable stench,

which caused indiscipline and bad temper, for an army that craps where it eats gets demoralised looking at flies green with shit, yet even the chaplain raised his cassock there amid the soldiers and was like a machine-gun firing liquid diarrhoea . . .

One is reminded of the British veterans of the Anglo-Boer war who claimed that they lost more companions from eating chapattis, made with stagnant veldt water on embers of buffalo chips, than from any 'Boer' sniper fire.

In 1917, while Portugal was fighting the real Germans in France, a new bout of fear seized Benguela when the forced migrants working on the coffee estates of South Kwanza rose up against the plantation overseers. Wild rumours spread through the white town, one rebellion became a dozen rebellions, one dead planter became a hundred dead planters. Volunteers signed up for military service and one loyal black in uniform suddenly became visibly recognised and was even offered a seat in the saloon section of the local bar. The rebellion was quelled, but the temporary racial truce in the town melted away and new fears, leading to new social violence, became the norm on the streets of Benguela.

Urban fears pitted the lowest ranks of poor whites, new European immigrants, illiterate Portuguese labourers, against the threatening achievements of the town's historic population of coloured mestizos. The structural forum for confrontation was the local football match and the brutal brawls that followed it. Alexander Semedo deplored this institutionalised violence which consumed all the passions of a loutish immigrant son-in-law who waged weekly war against the locally-born brown Portuguese. Alexander became increasingly alienated from his extended white family and rejoiced to discover that his banished natural daughter had borne him a mestizo grandson who later braved white contempt and ostracism to visit his grandfather.

The constant struggle for white survival in Benguela involved economic competition with neighbouring black societies, competition for trade, for cattle, for land, for water. Trade was the first African bastion to fall and the Semedo family, like many others, established a rural store where peasant produce was bought for goods and services. They sold textiles, cooking oil, and medicines; they hired out transport and negotiated on behalf of their customers with colonial authority; and they drove their African trading rivals out of business.

Cattle was the second field of fierce competition between Europeans and Africans and the younger Semedo generation acquired its initial capital by brutally engineering an armed confrontation with a Kuvale chief and then stealing his herd at gun point. Pepetela's writing is at is most graphic when recounting the mutual fears of the young whites, filled with bravado as they went out into the bush shooting anything that moved, and the old, watery-eyed chief, surveying the end of his civilisation from the summit of a rock *kopje*.

But raiding cattle without being killed by cattle minders or arrested by a colonial policeman was only the first step in building the modest Semedo estate. Land could be readily bought in the interior, dry land, marginal land, fallow land that was resting, but once bought the empire-building settlers gradually enclosed the lands of their black neighbours, the fertile lands, the wet lands, the riverside lands. Eventually the old farmers, like the old herders, became the targets of violence for the men from Benguela. Black landowners were artificially accused of disrespect, of disloyalty, of terrorist sympathy, of treason, and their lands were bloodily seized.

When in 1961 Angolan retaliation struck back against the colonial encroachment, after Sharpeville, after the Congo, after Mueda in Mozambique, Benguela observed the unfolding scene with curious detachment. In Alexander Semedo's house the debate was measured. Did the northern risings represent nationalism, or was it revenge for the rape of the land twenty years before. Old Benguela whites, who had been life-long opponents of the Portuguese dictator, were torn between their democratic credentials and their fear of anarchy. Loyal blacks, suspecting that they might be the first victims of terrorism, were caught between their colonial comforts and the draw of freedom. Young hotheads could not wait to run from home to join the armies, some as conscripts on one side, some as guerrillas on the other. But beneath the politics of mobilisation, and the rethinking of ideological positions, Pepetela identified a modest cultural and moral revolution which was stirring on this remote frontier of the Portuguese empire.

White youth in Benguela broke out of the post-Edwardian social constraints which still enmeshed their distant cousins in Europe. Alexander Semedo's grandchildren went to high school rather than being sent to work in the family shop; they discovered the music and dancing which revolutionised America; they organised unchaperoned beach parties and explored their sexuality with their peers rather than with their servant girls. The war, meanwhile, was far away, on the almost unimaginably remote streets of Luanda, in the cotton and coffee fields of North Kwanza. To Benguela it was a remote war, a phoney war, and only after the Lisbon revolution of 1975 did the now ancient and almost silent Alexander Semedo witness real change in the dynasty which he had founded.

Rivers of ink, mostly Anglo-Saxon ink, have flowed in the debates over the fall of colonial rule in Angola, but none of the brilliant band of journalists who witnessed the events had the vantage point enjoyed by Pepetela as his fictional family dynasty sought its various ways of coming to terms with being white Angolans. Some were immensely excited by the new dawn offered by the MPLA and, like radical young whites in Cape Town, they worked tirelessly for a revolutionary cause though they had little idea of what equality or austerity might mean. Others in Benguela expected the revolution to be just another temporary hiccough and they cheerfully watched an armoured column of white South Africans roll through the town on its way to Luanda, a way that in the event was blocked by an expeditionary force from Cuba.

When white power was not restored in Angola some of the Semedo family made hasty plans to decamp, loading the possessions of a life-time on to lorries that would retreat southward through the desert where old Alexander had been born 85 years before. But Alexander did not go with them. He was a Benguela man, and in Benguela he would stay regardless of all the shrieking of his household women. Old, wise, white, Africanised, he had outlived the monarchy, the republic, and the dictatorship, and he did not intend to move because the black bourgeoisie were now in the ascendant. He quietly confided his serene thoughts to his fetish, his Yaka with the amber eyes.

Notes

2 Colonisers and the African Iron Age

1. António de Oliveira de Cadornega, *História Geral das Guerras Angolanas* (Lisbon edition, 1940–2, 3 vols). These seventeenth-century soldier's memoirs are one of the richest pieces of Luso-African literature.
2. David Birmingham, *Trade and Conflict in Angola* (Oxford, 1966). This is the main source for this essay, and no further reference to it is given.
3. C. R. Boxer, *Portuguese Society in the Tropics* (Madison, 1965). This study of Portuguese colonial municipal government has an appended section on colonists.
4. The charter is in the Torre do Tombo archive in Lisbon and has been published, for instance in the third of the 13-volume work by António Brásio, *Monumenta Missionaria Africana* (Lisbon, 1952–). The oral evidence derives from G. L. Haveaux, *La Tradition Historique des Bapende Orientaux* (Brusells, 1954).
5. José Joaquim Lopes de Lima, *Ensaios sôbre a Statistica das Possessões Portuguezas* (Lisbon, 1846, vol. 3).
6. J. W. Blake, *Europeans in West Africa* (London 1942, 2 vols); David Birmingham, 'The Regimento da Mina', *Transactions of the Historical Society of Ghana* (Legon, 1971).
7. David Birmingham, 'Central Africa from Cameroun to the Zambezi', in *Cambridge History of Africa*, vol. 3 (1977).
8. Richard Gray and David Birmingham, *Pre-Colonial African Trade* (London, 1970).
9. A. G. Hopkins, *An Economic History of West Africa* (London, 1973) is a good source in which to find a balanced summary of this fraught subject.
10. Andrew Battell, *The Strange Adventures of Andrew Battell* (London, 1901) is an Englishman's eyewitness account of the early development of the Angolan slaving system.
11. Gerald Bender, *Angola under the Portuguese* (London, 1978).

3 The Regimento da Mina

1. For a discussion of Portuguese *regimentos* see A. da Silva Rego, *Portuguese Colonization in the Sixteenth Century: A Study of the Royal Ordinances (Regimentos)* (Johannesburg, 1959).
2. The interpretation of Portuguese monetary values is complex. An examination of the salaries of the citizens suggests that one *milreis* might have been very approximately equivalent to £10 in present-day [i.e. 1971, ed.] terms. Thus the captain would have been an £8000-a-year man, while his chief factor earned £1500 (150 *milreis*), the two factory

clerks and the doctor £700 (70 *milreis*), the vicar £500 (50 *milreis*), and his chaplains £300 (30 *milreis*). Most of the lesser employees earned the equivalent, on this scale of conversion, of £17 a month and £10 for women.

3. Severe regulations attempted to protect the virtue of the ladies in the castle. It was decreed that any officer or resident who took one of them as his mistress would lose all his salary. This was a severe penalty in a country where the only compensation for hardship and disease was a fat pay packet at the end of one's tour.
4. A gold coin of João II weighing 121 grains and worth 380 *reis*.
5. Diogo Lopez de Sequeira to King of Portugal, 22 December 1503, ATT, CC. 1–4–42, Brásio, *Monumenta Missionaria Africana* (Lisbon, 1952–) vol. 4, pp. 24–7.
6. 'The Voyage of Eustache de la Fosse', in J. W. Blake, *Europeans in West Africa* (Hakluyt Society, London, 1942) vol. 1, p. 210.
7. João Lobato to João III, 13 April 1524 in Brásio, vol. 1, p. 514.
8. Gonçalo Toscano de Almeida to King of Portugal, 14 April 1548, ATT, CC, 1–80–74.
9. This contractor was apparently not a Portuguese to judge by his name, which looks like the English, George Herbert. He may have been German.
10. Duarte Pacheco Pereira, *Esmeraldo de Situ Orbis* (Hakluyt Society, London, 1937) p. 128.
11. Blake, *Europeans in West Africa*, p. 1.
12. Historians working on this period of Ghanaian history must clearly be on the look-out for any document in which answers to these questions have been recorded.
13. A. Ott, 'Akan Gold Weights', in *Transactions of the Historical Society of Ghana*, vol. 9 (Legon, 1968).

4 Early African Trade in Angola

1. Walter Rodney, *A History of the Upper Guinea Coast 1545–1800* (Oxford, 1969).
2. Milan Kalous, 'Contribution to the problem of the hypothetical connection between Ife and the Gold Coast before the fifteenth century', *Archiv Orientalni*, vol. 35 (1967); D. Birmingham, 'The Regimento da Mina', *Transactions of the Historical Society of Ghana*, vol. 11 (1971).
3. António Mendes, 'Letter from the Court of Ndongo, 9 May 1563', in A. Brásio, *Monumenta Missionaria Africana* (Lisbon, 1952–68) vol. 2, pp. 495–512.
4. J. J. Monteiro, *Angola and the River Congo* (London, 1875) vol. 2, p. 148.
5. Francisco Gouveia, 'Letter from Angola, c.1563', in Brásio, *Monumenta*, vol. 2, pp. 518–21.
6. A. de O. de Cadornega, *História das Guerras Angolanas* (Lisbon, 1940) vol. 3, p. 219.
7. G. L. Haveaux, *La Tradition Historique des Bapende Orientaux* (Brussels, 1954) p. 47.

8. J. J. Lopes de Lima, *Ensaios sôbre a Statistica das Possessões Portuguezas*, vol. 3: *Angola e Benguela* (Lisbon, 1846) p. 24.
9. 'Carta de doação a Paulo Dias', in Brásio, *Monumenta*, vol. 3, pp. 36–51.
10. Monteiro, *Angola*, vol. 1, pp. 189–97.
11. Monteiro, *Angola*, vol. 2, pp. 190–1.
12. D. Birmingham, *Trade and Conflict in Angola* (London, 1966) p. 19.
13. Ralph Delgado, 'O Govêrno de Souza Coutinho em Angola', *Studia* (1960–2).
14. A more detailed discussion of this dating will be seen in D. Birmingham, 'The African Response to Early Portuguese Activity in Angola', paper presented to the University of California colloquium on Africa and Brazil, published under the editorship of R. H. Chilcote.
15. This spread of commercial information may be compared to the speed and subtlety with which the peoples of South-East Africa responded to changing trade situations at Delagoa Bay.
16. P. Pogge, *Mittheilungen der Afrikanischen Gesellschaft in Deutschland*, vol. 4, pp. 186–90, refers to Imbangala salt reaching the Lunda.
17. Dias de Carvalho, *Ethnographia e história tradicional dos Povos da Lunda* (Lisbon, 1890) p. 67.
18. Birmingham, *Trade and Conflict*, pp. 62, 66–7, 69, 98.
19. In 1586, for instance, Father Diogo da Costa reported that Monomotapa was very close and that 2000 armed men could easily establish communication across the two small intervening kingdoms: Brásio, *Monumenta*, vol. 3, p. 339.

5 Traditions, Migrations and Cannibalism

1. More recent traditions seem to have more historical substantiation: it seems that Noah might really have been caught in quite a nasty flood living where he did.
2. I and others have previously assumed, wrongly, that this was a long-distance war against the Teke of Stanley-Pool, rather than a war in the neighbourhood of the Matadi rapids. See Leite de Faria's new edition of Rui da Pina.
3. This statement appears to begin with Van Wing and to gain in strength as each subsequent historian adopts it unquestioningly, rather than in the manner of the Atlantic slave trade statistics recently exposed by Curtin.
4. The use of the term 'Kikongo-speaking peoples' may be as anachronistic as the reference to a fifteenth-century empire. It may be that Kikongo spread to the Kongo provinces as a trade language during the sixteenth century. We have no evidence one way or the other.
5. That unstudied but highly glamorised people from whom so many influences have been alleged to come, not only in West Central Africa, but also in East Central and Eastern Africa!
6. I am almost as guilty as anyone else of disseminating absurd speculations about the Jaga. I even found a reference in my own published writings to 'hordes of cannibals' descending on the Kongo kingdom. *Mea culpa*.

7. A recent parallel example is perhaps to be found in the activities of the Simba in Maniema. See Benoît Verhaegen, *Rebellions au Congo*, vol. 2.
8. Comment based on an unpublished MA dissertation: Anne Wilson, 'Long-distance Trade and the Luba-Lomami Empire' (London, 1970).
9. The answer to this question may be furnished by Joseph Miller at Wisconsin when working on the greatest of the Imbangala kingdoms, Kasanje.

8 Joseph Miller's Way of Death

1. Joseph C. Miller, *Way of Death: Merchant Capitalism and the Angolan Slave Trade, 1730–1830* (London: James Currey; and Madison, Wis.: University of Wisconsin Press, 1988), xxx, 770 pp.
2. Joseph C. Miller, *Kings and Kinsmen: Early Mbundu States in Angola* (Oxford, 1976); Joseph C. Miller (ed.), *The African Past Speaks: Essays on Oral Tradition and History* (Folkestone, 1980); Jan Vansina, *Oral Tradition: A Study in Historical Methodology* (London, 1965); Jan Vansina, *Oral Tradition as History* (London, 1985).
3. Philip D. Curtin, *Economic Change in Precolonial Africa: Senegambia in the Era of the Slave Trade* (Madison, Wis., 1975).
4. Miller, *Way of Death*, p. 40.
5. *Ibid.*, p. 70.
6. *Ibid.*, p. 75.
7. *Ibid.*, p. 91.
8. *Ibid.*, *passim.*
9. *Ibid.*, p. 224.
10. Philip D. Curtin, *The Atlantic Slave Trade: A Census* (Madison, Wis., 1969).
11. Miller, *Way of Death*, p. 232.
12. *Ibid.*, pts 2, 3.
13. *Ibid.*, title, ch. 10.
14. *Ibid.*, p. 453.

9 The Coffee Barons of Cazengo

1. J. J. Lopes de Lima, *Ensaios sôbre a statistica das possessões portuguezas*, vol. 3: *De Angola e Benguella* (Lisbon, 1846) pt I, p. 76. In that year exports of £50 000 were dominated by 50 tons of ivory and 400 tons of lichen dye plants.
2. Production commonly exceeded permissible exports under international agreement. Some of the surplus may have been sold on the Zaïre coffee quota.
3. 1941 exports were 14 000 tons.
4. For an analysis of changes in Portuguese imperial economic strategy see Keith Middlemas, *Cabora Bassa* (London, 1975), which describes the process from the Mozambique perspective.
5. David Birmingham, 'Themes and Resources of Angolan History', *African Affairs*, vol. 73 (1974).

6. Arquivo Histórico de Angola, 13–2–23, fo. 14^v.
7. *Ibid.*, fo. 58^v. It is not ascertained whether this man was white, black or mestizo.
8. *Ibid.*, fo. 37.
9. Arquivo Histórico de Angola, 32–2–24, fo. 62^v.
10. Letter from Cazengo dated 19 July 1846 published in the *Boletim Official* (BO) of 8 August 1846. Crude sterling equivalents of 4500 *reis* per £ have been given throughout. Pereira Cardozo was an all-round entrepreneur; he also reported on the small iron foundry which he had set up 'with little vexation to the local populace'.
11. Arquivo Histórico de Angola, 32–2–23, fos. 22, 55^v, 61.
12. The published reports of the BNU (available, for instance, in the library of the Banco de Angola which took over as both the commercial and issuing bank of Angola in 1926) are disappointing. Fuller unpublished reports and correspondence are held by the Arquivo Histórico Ultramarino in Lisbon on limited access.
13. Dona Ana Joaquina is clearly a figure worthy of serious study. Her town residence survives as a dilapidated architectural monument in Luanda. She was more than a *grande dame* of high society, however, and Mário António claims that she sent an envoy of her own, António Bonifácio Rodrigues, to forestall the great embassy which Rodrigues Graça led in 1843 to the royal Lunda court of the *muata yamvo*. See Mário António Fernandes de Oliveira, 'Alguns aspectos da administração de Angola em época de reformas 1834–51' (unpublished dissertation, Lisbon, 1971).
14. Arquivo Histórico de Angola, 32–2–24, fo. 98^v, 11 August 1876.
15. In 1875, for instance, Norton Carnegie & Co. were allocated one convict to work in Cazengo. Arquivo Histórico de Angola, 18–1–4. The convict register for 1887 to 1910 lists about 100 men assigned to Cazengo. Arquivo Histórico de Angola, 32–1–39.
16. Arquivo Histórico de Angola, 18–7–4, 1 February 1894.
17. Arquivo Histórico de Angola, 32–1–41, 1887–1904.
18. Arquivo Histórico de Angola, 18–7–3, 14 May 1894. Chicanery in plantation shops remained a serious grievance in Angola until recent times, but it was unusual to find such detailed complaints about the system as are contained in the gruesome report on the death and burial of Bernardo.
19. Arquivo Histórico de Angola, 18–12–2, 4 July 1906.
20. Arquivo Histórico de Angola, 18–11–4, 27 November 1908. For more about the Kabuku, see the important article based on the Luanda archives by Jill R. Dias, 'Black Chiefs, White Traders and Colonial Policy near the Kwanza: Kabuku Kambilo and the Portuguese, 1873–1896', *Journal of African History*, vol. 22 (1976).
21. Arquivo Histórico de Angola, 18–12–2, 20 July 1906.
22. Arquivo Histórico de Angola, 18–6–4, 22 June 1892.
23. *Ibid.*, 2 July 1892. The charges on which de Freitas was wanted included torture, private incarceration, homicide, rape of his own daughter, highway robbery with violence, abuse of the civil administration, insults to the judicial authorities, kidnapping and malicious wounding.

Other barons were less spectacular in their criminality, but Arquivo Histórico de Angola, 18–5–4, 4 December 1886, also illustrates the violence of the society.

24. Arquivo Histórico de Angola, 18–7–2, 10 September 1895.

25. Arquivo Histórico de Angola, 18–7–4 lists the 75 administrators of Cazengo between 1843 and 1894. The sixteenth was a member of the Van Dúnem family, António Pereira dos Santos Van Dúnem Junior. He was probably an army officer, like Balthasar Van Dúnem in the eighteenth century, and the famous revolutionary José Van Dúnem in the twentieth century. See Carlos Couto, *Os Capitaes-Mores em Angola no Século XVIII* (Luanda, 1972), p. 63. According to Martins dos Santos, *Primeiras Letras em Angola* (Luanda, 1974), p. 47, Teresa Van Dúnem was the village schoolmistress of Cazengo at an unspecified date. In 1896 another Van Dúnem, vulgarly known as Cangraiamvulla, was heavily in debt in the town of Dondo and stole a slave. (Arquivo Histórico de Angola, 18–8–2, 28 May 1896.)

26. For details of the Angolan military structure in the nineteenth century see the very recent work of René Pélissier, *Les Guerres Grises: Résistance et Révoltes en Angola (1845–1941)* (Montamets, 1978). This is the first volume of his two volume opus on the military history of Angola.

27. Arquivo Histórico de Angola, 18–7–4, 1 February 1895.

28. Arquivo Histórico de Angola, 18–12–2, 24 March 1906. (This is the first typewritten document in the archive and heralds an era not of legibility but of chewed flimsies.) Sleeping sickness hit Cazengo hard, and like other aspects of the medical history of Angola is in need of research. It reached the district by 1901 and had not quite burnt itself out by 1910. Plantations obviously suffered particularly from epidemics and by 4 May 1901 anxiety was being expressed about the labour supply already depleted by São Tomé competition (Arquivo Histórico de Angola, 18–10–3). Medical anxieties about the threat to the whole population were sent to Luanda on 16 September 1901 (Arquivo Histórico de Angola, 18–10–2). In the early 1870s and again in 1890 Cazengo had suffered smallpox epidemics. As late as 1910, however, the district had no clinic or chemist and relied on herbalists to fight against the leading diseases cited as leprosy, syphilis, elephantiasis, tuberculosis, alcoholism and malnutrition (Arquivo Histórico de Angola, 18–12–3, annual report for 1910).

29. *Boletim Official*, supplement for 11 February 1846.

30. Cited in João de Andrade Corvo, *Estudos sobre as províncias ultramarinas* (Lisbon, 1883).

31. Published on 4 March 1900 in the journal *Dia* and cited in *Memória explicativa e justificativa dos actos da situação da Companhia Real dos Caminhos de Ferro Atravez d'Africa* (Porto, 1909), 31. Another commentator remarking on the huge sums of metropolitan public money risked in the Cazengo chimera and the Ambaca 'Trans-Africa' railway said that soon the map of Europe would no longer show Portugal but 'The Territory of the Ambaca Company – formerly Lusitania'.

32. Arquivo Histórico de Angola, 18–6–3, 1889.

33. Arquivo Histórico de Angola, 18–1–4. Christianity was very nominal and priests or missionaries were rare. In 1854, however, it was recorded in letter-book number 32–1–24 that David Livingstone passed through the district. He carried with him two guns and some scientific instruments but 'made no converts among Portuguese subjects'. See David Livingstone, *Missionary Travels* (London, 1857), chs 19–21, for a less laconic account of his visit to Cazengo.
34. Arquivo Histórico de Angola, 32–1–22, 27 June 1888.
35. Arquivo Histórico de Angola, 32–2–6, 27 November 1882.
36. Arquivo Histórico de Angola, 32–2–12 about 1856.
37. Arquivo Histórico de Angola, 18–7–1, 19 April 1893.
38. A British resident in Angola in 1973 remembered stones rattling on his windows in a Pungo Andongo farmhouse when he was four years old.
39. Arquivo Histórico de Angola, 32–1–48, 23 June 1917.
40. António d'Assis Junior, *Relatório dos Acontecimentos de Dala Tando e Lucala* (Luanda, 1917, 2 pamphlets). He came back from exile, however, and published a fascinating historical novel entitled *O Segredo da Morta*, about the Mbundu during the old colonial period.
41. Next to coffee and cotton, the Angolan sugar cane industry is the economic sector most in need of historical investigation, and the one most important to the postcolonial state. In Cazengo 95 hectares of cane were planted between 1890 and 1895. Seven estates had water or steam-powered mills and some of the rum stills exceeded 1000 litres in capacity. The industry was closed down in 1907 and John Gossweiler wrote a comprehensive report on it for purposes of compensation. (Arquivo Histórico de Angola, 18–12–3, 14 January 1910.)
42. Arquivo Histórico de Angola, 18–17–4, 22 November 1916. The Angolan Secretary for Native Affairs suggested that villages be set up in Cazengo for Luba and other returnees from São Tomé.
43. See Paul E. Lovejoy, 'Plantations in the Economy of the Sokoto Caliphate', *Journal of African History*, vol. 13 (1978), pp. 341–68.
44. For a short while Cazengo district was subordinated to a regional governor in Golungo Alto. The changes in the Angola administrative structure were many and complex, and greatly affect the location of archival material. There is a useful, though not always reliable, guide by the former archivist, Mário Milheiros, *Indice Histórico-Corográfico de Angola* (Luanda, 1972).
45. Difficulties in recruiting the harvest brigades in Luanda were a factor in the attempted *coup d'état* of 1977. See David Birmingham, 'The Twenty-Seventh of May', *African Affairs*, vol. 77 (1978).

11 Colonialism in Angola: Kinyama's Experience

1. Officially government recruiters mainly enrolled conscript workers for government services such as road maintenance; in practice the government supplied forced labour to many private employers as well.
2. In 1957 the PIDE political police, which ruthlessly suppressed freedoms in Portugal, was introduced into Angola. Its methods of intimidation became world famous over the next 17 years and the association of

brutality with policemen spread in part to the other police services in Angola such as the fictional valley constable portrayed here.

3. John Marcum in *The Angolan Revolution*, vol. 1 (Cambridge, Mass., 1969) p. 19, cites the hope of an army officer in 1966 that each Portuguese white conscript soldier would father six illegitimate mulatto children before returning to Europe. The degree of violence, pain and trauma thereby officially sanctioned would be hard to exaggerate.

4. Elsewhere in Africa, even in South Africa, the late colonial period saw new and more skilled jobs becoming available to Africans. In Portuguese Africa these jobs were offered to migrants from Europe and the Atlantic islands of Madeira and Cape Verde whose education and skills were often little higher than those of rural Angolans.

5. Gerald J. Bender, *Angola under the Portuguese* (London, 1978) has a good account of white peasant colonies in the southern highlands.

6. The Spanish hospital was up country from Huambo, near the Benguela Railway on which patients were regularly to be met. As late as 1973, when the colonial presence was at its height, sick Angolans, black and white, often travelled several hundred miles to find a trustworthy doctor.

7. The 1945 rejection of all protests against compulsory cotton growing was signed by President Carmona, Prime Minister Salazar and Colonial Minister Caetano.

8. Reports of genuine historical events of a similar nature taking place in the south were given to the author in New Lisbon (now Huambo) in August 1963.

9. The Cela white colony in the northern part of the Benguela highlands was planned in the 1950s for 8400 families. In 1960 about 300 were there and 122 had already left 'either through their own volition or by being expelled for offenses ranging from alcoholism and refusal to work to theft or even rape'. Gerald J. Bender, 'Planned Rural Settlement in Angola 1900–1968', in F. W. Heimer, *Social Change in Angola* (Munich, 1973) p. 242.

10. Although this story is allegorical, this is of course the real date of the military *coup d'état* in Lisbon. This coup toppled the 40-year-old dictatorship of the Salazar–Caetano corporative government which, between the world wars, had created the Portuguese New State, somewhat along the lines of Mussolini's fascist state in Italy.

11. See Robin Hallett, 'The South African Intervention in Angola 1975–76', in *African Affairs*, vol. 77 (July 1978). For a wider view of the war of intervention in Angola, see Ernest Harsch and Tony Thomas, *Angola: the hidden history of Washington's war* (New York, 1977).

13 The Twenty-Seventh of May

1. *Angola: a tentativa de golpe de estado de 27 de Maio de 77* (Lisbon, 1977) pp. 9–10.
2. *Facts and Reports*, vol. 7, no. 25, item 2193, citing Prensa Latina.
3. *Afrique-Asie*, 11 July and 25 July 1977, contained detailed accounts of the May events by Simon Malley.
4. A third confrontation occurred later, in May 1978.

Index

Milton Keynes UK
Ingram Content Group UK Ltd.
UKHW031101010824
446387UK00001B/69